Monsters in the Machine

MONSTERS IN THE MACHINE

Science Fiction Film and the Militarization of America after World War II

Steffen Hantke

University Press of Mississippi / Jackson

www.upress.state.ms.us

The University Press of Mississippi is a member
of the Association of American University Presses.

Copyright © 2016 by University Press of Mississippi
All rights reserved

First printing 2016

Library of Congress Cataloging-in-Publication Data

Names: Hantke, Steffen, 1962– author.
Title: Monsters in the machine : science fiction film and the militarization
   of America after World War II / Steffen Hantke.
Description: Jackson : University Press of Mississippi, 2016. | Includes
   bibliographical references and index.
Identifiers: LCCN 2016002840 | ISBN 9781496805652 (hardback)
Subjects: LCSH: Science fiction films—United States—History and criticism.
   | Motion pictures—United States—History—20th century. | Armed Forces in
   motion pictures. | BISAC: PERFORMING ARTS / Film & Video / History &
   Criticism.
Classification: LCC PN1995.9.S26 H28 2016 | DDC 791.43/615—dc23 LC record
available at http://lccn.loc.gov/2016002840

British Library Cataloging-in-Publication Data available

Contents

vii   Acknowledgments

3   **Introduction**
      A Bright New Future, With Monsters

47   **Chapter One**
      Military Stock Footage

85   **Chapter Two**
      Veterans

121   **Chapter Three**
      The Southwest

153   **Chapter Four**
      Decolonization

185   **Conclusion**
      The Long Shadow of the Fifties

203   Notes

221   Works Cited

229   Index

Acknowledgments

Many of the ideas that found their way into this book were first tried out at conferences and invited guest lectures. For these opportunities I am grateful to Agnieszka Soltysik-Monnet at the University of Lausanne, Lars Schmeink at Hamburg University, Frank Hentschel at the University of Cologne, Roger Lüdeke at the Universität Düsseldorf, Naoyuki Mizuno at Kyoto University, Chiho Nakagawa at Nara Women's University, and Meike Uhrig at Tübingen University. I would also like to express my gratitude to the Southwest Popular Culture & American Culture Association; for well over a decade, its annual conference has provided a home away from home. For their invaluable help with the research, I am grateful to my friend and colleague David Schmid and the staff at the University at Buffalo Library and Annex. For their critical comments on military stock footage, I am indebted to Mark Levy, John Rieder, and Mark Bould. For patiently and generously answering questions about *Welcome to Mars* and 1950s retrofutures, I owe thanks to Ken Hollings. Over the years, many editors have put up with my writing and patiently tried to improve it (an ongoing struggle); among them, I owe a special debt of gratitude to Rob Latham, Linnie Blake, Xavier Aldana-Reyes, and Harry Benshoff. Among the many colleagues and friends who have been inspiring and encouraging just by being themselves, I would like to thank David Willingham, Donald Bellomy, and Dan Disney.

My heartfelt thanks also go to Leila Salisbury, for bringing me back to the University Press of Mississippi, to Valerie Jones, for her tireless work in steering me patiently through the production process, and to Peter Tonguette, for bringing a sharp eye to all errors great and small.

In 2010, an essay of mine on *The Time Machine* was published in *ZAA: A Quarterly of Language, Literature and Culture*; my thanks go to the journal's editorial staff for giving permission for a revised and expanded version of that essay to be included here.

Work on this book was supported by a Sogang University Research Grant in 2014.

Finally, and most importantly, this book is dedicated to Aryong, the queen of outer space, the fifty-foot woman, for being brave enough to have married a monster from outer space.

Monsters in the Machine

Introduction
A Bright New Future, With Monsters

Fifties Science Fiction: Fondly Remembered, Critically Dismissed

This book is about American science fiction films of the 1950s. Many of these films are fondly remembered, yet critically dismissed. If you are in your fifties or sixties, the films might be part of your childhood memories, of evenings spent at the local theater or at the drive-in. If you are in your fifties or younger—that is, if you are a member of the baby boomer generation—they might remind you of afternoons spent in front of the television set; after the studios had sold these films off, this is where many of them would enjoy a long second life. If you are not in your fifties yet, you would, of course, have no way to remember these films at all. But you might be aware of them. They might occasionally play in the background, on a TV or movie screen, in a scene from one of your favorite films, where a director has planted them as an affectionate nod to an earlier, more innocent time in Hollywood history. Except for some notable titles, many of these films are not very well known. There are no cinematic milestones here, no entries on the British Film Institute's top ten list of the greatest films ever made. This goes for their directors as well, who tended to be skilled craftsmen at best and more or less ambitious entertainers at least. There were too many of these films during the 1950s, and too many of them were, to be perfectly honest, eminently forgettable. And yet they endure. To be precise, their vocabulary endures. Their tropes and metaphors, their memorable characters, their spectacular settings, their plot twists, the way they mix science fiction and horror, and, most of all, their bestiary of madmen, mutations, and monsters—all of this is still very much with us.

As a distinct cinematic cycle, the films discussed in this book come into focus in a series of iconographic snapshots. There is the fifty-foot woman and the incredible shrinking man. There are the prehistoric dinosaurs, ants, spiders, and grasshoppers, all grown to grotesque proportions. There are the brilliant scientists, some of them quite obviously mad as they delve into forbidden realms of knowledge, others working in fruitful collaboration as they advance the amazing potential of new technologies for a better, safer world. There are the space aliens, some arriving in flying saucers to prevent humanity from destroying the world, others to invade, conquer, and occupy it (some attacking humanity in vast military campaigns, others insidiously sneaking into human hearts and minds). And, time and again, there is the American military coming to humanity's rescue. There are the convoys of tanks and trucks rolling out to meet the menace; the heroic officers and enlisted men taking experimental planes, nuclear submarines, and spaceships out into territories, both in space and time, where no one has gone before. There is battlefield camaraderie, frontline courage, strategic and tactical planning, and grunts grumbling about the brass. The military: this is the basic flavor, the tone or tenor, the glue that holds all these other iconic images together. Seen as a distinct cinematic cycle, the films rearrange and recombine familiar elements in a creative process that gradually reveals the larger cultural and political landscape of America in the 1950s. It is the repetitive urgency of these films, their almost obsessive return to the same central moods and motifs, that makes them such eloquent testimony to a deeply felt, shared cultural moment. That the military should happen to be such an essential part of these films is the focus of the critical discussion in this book.

"I bid my hideous progeny to go forth and prosper":
Fifties Science Fiction and its Gothic Roots

In trying to trace back 1950s science fiction films to their historical and generic origins, one will inevitably encounter the gothic tradition of the late eighteenth and early nineteenth centuries. In its richness and flexibility, the gothic may be responsible for a wide array of genres across different media. But when it comes to science fiction films from the 1950s, the genealogy harkens back to one canonical text of the gothic in particular, Mary Shelley's *Frankenstein, or the Modern Prometheus* (1818). More than any other canonical gothic text or author—from Walpole to Radcliffe, Lewis, and Maturin—Shelley breaks new ground in the amalgamation of what were to become separate cinematic genres: science fiction on the one hand, horror on the other. Fifty-odd years since the inception of the gothic with the publication of Horace Walpole's *The Castle of Otranto* (1864), Shelley's novel marks the watershed moment when those two genres—until then united under the umbrella of the gothic—finally part ways. As a strategy for granting legitimacy to those textual elements that violate ontological ground rules (e.g., the re-animation of dead matter), Shelley draws on the rhetoric of science and its social power.[1] As for the many science fiction writers that were to follow in her footsteps, scientific accuracy is of minor importance to Shelley. Notoriously evasive about the actual science involved in reanimating dead matter, Shelley is more interested in its mythical resonance and in its impact on individual lives and social interactions. In its powerful use of science as a source of potent metaphors, *Frankenstein* anticipates a tradition of science fiction that includes films from the 1950s populated by those very same metaphors. Even the scientists in 1950s science fiction film never completely shed this mythological burden they are made to carry. But they mark a departure from mythology toward something more akin to modern technoscience, which looks at the once-mythical activity of scientists in historically specific institutional and ideological contexts.[2] Unlike Shelley's promethean loner, 1950s scientists perform heroic work as institutional employees. "The *scientific and military experts*," Andrew Tudor reminds us, "who spent so much of the decade [i.e., the 1950s] prevailing over threats from space, from beneath the sea, or from other dimensions, were allowed to be heroes in ways almost unique to the period" (114, italics added). From the gothic castle keep in *Frankenstein* (James Whale, 1931) to Dr. Moreau's *Island of Lost Souls* (Erle C. Kenton, 1932), the isolated location of scientific research is a staple of 1930s science fiction films. Scientists in 1950s films, like the ones in *Creature from the Black Lagoon* (Jack Arnold, 1954), work in teams. They tend to be employed by universities, which, according to Tudor, are often funded by or cooperating with the military. They worry about getting published, have international networks of colleagues, and their teams feature designated members who specialize in fundraising and public relations.

> No longer the special quasi-magical activity of thirties mad science tucked away in old houses and Gothic castles, science is more prosaic and more all-embracing. Penetrating into every corner of our lives, the science developed in fifties horror movies is a constitutive part of our everyday world, its admired and feared exponents harbingers of both progress and disaster, its most common threat—radiation—unseen, but a potential invader of any area of our activities. (Tudor 147)

While Shelley's novel paves the way for science fiction by providing the mythological backdrop to the scientist as an emblematic Enlightenment figure, *Frankenstein*'s ambivalence about science also opens a rich vein of anxiety, paranoia, and abjection. As the frequent confusion between the name of the creator and the name of the creation suggests, the novel's monster is at least as important as its eponymous mad scientist. Shelley's "hideous progeny" is a walking, talking corpse, after all; and it is this corpse that focuses attention on certain genre elements that might overlap with science fiction but also exceed that genre and deviate from it. The corpse at the heart of *Frankenstein* infects the world of the novel with death—from locations and activities (cemeteries and grave robbing) to plot twists (abandonment and revenge), and, most important, the affective response of the audience (horror, terror, disgust). The inclusion of abjection in *Frankenstein* does not mean that this branch of the gothic is necessarily technophobic—the flip side of the walking, talking corpse is, after all, its promethean creator. Thus, gothic writers and filmmakers on the liberal, progressive end of the spectrum—one might think of Clive Barker or David Cronenberg—have been open to explorations of the abject that embrace and even celebrate all that which abjection rejects, vilifies, and expels. But given the predominant embrace of abjection as a subject to inspire fear and disgust, it is hardly surprising that *Frankenstein*, and its many adaptations, have figured prominently not only in textbooks of science fiction, but also (or perhaps even more so) in textbooks of horror cinema.

The two genres may have periodically parted ways, with horror veering toward the supernatural and science fiction embracing the technological sublime rather than the abject. Generic differentiation aside, though, Shelley's impure hybrid dynamic is what drives 1950s science fiction cinema. With few exceptions, 1950s films deploy science and technology—not the supernatural nor the deeply subjective psychological—as the legitimization for the reversal of ontological ground rules. Science makes it possible to step beyond strict realism. Monsters and mutations are always and inevitably the product of technoscience, just as technoscience is always and inevitably in bed with the military. Again, with few exceptions, the films tend to share Shelley's ambivalence toward science and technology, coming down far less frequently on the side of the technological sublime than on the side of abjection. As I have said, this does not mean that they are invariably technophobic; science and technology save the day as frequently as they ruin it, depending on the political stance of each individual film. Rather, in their affective structure, the films aim for suspense and shock and even for disgust. In fact, many of them go quite deliberately for the moment Stephen King has famously called "the gross-out." Far more alien creatures

Human Perfection: The Face of Technoscience in *This Island Earth*

The Abject Underbelly on Technoscience: Monstrosity in *This Island Earth*

Heroic American Masculinity in *The Atomic Submarine*

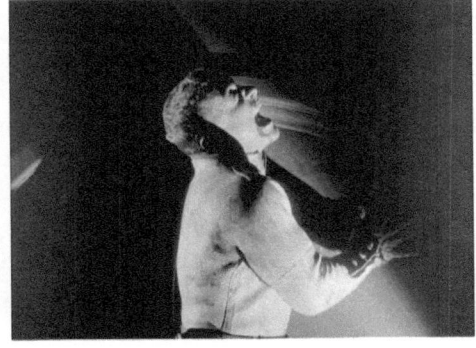

Heroic American Masculinity Amputated by Technology in *The Atomic Submarine*

in 1950s films are grotesque and repulsive than sublime (or even just cute). Far more of them come to conquer, lurk, menace, dissolve, absorb, and destroy humanity than to aid or guide or expedite humanity in projects of individual bodily or collective spiritual transcendence. One look at a film like *This Island Earth* (Joseph M. Newman, 1955) and it becomes clear that for every image of potentially sublime reason and transcendence, there is an image of monstrous abjection. Jack Arnold's *Tarantula* (1955) goes from the awesome possibilities of nuclear medicine to the grotesquely disfigured features of the scientist experimenting with it, just as Spencer Gordon Bennet's *The Atomic Submarine* (1959) celebrates cutting edge US naval technologies one moment, and shocks the audience the next when it shows a sailor's body sliced in half by an automatic spaceship door relentlessly closing on him. This combination of science fiction and horror—a hallmark of the 1950s cycle of films—has triggered some useful critical debate. In order to understand the films more clearly, it is worthwhile to look at some of the positions taken by critics in this debate.

Leading the debate to date is Mark Jancovich, who has provided an excellent overview of some of the critical arguments made to distinguish horror and science fiction in the 1950s cinematic cycle from each other. Jancovich points out that, for viewers during the 1950s, the distinction between the two genres would have been irrelevant because the films "were more usually simply referred to as 'monster movies'" (*Rational Fears* 11). The suggestion that 1950s films were "distinguished from science fiction due to their supposed inaccuracy or implausibility of their action or locations" or for "being anti-scientific in their attitude" (11) may move them closer to horror. But this supposed attitude does not really discount genre theories of science fiction that demand a similarly strict Campbellian pro-scientific ethos. Jancovich also weighs arguments about the political stance of both genres made by Warren Luciano and Vivian Sobchak. Between the two, Sobchak arrives at the conclusions that 1950s films constitute 'hybrids' of both genres (14) while Luciano gravitates more toward science fiction as a broad, all-inclusive category. On Sobchak's side, one might also cite Andrew Tudor, who recognizes hybridity by referring to the films as "SF-inclined horror movies" [93]).[3] When nudged toward the science fiction side of the hybrid mix, 1950s films gravitate toward the dark, cautionary, dystopian strain in science fiction. When nudged toward the side of horror, they gravitate toward the subgenre of technohorror, with its out-of-control machinery. Jancovich eventually abandons the debate without assigning the films in question a proper genre. Instead, he focuses his critical attention on the central significance of science and technology shared by all films in the cycle regardless of whether science fiction or horror dominates the hybrid mix from one film to the next. With this critical agenda, Jancovich reads the films in response to the tightening of Fordist control over the state and its institutions, private corporations, and private lives in the postwar years. This thematic rather than generic focus permits Jancovich to expand the canon of primary texts to include, among the films he discusses, novels and short stories by American pulp fiction authors (Ray Bradbury, Robert Bloch, Richard Matheson). This is a useful decision since the work of exactly those writers intersected practically and thematically with cinema and television throughout the 1950s, with all three of them writing for, or being adapted by, anthology television series like *Thriller* (Bloch), *Alfred Hitchcock Presents* (Bloch and Bradbury), and *The Twilight Zone* (Bradbury and Matheson). In my own discussion, I will follow Jancovich's lead, albeit less in regard to the literary culture of the 1950s and more with an eye on television, which, by the 1960s, was going to pick up where cinema was about to leave off.

Jancovich's reading of science fiction films responding to 1950s anxieties about conformism and dehumanization suggests the presence of the military as one cog in the institutional machinery of postwar America. It is not singled out as the most important cog in the machine or as its basic organizational principle. This is not an oversight on Jancovich's part. But it is an opportunity to shine a spotlight on exactly this aspect of postwar American life. By focusing thematic attention specifically on the military—on what, in the following pages, I will describe as "the military-industrial complex— this book will try to reshape the cinematic canon slightly the way Jancovich did when he included pulp writers in his own analysis. Aside from a few references to fiction and television, my own reshaping of this canon is determined by the various degrees to which any given film tilts the balance more toward the horror or more toward the science fiction side of the generic hybrid. I will also try to balance this hybrid as Jancovich and Sobchak describe it against representations of the military-industrial complex that have little or no relationship to either horror or science fiction. For example, on the science fiction end of the spectrum would be films like Irving Pichel's *Destination Moon* (1950) and Byron Haskin's *Conquest of Space* (1955). Both films are technophilic celebrations of American progress in which the abject plays little or no role at all. Ideologically aligned with these science fiction films would be male melodrama like Gordon Douglas's *Bombers B-52* or Anthony Mann's *Strategic Air Command*, or war films like *Twelve O'Clock High*. Set apart from the strict realism in something like *Bombers B-52* are films that still qualify as science fiction because they take a minor extrapolative step but otherwise stay within the bounds of contemporary settings; Alfred E. Green's *Invasion U.S.A.* (1952) would be an extreme example of this type of film, while Sidney Lumet's *Fail Safe* (1964), Stanley Kubrick's *Dr. Strangelove* (1964), or James B. Harris's *The Bedford Incident* (1965) would be more moderate examples. A cluster of films using conventions of the disaster film would fall into the same category, with examples ranging from some of the giant creature films like *Them!* (1954) and *The Beginning of the End* (1957) to apocalyptic films like Val Guest's *The Day the Earth Caught Fire* (1961). Distributed along this spectrum are also films borrowing from classic adventure narratives that feature travel and exploration. Examples of this type of film would be Richard Fleischer's *20,000 Leagues Under the Sea* (1954) and *Fantastic Voyage* (1966), George Pal's *The Time Machine* (1960), Irwin Allen's *The Lost World* (1960), Irwin Allen's *Voyage to the Bottom of the Sea* (1961), and Ib Melchior's *The Time Travelers* (1964). Each film in this category is adjusted to various degrees to the presence of fantastic elements within a more or less realistic setting.[4] Finally, Francis D. Lyon's *Cult of the Cobra* (1955), Jacques Tourneur's *Night of the Demon* (1957), and Mervyn LeRoy's *The Bad Seed* (1956) stand out as films that gravitate toward supernatural horror, a rather atypical subgenre in 1950s cinema. All three films struggle with the supernatural, and the latter two reign in their flirtation with the supernatural and return to the scientific discourses of anthropology and psychology (in the case of *The Bad Seed*, this happens somewhat tongue-in-cheek). *Cult of the Cobra* is still of interest because its characters are World War II veterans and its setting is the world of postwar normalization. To make matters even more complicated, the science fiction genre also operates in a broader environment of genre differentiation, in which it conducts lively stylistic and thematic exchanges with the Western and film noir, as well as with the spy thriller and the paranoid conspiracy thriller.

At first glance, the type of science fiction that emerges from this intersection of various genres seems to be a mishmash of anything and everything. Travel narratives, disaster films, war and combat films, spy films, and Westerns—it all finds its way into the mix. And yet two characteristic features prevail: 1950s science fiction films are tonally and affectively keyed into the horror film, just as thematically they all share a common link, that with the military-industrial complex. This central theme is represented in a vernacular that eschews the supernatural over the scientific, that relies to varying degrees on images of abjection, and that tends to prefer to shock its audience rather than to awe it. Though I acknowledge that these films cut across a variety of genres, and that they revolve around the hybridization with the horror film, I am going to refer to them as science fiction. To some extent, the term does not claim to capture and pinpoint them in their generic essence. Genre, as many critics have argued, has always been more flexible in practice than those devoted to its theoretical description have admitted. The label of "science fiction" fits quite well with the elements in the mix that tend to remain dominant even when films operate in the borderlands between genres.

Historical Contexts: Popular Culture in the 1950s

As I am taking on these films as reflections of—and interventions in—the political, social, and cultural life of America during the 1950s, I need to acknowledge that this nation and this era are, of course, too vast and too diverse to be summarized neatly by a single cycle of films. Some of the existing literature, which might help me paint a picture of the time and the place, makes explicit concessions to the diversity of the 1950s. Even in its narrow focus on a single year at the end of the long 1950s, Fred Kaplan's book *1959: The Year Everything Changed* (2009) goes through a dizzying array of historical events and figures. It starts with notorious "sick comics" like Lenny Bruce and Mort Sahl, the radical musical stylings of Ornette Coleman and Miles Davis, and Beat Generation writers like Jack Kerouac and Allen Ginsberg, and moves on to literary heavyweights like William Burroughs and Norman Mailer, avant-garde artists like Pollock, Rauschenberg, and Johns, and political, artistic, and scientific mavericks like Frank Lloyd Wright, Robert Frank, C. Wright Mills, and the inventors of, respectively, the microchip and the birth control pill. The scope of these figures and events already exceeds what science fiction cinema might be able to say about the 1950s. Even discussions that come closer to the heart of science fiction cinema tend to cast a wider net than this book ever could. For example, in the course of his "unscripted reflections on the fantasy of science in the early years of the American Century," Ken Hollings's astounding radio serial *Welcome to Mars* lays out a phantasmagoria of the 1950s assembled from the more dubious aspects of the time. Hollings covers the CIA's experiments with psychotropic drugs, as well as the sighting of unidentified flying objects that would build up into a pervasive though short-lived flying saucer craze. He also discusses the neurological research into memory and identity conducted by independent think tanks like the RAND Corporation, and the strange prolonged influence on the culture of charismatic charlatans like Aleister Crowley. A special place in the series is reserved for the designers and visitors of state fairs and exhibitions promising glimpses of utopian futures as the American Century was unfolding. Echoes of Hollings's phantasmagoric montage of serendipitous intersections and unexpected confluences also reverberate through the parts of Adam Curtis's documentary work devoted to the 1950s, both in America and in Britain. Curtis's serial *The Living Dead* (1995), for example, traces the intersection of memory and authority by looking at the Allied victory over Nazi Germany, the Nuremberg trials, and the troublesome logistical continuities between the Nazi war machine and the advent of the American Century. All of this work tries to defamiliarize America in the 1950s and to reveal the cultural weirdness of a period that is all too easily assimilated into a narrative of uneventful, unadventurous, and conservative postwar complacency und uniformity.

While Kaplan's notes on the year 1959 operate closer to mainstream history, Hollings's, and to a lesser degree Curtis's, phantasmagoric musings on the 1950s offer a more insightful commentary on the peculiar position of science fiction cinema during the 1950s. The emblematic status of science fiction may be more a product of historical hindsight than of a cadre of producers, writers, and directors uncannily attuned to the zeitgeist. Yet the films themselves were wildly popular; it is hardly an exaggeration to say that science fiction constituted "a major Hollywood genre in the 1950s [considering that] by one estimate, five hundred film features and shorts were produced between 1948 and 1962" (O'Donnell 169). Andrew Tudor goes one step further, calling it "the Fifties boom" that was to produce "a sustained upsurge in horror-movie distribution [between 1956 and 1960]" (25).[5] Part of this boom was the establishment of a recurring cast of characters both behind and in front of the camera. Many of the actors would become deeply familiar in their association with the genre to an audience far beyond the boundaries of fans and aficionados. Nonetheless, these Hollywood stars seemed to exist in a cinematic universe parallel to Hollywood's official definition of itself. While actors like Richard Carlson, Kenneth Tobey, Whit Bissell, or Faith Domergue are now considered icons of 1950s science fiction film, mainstream Hollywood at the time would celebrate John Wayne, Bob Hope, Rock Hudson, Doris Day, and Dean Martin and Jerry Lewis as the top moneymakers of the decade.[6] The dissociation between the two groups is striking enough to corroborate Hollings's assertion that the 1950s were not merely as culturally diverse as Kaplan suggests, but that there was an underside to the culture which, in its peculiar position of being highly visible and yet largely ignored, suggests a rich and conflicted collective unconscious.

Deeply embedded in both Kaplan's and Hollings's kaleidoscopic discussions of 1950s America are the two themes that have tended to dominate the popular understanding of science fiction films from the period—communist hysteria and paranoia on the one hand, fear of an imminent catastrophic nuclear attack from the Soviet Union on the other. Kaplan, Hollings, and Curtis describe, for example, Fidel Castro's and Nikita Khrushchev's respective goodwill tours of the US, just as they comment on the suburban domestic architecture of fallout shelters and fantasies of urban nuclear panic and post-nuclear desolation. They also remind their audiences of enigmatic yet likely-to-be-forgotten historical figures like Herman Kahn, the professional prophet of nuclear doom immortalized in fictional characters like the eponymous Mephistophelian enigma Dr. Strangelove in Stanley Kubrick's 1964 film, or the character of Prof. Groeteschele in Eugene Burdick and Henry Wheeler's novel *Fail Safe* (1962). Textbook accounts of 1950s science fiction cinema, like the one by Victoria O'Donnell in Peter Lev's overview volume of the 1950s (*The Fifties: Transforming the Screen, 1950–1959*), still come with programmatic titles like "Science Fiction Films and Cold War Anxiety," and rightly so. Holding together the cultural diversity, the rich phantasmagoric tapestry, of 1950s America is the tight framework of the Cold War, and thus of the military.[7]

If American popular culture of the 1950s is framed by the Cold War, then it is hardly surprising that science fiction films of the period would have the military on their mind. In Robert Wise's *The Day the Earth Stood Still* (1951), it is the military that places Washington, DC, under lockdown when the alien ambassador, having landed on the White House lawn, goes AWOL. In Gordon Douglas's *Them!* (1954), it is the military, in collaboration with state and federal law enforcement, that goes up against the giant mutated ants nesting in the Los Angeles sewer system. In Christian Nyby's *The Thing from Another World* (1951), it is the military—with help from scientists, newspapermen, and assorted civilians—that discovers, unleashes, and then destroys the alien creature. Some films get even more specific when it comes to the different branches of the military. Thus, it is the US Air Force which heroically and tragically launches Robert Day's eponymous *First Man into Space* (1959), just as it is the US Navy which sends Spencer Gordon Bennet's *The Atomic Submarine* (1959) on its mission below and across the polar ice. Even the crew of the spaceship in Fred M. Wilcox's *Forbidden Planet* (1956), which is never explicitly identified as a military vessel, is a tight unit organized by military rank and discipline. Francis D. Lyon's *Cult of the Cobra* (1955) features a group of American GIs at the end of World War II and the exotic creature wreaking havoc among them after their return to civilian life, just as Roy Del Ruth's *The Alligator People* (1959) tells the story of a couple of newlyweds who, having met during their military service in World War II, must now face the monstrous consequences of their past experiences. Taking its cue from cinema, television does not stand aside either. Vast and secret projects conducting cutting-edge research—from the various scientific projects scattered across episodes of *The Outer Limits* (1963–65) to the eponymous *Time Tunnel* (Irwin Allen, 1966–67)—are always and inevitably financed and overseen by the military. In some films, the military comes in late in the game or hovers around the edges of the story; Don Siegel's *Invasion of the Body Snatchers* (1956) ends with the prospect of national mobilization against the alien invasion (thanks to a framing device famously added as an upbeat afterthought to a downbeat story). There are a few films from which the military is conspicuously absent, though. In Gene Fowler Jr.'s *I Married a Monster from Outer Space* (1958), for example, a group of red-blooded male vigilantes drives back an alien invasion; no military intervention is necessary. More representative for the cycle as a whole, however, are films like William Cameron Menzies's *Invaders from Mars* (1953) or Byron Haskin's *War of the Worlds* (1953), which offer their audience extended and spectacular military action.

While science fiction in general does not come with a built-in affinity for military action, some 1950s films are borrowing prodigiously from the war film. *War of the Worlds* and *Invaders from Mars*, for example, feel almost as much like war films as science fiction. They feature soldiers as characters, portray military life in general, are preoccupied with combat and violent conflict, and are structuring their respective narratives around invasion and conquest. Other genres lend themselves to the same cross-fertilization. Depending on their historical backdrop, period drama and even the biblical epic allow for military themes. Similarly, the Western has a special niche reserved for stories about the Indian wars, or it draws on the American Civil War, or it explores the Spanish American War. Just as these genres discuss issues of the day by displacing them on to other historical periods, science fiction films from the 1950s resort to imaginary conflicts and imaginary enemies, be they invading space aliens or giant mutated creatures. Whenever the actual realities of war might sour an audience on the enjoyment of imaginary wars, cinematic genres capable of generic displacement seem to flourish. From the safe distance of metaphor or allegory, they comment on historical events that are too close to discern clearly, too frightening to contemplate, or too painful to remember for any literal representation.[8] All around and right behind the 1950s allegories of war, there is the lived experience of an audience that remembers World War II and the Korean War and is immersed in the prolonged, excruciating suspense of the Cold War.

To be clear, with their strong and pervasive military theme, science fiction films of the 1950s do not offer a substitute for the war film per se. Thomas Schatz has drawn attention to the "rapid phasing out of the war film, and particularly the combat drama," which meant that "by the summer of 1946 not a single war film was in release or in production" and that, after 1946, "war film production stalled completely for several years" (368). This slump testifies to the American audience's fatigue with the war and thus with stories about the war. With the run-up to the Korean War, however, the slump was over. David Halberstam calls that war "a godsend" for those who had "badly wanted a massive increase in the defense budget" (*Coldest Winter* 95). The war film's comeback marks the start of the remilitarization of American life after these few exceptional intermediary years. This return to a war footing also happened to coincide with the horror genre looking for a new mode, a new relevance, after wartime horror films had run their course (and finding that mode when they would merge with science fiction, a genre that had not yet come into its own and, consequently, had enjoyed little attention in the cinema in previous years).[9] The fact that the return of the war film as a viable Hollywood genre and the start of a new cycle of science fiction films happen to occur more or less simultaneously around the transition from the 1940s to the 1950s testifies to a broader remilitarization of American culture marked by the Korean War. War films of the late 1940s and early 1950s remain rooted in the experience of World War II, even after the genre's half decade long hiatus; the Korean War's visual similarity to World War II may have helped this trend along. To the degree that the 1950s war film failed to get updated by confronting the new military and political idiosyncrasies of the Cold War, the films' ideological content, transferred from one genre to the other, also reached back to the experience of World War II—a strange anachronism, if you think about it. A certain type of war provides the paradigm for the late 1940s war film, and that paradigm is World War II and not the Cold War.

Just as in the case of the war film, science fiction films of the 1950s come as hawks and doves. As Tom Engelhardt notes, in

> the science fiction films that prospered in the 1950s, exclusionary villains came from the other side of borders previously unimagined and unerringly headed for (or burst to life in) the United States with mayhem in mind [. . .] On the other hand, in the inclusionary mode, similar beasts or robots or space aliens turned out to be, if not lovable, then far wiser than Americans [. . .] The

exclusionary films were apocalyptic and hysterical about them; the inclusionary ones about us. In either case, every stand in these films was potentially the last one. (102)[10]

For every film like *Invaders from Mars* (1953), in which the tone is triumphant and complimentary, and in which the military comes in to fight the decisive battle on behalf of humanity, protect innocent civilians, and save the day, there is a film like *The Day the Earth Stood Still* (1951), in which a nervous soldier pulls the trigger when the alien visitor in front of the White House pulls out what looks like a gun, gunning down a peaceful ambassador about to make a gesture of interstellar goodwill. Understandably, the US Army declined to support the making of *The Day the Earth Stood Still*; its portrait of the military—aided by an equally hysterical law enforcement community, which, in turn, is aided by an upstanding citizen the film makes out to be a morally corrupt informer—is far from complimentary. *War of the Worlds* (1953), meanwhile, imagines a prolonged battle of the military against the Martian invaders. Ultimately the military fails in its mission, and humanity is crushed and overrun in one humiliating defeat after another. In films less geared toward spectacular combat, like *Cult of the Cobra* (1955) or *The Thing from Another World* (1951), the military provides the space for action—an air force base, a scientific research station in some far-flung corner of the globe—or the space for community, as army buddies bond with each other and bicker about their superiors and the army's way of doing things. In the final instance, all of these films depend on the military: as an indispensable principle of organization (effective or wastefully authoritarian), camaraderie (authentic and spontaneous or institutionally mandated and compelled by shared danger), and source of moral communal values (loyalty, reliability, discipline, and so forth).[11]

If we search 1950s science fiction films for such representations of the military, the pattern that emerges could hardly be clearer. Steadily and with increasing popular success, they incorporate the military into their generic repertoire. This happens at the same time when the war film is regaining its popularity, after an immediate post-World War II slump, around the time of the Korean War. Military themes may have flickered through science fiction cinema prior to the 1950s, but they were not a dominant concern. In the horror film, they played no significant role at all. Only when science fiction and horror merge in the 1950s would their hideous progeny show an interest in the military unprecedented by each genre separately. Science fiction during the 1950s would thus participate in, and presumably contribute to, the remilitarization of American culture, first in the cinema and then on television. Just as in the Western, the enemy might have been a figure of displacement, thinly allegorized as Indians or space aliens, standing in for Germans and Japanese, North Koreans, Russians, or Chinese. The American military standing up to them, however, would be all too real, literally and recognizably itself.

Historical Context: The Military-Industrial Complex at Home

Any overview of the US after World War II that tries to answer the question of what role the military played in the life of the nation will have to pay attention to what was on television on January 17, 1961. On that date, the TV audience was treated to President Dwight D. Eisenhower's farewell address. After two terms in office, the president was looking back over nearly a decade in which he had been the face of the nation. Far from waxing nostalgically, however, Eisenhower took the opportunity to introduce a new term into the public debate that was to have tremendous staying power. That term was the "military-industrial complex." Though Eisenhower was hardly the first to recognize what was to become a serious political issue, the naming of this phenomenon by such a highly visible, prestigious political figure resulted in the term's resonance in decades to come. Though it would drift in and out of focus with the shifting circumstances of US foreign policy, its lack of precision might have ensured its longevity as much as its continuing relevance. Though defined broadly enough to inspire a scholarly debate about what exactly Eisenhower had meant (or, for that matter, who among his script writers had been responsible for coming up with it), the term nonetheless came to define primarily the period summarized in the address, the 1950s Eisenhower himself oversaw as Commander in Chief.

"We now stand ten years past the midpoint of a century," Eisenhower reminds his audience, "that has witnessed four major wars among great nations. Three of these involved our own country. Despite these holocausts, America is today the strongest, the most influential, and most productive nation in the world" (qtd. in Ledbetter 212–13). Following this reference to the collective memories of World War II and the Korean War is an evocation of America's Cold War enemy, a "hostile ideology," as Eisenhower calls it, "global in scope, atheistic in character, ruthless in purpose, and insidious in method" (213). The phrasing leaves no doubt that, against such enemy, the US must guard itself with a standing army and an extensive arsenal.

The Friendly Face of Post-World War II Remilitarization: Dwight and Mamie Eisenhower. Source: Eisenhower Presidential Library.

The deployment of this arsenal at short notice must, in turn, be advertised by way of an assertive, maybe even aggressive foreign policy posture. To this end—and this is where the address turns a corner both thematically as well as tonally—America has "been compelled to create a permanent armaments industry of vast proportions," aided by "three and a half million men and women [. . .] directly engaged in the defense establishment" (215). It is this network of military hardware, advanced technology, and a vast and diverse array of human resources, grounded in the interaction between politics and private industry, which emerges as the target of Eisenhower's concern. "In the councils of government," he continues in what is perhaps the address's most famous and frequently cited passage,

> we must guard the acquisition of unwarranted influence, whether sought or unsought, by the military-industrial complex [. . .] We must never let the weight of this combination endanger our liberties or democratic processes [. . .] Only an alert and knowledgeable citizenry can compel the proper meshing of the huge industrial and military machinery of defense with our peaceful methods and goals, so that security and liberty may prosper together. (216)

Historians who have pondered this speech have arrived at a variety of conclusions about Eisenhower's intentions. It is safe to say that, at the most basic level, the "unwarranted influence" Eisenhower warns against stems from individual and, more important, corporate economic power parlayed into political influence. This force might steer processes of decision-making that should, constitutionally, be regulated by democratic elections, creating, as James Ledbetter puts it, "a network of public and private forces that combine a profit motive with the planning and implementation of strategic policy" (6). Obviously, it "is either ironic or contradictory or hypocritical that the man who first sounded a warning against a 'military-industrial complex' was, by any definition, a leading figure in that complex" (4). In fact, John Bodnar concedes that, in historical hindsight, Eisenhower would come "to represent the idea that it was acceptable to hold deep reservations about American military power and about the very idea of war" (81). With this systemic insight, Eisenhower did provide a useful model for understanding how America went from the systematic militarization of virtually all aspects of life during World War II, through the wholesale demilitarization of the American economy immediately following the end of that war, only to return to the "total war footing" of World War II during the Korean War (Ledbetter 57). This newly re-established "total war footing" was to become entrenched as the permanent state of crisis, the indefinitely suspended apocalyptic catastrophe, the unnatural state of affairs that was the Cold War.

To be absolutely clear: Eisenhower's remarks are tailored to a narrow range of interactions between corporate, military, and political power yoked together by the Cold War's imperatives. Starting from this foundation, however, other political thinkers of the period would then extend that range of interactions in their own analysis to describe a more far-reaching militarization of American life—one in which corporate, military, and political forces are surrounded by a larger social, cultural, and ideological realm. C. Wright Mills, in his book *The Power Elite* (1956), for example, devotes two chapters ("The Warlords" 171–97; "The Military Ascendency" 198–224) to the newly increased significance of the military as one of America's ruling elites, taking its place among chief executives, heads of corporations, celebrities, or good old "high society." While economic forces "and political climate [. . .] have historically favoured the civilian devaluation of the military as an at-times necessary evil but always a burden" (176), Mills writes, the broad prospect of being permanently and "technically open to catastrophic attack upon the national domain" (183) has transformed this cautious attitude toward the military. What used to be a "parasitical" class (175)

Chrysler Advertisement in *Life* Magazine: An Economy on Permanent War Footing

has now grown into a class invested with broad political powers to match the economic ones brought to the table by private companies, especially in the arms industry, which function as its corporate sponsors. Beyond this recapitulation of Eisenhower's political and economic argument, Mills goes one step further. He argues that, in effect, "virtually the entire population is involved in war, as soldiers or as civilians—which means that they are disciplined in a hierarchy at whose head there sit the warlords of Washington" (189). In other words, American postwar militarization occurs not just as a political and bureaucratic phenomenon. It also involves a broad ideological foundation—something that Mills refers to, in all its inevitability, as "military metaphysics" (202). The final product of these shifts and changes is "a nation whose elite and whose underlying population have accepted what can only be called a military definition of reality" (198).

Unlike Eisenhower's cut-and-dried political and economic critique, Mills's insistence on "the military definition of reality" or "the military metaphysics" refers more to an outlook, a frame of mind, and a set of social and cultural practices. Mills helps to produce a broader concept that aligns itself with the term "military-industrial complex" as brought into circulation by Eisenhower. In other words, Mills extends and broadens the concept from the economic, political, and social toward the cultural and, more broadly, ideological. Mills defines the militarization of American society as

Life in 1950s America: The Comfortable Coexistence of Consumerism and Apocalypse

something manifesting itself not only in surface phenomena (e.g., defense budgets, the reliance on military force in matters of foreign policy, etc.) but also on a more fundamental level, and thus with more pervasive power (e.g., in the adoption on military discipline as a basic model of social organization, the acceptance of state secrecy as a foundational principle of spatial and institutional organization, etc.). This newly defined concept is extremely useful for the analysis of American culture because it allows for the critical consideration of uniquely American forms of militarization, forms that deviate from popular ideas of what militarism ordinarily looks like. Throughout the 1950s, for example, *Life* magazine would run stories about military matters—the launching of America's first nuclear submarine by Mrs. Eisenhower, the construction of Arctic listening stations, the invention of new super-weapons, the torturous testing of physical and psychological endurance limits in air force pilots. These stories would run side by side with celebrity gossip, fashion reports, and sentimental human interest pieces.¹² Conversely, military manufacturers like Lockheed Martin would place advertisements in the magazine which, at times, were difficult to distinguish from official reporting about military hardware. The same blurring of boundaries would also take place on television. An episode of the show *Tales of Tomorrow* (ABC, 1951–53) entitled "Blunder" (August 10, 1951) would feature a commercial during the lead-in. The commercial would be asking viewers to sponsor CARE packages for the starving refugees streaming into West Berlin and West Germany from behind the Iron Curtain. At midpoint, the program would then run a commercial for United States Savings Bonds, referred to as "Defense Bonds," as part of a Payroll Savings Plan, which linked the assurance of steady employment directly to the arms industry. All of this would be tied together with the episode's plot about a nuclear scientist inadvertently blowing up the Earth after efforts by the scientific community had failed to warn him in time against the dangers of his experiment (written by Philip Wylie). Just as in *Life* magazine, the flow of ABC's programming consistently erased boundaries between science, the military, and Cold War politics in advertising and programming.

The casual coexistence or even mutual interpenetration within the same media space of civilian and military matters might serve as an index of the military-industrial complex's pervasiveness. Within the framework of what Mills calls the "military definition of reality," the normalization of military matters as an indispensable part of American life might take idiosyncratic forms. Whereas, for example, the introduction of mandatory loyalty oaths for certain professional groups during the 1950s fits into the stereotypical conception of a militarized society, the general absence of mandatory school uniforms from public education during the same time does not.¹³ The nation throughout most of the 1950s might have had a president in the White House whose political career was launched by his substantial achievements during World War II (rather than his brief stint as president of Columbia University), and yet voters rejected another general—Douglas MacArthur, celebrated on the political right, especially after being dismissed from his post by Eisenhower during the Korean War—in his brief bid for a political career. While US Cold War imperialism is hardly debated as an adjunct to the military-industrial complex, the American avoidance of military invasion and occupation as a method of such imperialism, especially after the experience of the Korean War, is not. Critics have had to contend with the peculiar fact that US foreign policy initiatives for winning "hearts and minds" would usually take place at the point of someone else's bayonet.¹⁴ Only a concept as broad and flexible as Mills's "military metaphysics" can accommodate the

MacArthur Speaking at Soldier's Field, Chicago: A General's Aborted Political Career. Source: National Archives via pingnews.

idiosyncratic methods and manifestations of the military-industrial complex in postwar America. This is, to be clear, not a conspiracy theory about a secretive cabal taking over the nation. At their worst, theories enthralled by Eisenhower's concept can have a decisively paranoid touch. Extended by Mills's, though, Eisenhower's provides a useful tool for reading large political, economic, and cultural trends, playing themselves out in the open arena of political debate and popular entertainment during the 1950s. To avoid all confusion, let me be clear about it: for the purposes of all further discussion, this expanded definition—a definition which relies primarily on Mills's revision of Eisenhower's concept to include social, cultural, and ideological matters beyond those that strictly and narrowly apply to economics and politics—is the one I have in mind whenever I will be using the term "military-industrial complex" in this book.[15]

Historical Context: The Military-Industrial Complex Abroad

No one paying attention to the economics of the military-industrial complex could have been surprised that the domestic sphere would not be able to contain its "unwarranted influence." Predicated on the capitalist imperative of growth and expansion, the military-industrial complex would claim for itself a far more extensive sphere of operation than the US itself. After the US cast off the last vestiges of its pre-World War II isolationism, it would conduct rehearsals for the American Century on the beaches of Normandy, during the island-hopping campaign in the Pacific, and during its lasting military presence in parts of Europe, Asia, and Africa after the conclusion of World War II. As Chalmers Johnson points out, at "the height of the Cold War," the US' territorial moves during World War II would be cemented as "a chain of military bases stretching from Korea and Japan through Taiwan, the Philippines, Thailand, and Australia to Saudi Arabia, Turkey, Greece, Italy, Spain, Portugal, Germany, England, and Iceland—in effect ringing the Soviet Union and China with literally thousands of overseas military installations" (*Blowback* 36). Just as the war had reordered domestic space in the interest of the emergent military-industrial complex, it would expand the reach of American military power and political influence across the globe. This expansion proved so successful that the bitter rivalry with the Soviet Union, as the central fact of global politics after World War II, would hardly be able to account for the workings of the military-industrial complex as manifested through US foreign policy.

Conservative historians reading American engagement with the rest of the world during the Cold War still subscribe to the bipolar rivalry as the basic structuring conflict at work. Ideology, within this model, precedes politics. Odd Arne Westad in his book *The Global Cold War: Third World Interventions and the Making of Our Times* (2007), for example, argues for an ideological equivalence of the US and the Soviet Union, based upon "the ideologies inherent in their politics" held with equal honesty and conviction on both sides (4). Both systems, according to Westad, were poised against each other as rival models of modernity. Each employed similar strategies ("the political and cultural seduction of local elites, access to local markets, and military aid and training" [25]). And in their zeal and sense of historical messianic self-importance, both were willing to overlook without "the slightest hint of irony given their own practices" (32) the difference between authentic ideals and self-serving pragmatism. Westad even cites the historical timeline as evidence for this equivalence: just as Henry Luce's famous editorial on the American Century would predate US military victory in Europe and the Pacific, "Soviet planning for the postwar world began as soon as the German offensive ground to a halt in 1942" (57).

Regardless of this theory's persuasiveness, however, even Westad's acknowledgment of the shared aims, methods, and conflicts of the US and the Soviet Union contains the seeds of a different historical narrative. In this alternative story, as Dale Carter tells it, "the emergence of the Cold War may be interpreted not simply as a tragic conflict between powers but also as a form of international organization required inside the post-imperial structure" (28). This version of the story de-emphasizes the rivalry and aggression between both superpowers and instead focuses on the collaborative aspects of their relationship. Unlike the violent and costly crushing of Japanese imperial ambitions that began at Pearl Harbor in 1941—the geographic flashpoint where the US' military foray westward across the Pacific and the Japanese expansion of the Asian Pacific Co-Prosperity Sphere eastward would violently collide with each other—US Cold War policy regarding the Soviet Union successfully avoided direct military conflict for decades. Moments of escalation, such as the Cuban Missile Crisis, may be cited as evidence for how close the world would perpetually be to the brink of war. But in its actual historical progression, even the Cuban Missile Crisis ultimately represents a moment of the two nations *not* going to war. Just as World War III would never happen as the result of the Cuban Missile Crisis, conflicts between both superpowers were, at best, resolved in proxy wars. The failed invasion of Cuba at the Bay of Pigs, for example, is a far more representative moment in Cold War history than the Cuban Missile Crisis. More often than not, however, the US would avoid even those proxy wars, whenever they would become costly. For every covert engagement in response to, for example, the Soviet invasion of Afghanistan, there would be a relatively moderate (some might say shamefully toothless) diplomatic response to the Soviet invasion of Hungary, the Prague Spring, or the worker's uprising in East Germany. Despite various labels like "containment" or, more aggressively, "rollback," the collaborative aspect of the Cold War balance successfully installed and maintained political, bureaucratic, and technocratic elites on both sides of the Iron Curtain. These elites were, after all, mutually dependent upon a sustained rhetoric of threat and crisis. The stability of this global system would then allow each supposed rival to expand its respective sphere of influence to the point where expansion would not destabilize the larger balance. Within this carefully counterbalanced sphere it would then be possible to implement policy with unrestrained self-interest. What Carter calls "a form of international organization required inside the post-imperial structure" was, therefore, not so much a bitter struggle between mortal enemies. Instead, it was a convenient power-sharing arrangement of competitors who knew all too well that symmetrical warfare in the age of nuclear weapons would yield no useful result.

In a detailed analysis of "the basic US Cold War document, NSC 68" (10), Paul Nitze's position paper on US foreign policy released in April 1950, Noam Chomsky agrees with Westad's equivalency argument. Chomsky explains that, on the side of the Soviet Union, "the Cold War served to entrench the power of the military-bureaucratic elite whose rule derives from the Bolshevik coup of October 1917" (20), while, on the side of the US, "the domestic counterpart has been the entrenchment of Eisenhower's 'military-industrial complex'" (21). Not surprisingly, however, Chomsky disagrees with Westad when it comes to the idealistic, and frequently illogical, tautological, and self-fulfilling rhetoric in a document like NSC 68. For Chomsky, pragmatic self-interest overrides ideology. Hence, he argues that "the Depression was overcome [not by the New Deal, but by] far more massive state intervention during the war"—an intervention that was to produce a "quasi-totalitarian wartime command economy" (21). Consequently, the US would not aggressively and militarily intervene to contain Soviet ideology, but would do so only to shore up its own economy by creating, defending, and expanding manufacturing bases and foreign markets for its own domestic exports. The battleground for such interventions would never be the Soviet Union or its satellite states, but, by and large, would be the so-called Third World. In the final instance, Chomsky concludes his analysis,

> for the USSR, the Cold War has been primarily a war against its satellites, and for the US a war against the Third World. For each, it has served to entrench a particular system of domestic privilege and coercion. The policies pursued within the Cold War framework have been unattractive to the general population, which accepts them only under duress [. . .] The Cold War has a functional utility for the superpowers: one reason why it persisted. (28).[16]

The real threat to the United States during the Cold War, Chomsky concludes, were nations that refused to align themselves with the US and its global ambitions; "economic nationalism" rather than communism is the prime target of Cold War containment. Wherever it arises, it "elicits US hostility," and whenever possible, "the culprit is assigned to the Bolshevik conspiracy to destroy Western civilization" (45). The result of these priorities is thus not symmetrical warfare against an enemy of equal strength, but asymmetrical warfare against a host of lesser nations unwilling to comply. The arsenal for these wars is conventional, not nuclear.

The difference between Westad's and Chomsky's reading of Cold War history opens up a gap between the ideological view of political agency on the one hand, and its pragmatic reality on the other. If Chomsky is correct in his assessment that "policies pursued within the Cold War framework have been unattractive to the general population, which accepts them only under duress," then the ideological framework to which Westad is attaching so much importance is not likely to be the causal force behind foreign policy. They may, however, provide a public narrative that legitimizes (unattractive) foreign policy. As long as the general population consents to the ideological legitimization—accurate or not—the high costs of imposing actual "duress" on the population may be minimized. In this sense, Westad's story about the bitter ideological rivalry between the US and the Soviet Union would be simple and morally self-righteous, driven by a clear fable about combating a demonized other. In contrast, Chomsky's story about asymmetrical warfare by the US against Third World nations in the interests of an economic elite and in balanced cooperation with a corresponding elite in the Soviet Union is not only morally dubious, it also challenges the comfortable distinction between us and them, as well as the simplicity of simple and straightforward bipolar global politics. Given the intense preoccupation of 1950s popular culture with nuclear war and communist subversion, it seems clear that Westad's—not Chomsky's—historical narrative is the one capturing the zeitgeist of America in this phase of the Cold War. If Chomsky's historical analysis can be considered a counter-narrative to the dominant one, it is, in fact, the ideological function of the conservative Cold War narrative to distract from, drown out, or repress its uncomfortable alternative. The question that arises is whether popular culture, to the degree that it aligns itself with the dominant ideological reference points in its historical context, can be expected to express alternative views, especially if they are disturbing and undesirable.[17]

Given Eisenhower's concerns about the spread of the military-industrial complex's "unwarranted influence" and Mills's indictment of the "military metaphysics" that goes hand in hand with it, no one can be surprised that 1950s American cinema had the military on its mind. That this cultural centrality of the military would spring from World War II is not surprising. What is surprising is that it would endure during the postwar years, a period in which, with the brief exception of the Korean War, no direct military confrontation was to take place. The historical trajectory of these years is strangely suspended between rising and falling interest, support, and enthusiasm versus all things military. There is the initial triumph in World War II, followed by a brief interval of substantial demobilization. This is followed by remilitarization on the vague and problematic pretext of the Korean War, and eventually by permanent militarization by way of the military-industrial complex in the indeterminate and ambivalent state of imminent conflict during the Cold War. Incoherent and multifaceted as this period of transition from World War II via the Korean War and into the Cold War might appear, it is culturally overshadowed by one central emblematic military technology—the bomb. Again, all three periods mark a transition: from America's acquisition and deployment of nuclear weapons against Japan at the end of World War II (August 1945), to their acquisition by the Soviet Union (August 1949), their serious political consideration of their use during the Korean War (1950–53), and their rapid proliferation on both sides, and eventual acquisition by other nations (Britain in 1956; France 1960; China 1964), during the Cold War. Given the increasing significance of nuclear weapons in the arsenal of the US military after 1945, and the concomitant anxieties caused by the Soviet Union's acquisition of the bomb by 1949, the hyperbolic cultural response they triggered within postwar American culture is easily understandable. Just as the bomb cast a long shadow over all military matters within the first decade after World War II, realigning American foreign policy and military strategy alongside its possibilities and limitations, it also casts a shadow over 1950s popular culture, whether explicitly interested in military matters or not.

Flashblindness: The Representational Challenges of Nuclear War

The advent of the bomb seemed to turn the end of World War II into a kind of Zero Hour, a watershed moment that radically cut the present and the future off from the past. Historical continuity had become yet another casualty of the bomb, and cinema stepped up to recognize this fact. In a scene from William Wyler's *The Best Years of Our Lives* (1946), a returning veteran hands his son some trophies he has collected from Japanese soldiers. Well-intentioned, the gesture is greeted with incomprehension from the boy. Instead of showing interest in his father's World War II experiences, he expresses fascination and dread with the Cold War. Talk about nuclear war had been a subject in school while his father was absent, and it is nuclear war, not World War II, that now preoccupies the boy. Similarly, Stanley Kramer's *Judgment at Nuremberg* (1961) ends with the Nuremberg war criminal trials being overshadowed by the incipient blockage of West Berlin by the Soviet Union in 1948. The film leaves open the question about the historical significance of the criminal proceedings against leading Nazi functionaries, but it is clear that the more pressing issue of the day is the rising tensions between the US and the Soviet Union. The Cold War takes precedence over World War II; concentration camps and genocidal war are replaced in public consciousness by the atom bomb.[18]

Given how much the bomb looms over 1950s American culture, it is hardly surprising that science fiction films of the period—especially since they already show such great interest in military themes—seem as obsessed with the bomb as American popular culture at large appears to be. As mushroom clouds hover over alien invasion and giant creature films, radioactive fallout caused by nuclear testing comes to the rescue of every scriptwriter in need of a plausible explanation for grotesque human deformities, animal gigantism, and a grab bag of other inexplicable phenomena and transformations of the modern world. For writers and directors, the bomb's practical uses seem endless. In many films its appearance is surprisingly casual. Nuclear fallout can be mentioned in a throwaway line of dialogue or a passing reference that is barely explored. Its presence can be sanctioned with a nod, as if to say, "Oh nuclear fallout: that again!" Given this matter-of-factness, one would assume that the bomb had quickly become a normal part of daily lives. Still, even the most casual reference betrays a deeper level of concern if it appears in a culture that, on the whole, cannot stop talking about the bomb. All this attention is a sign of insecurity in the face of subject matter that resists representation and, even worse, proves to be difficult to put on film. However, the nature of nuclear weapons itself, in combination with the political context of their deployment, creates just such representational challenges.

Critics who read 1950s science fiction films primarily as hyperbolic responses to the rise of the nuclear age have to contend with the fact that "Americans in general remained largely ignorant of the details of nuclear war throughout the decade [i.e., the 1950s], as the American government maintained an extremely restrictive, even repressive control of the dissemination of such information" (Booker, *Monsters* 66). In addition, nuclear weapons pose representational problems for conventional Hollywood narratives. Ubiquitous as Geiger counters, atom bombs, and references to radiation are in these films, nuclear discourse does not translate easily into cinematic images. As David Halberstam has put it, "Given the fact that in all World War Two only 3 million tons of TNT had been used, *the imagination could scarcely comprehend* this new destructive power [of the hydrogen bomb]" (*The Fifties* 29, my emphasis). Before addressing historical specifics, let me begin with a more abstract formal and aesthetic consideration, which, nonetheless, grounds much of the historical context that follows. Summarizing arguments made at "'the institution of Nuclear Criticism', proposed at a Cornell University conference and in a subsequent *diacritics* special number in 1984" (45), Aaron Rosenberg points to the obvious fact that "total nuclear war names an event that has never as yet happened in history, an event about which there cannot be any direct experience" (46). In the absence of a concrete historical referent, nuclear discourse finds itself confronted with the problem of having to perform a task of representation in which an event must precede its textual account, even if that account announces itself as occurring within the realm of fiction. Hence, the reality produced by nuclear discourse is a specifically *textual* reality. It evokes and shapes reality as much as it can be said to "reflect" it. Taking his cue from Jacques Derrida, one of the contributors to the project, Rosenberg acknowledges the close proximity of language and nuclear weaponry by recognizing "the unprecedented capacity [of nuclear weapons] to weaponize language itself" (46). He concludes that "nuclear weapons systems expose themselves to the same aporias that belong to language practices in general." Or, as Charles Gannon puts it, the bomb is "an absolute destroyer both of physical and conceptual boundaries and restraints" (112). From this otherwise lamentable fact, Derrida derives the hope for the "the rigorous application of *textual* criticism and interpretation [as] essential to developing an understanding of the cultural logic of the 'nuclear age'" (Rosenberg 45). In visual terms, the appropriate metaphor for this complex of representational challenges might be "flashblindness": given "the visual intensity of a nuclear explosion, which reaches the brilliance of thousand midday suns," any human observer trying to look directly at the phenomenon will suffer "lesions on the eye and permanent blindness" (Masco 9–10). Barring the intervention of representational technologies, direct perception is impossible.

In reading the science fiction films of the 1950s said to be obsessed with the nuclear age, we might want to expand Rosenberg's thumbnail sketch of the representational challenges posed by the "cultural logic of the 'nuclear age'" from language to other forms of representation, especially that of the cinematic image. One would have also have to factor in the concrete political and historical conditions under which cinema meets the challenge of speaking the unspeakable, imagining the unimaginable, and making real that "event about which there cannot be any direct experience" (Rosenberg 46). Ironically enough, starting in 1945, it was not the overabundance of detailed and accurate information on nuclear weapons that imposed restrictions upon representation, but the lack thereof, specifically in regard to the bombs dropped, respectively, on Hiroshima and Nagasaki.[19] Their development by way of the Manhattan Project had taken place under the strictest measures of national security. Research and production facilities had been spread out across different states. Scientists and other personnel were kept in the dark as to the overall shape of the project to which, individually, they would be contributing ideas and labor. This lack of specific information would not be remedied significantly with President Truman's televised announcement of the deployment of this new and awesome weapon on August 6, 1945. Though the US military brought in scientists to the two drop sites to study the effects of the weapons, the information they gathered would remain largely classified. The occupational military government of defeated Japan, under the leadership of General Douglas MacArthur, would extend this policy of information control and containment for months afterward, especially in regard to visual documentation of the specific impact of the bomb on the human body.[20]

When television became a more widespread medium starting in the early 1950s, its reporting on nuclear tests were riddled with the same tension between the audience's desire to see and the medium's ability to deliver satisfactory images. In his study of American television during the McCarthy era, Thomas Doherty provides a brief history of American television broadcasts of nuclear detonations in the early 1950s (8–13). The first of these broadcasts, by Los Angeles stations KTLA and KTTV on February 6, 1951, produced images for broadcast via a television camera at a distance of roughly 250 miles from the explosion itself. Disappointingly, "the cameras caught 'the flash of eerie white light,'" and little else (Doherty 8). The next broadcast was on April 22, 1952, from an explosion in Yucca Flats, Nevada. It resulted in

> a flash that, for a few seconds, blackened TV screens with a dark penumbra around the central point of light that was the blast, as was reported by the trade magazine *Broadcasting/Telecasting*. Viewers squinted to discern a tiny white spot in a wall of pitch black, unaware that the white pinhole centered in the blackness resulted from an optical malfunction: the orthicon tube in the pickup camera had blacked out under the blinding light of the blast. (9)

Viewers complained about the bad quality of the image. March 17, 1953, saw another broadcast from Yucca Flat, emceed by Walter Cronkite for CBS, Chet Huntley from ABC, and Morgan Beatty for NBC. The explosion was staged in "a fabricated two-household community dubbed 'Doom Town' [...] with nuclear family mannequins occupying each abode, standing upright, not sitting around a television set" (10). Again, Doherty notes, the television image was reported to have "wobbled" and "blacked out" temporarily, though the image returned soon enough for viewers to catch a glimpse of the mushroom cloud forming in the aftermath of the blast.[21]

Aside from the lack of concrete information, films from the 1950s also had to contend with the problem that Hiroshima and Nagasaki posed in regard to the historical narrative that separated the end of World War II from the Cold War. These narratives would have been essential in establishing a categorical distinction between the actual deployment of nuclear weapons against Japan and the projected deployment of nuclear weapons either by the Soviet Union or by the US against the Soviet Union. The defensive posture of US nuclear strategy at the time was clear; after all, what had been called the Department of War during World War II had, as part of the reorganization mandated by the National Security Act of 1947, been renamed the Department of Defense. Hence, postwar scenarios that would feature the use of nuclear weapons by the US needed to imply a prior attack on the nation, presumably with nuclear weapons as well. Ruling out any narratives that would involve nuclear weapons used in the course of conquest or territorial expansion, the remaining scenarios would have to be limited to the ones in which the US is victimized by a sneak attack before retaliating righteously. Narratives predicated on the US' victimization—a trope that extends from 1950s science fiction films all the way to films like *The Day After* (Nicholas Meyer, 1983) or *Red Dawn* (John Milius, 1984)— lend themselves to casting the world's leading superpower in the role of the underdog. It's fair to say that this is a vision of America so useful to domestic and foreign policy as to be virtually indispensable for the nation's image of itself.[22] However, this option carries unwelcome connotations of a masochistic surrender to another nation's force that is difficult to reconcile with nationalistic pride in the superior US military arsenal. Inevitably, though, the subsequent rise of the underdog would allow that narrative to conclude with the reassurance that a masochistically victimized nation would eventually be re-masculinized by an act of violence and thus returned to a state of aggressive agency. Nonetheless, such narrative closure would have to work hard to erase any lingering sense of the prior victimization needed to justify the resurgence and retaliatory sadistic violence.

As information about the bomb gradually became more widely available throughout the late 1950s, the growing awareness of its peculiar qualities proved to be problematic. This was especially true for a cinematic tradition of representing combat in war films based on conventional weapons, a genre that had come into its own during World War II. There were persistent fantasies within the military and the larger population about so-called tactical nuclear weapons—that is, devices with limited range, to be deployed by tanks or even by hand-held battlefield weapons. These scenarios would give rise to the idea of a limited, winnable war. In reality, though, nuclear weapons proved to be useful only for deployment by way of strategic bombers and missiles against civilian populations.

> In June 1947 the Joint Chiefs of Staff sent a top secret report, "The Evaluation of the Atomic Bob as a Military Weapon," to President Truman [. . .] "Ships at sea and bodies of troops are, in general, unlikely to be regarded as primary bomb targets," the report concluded. "The bomb is pre-eminently a weapon for use against human life and activities in large urban and industrial areas." The report suggested that a nuclear attack would stir up "man's primordial fears" and "break the will of nations." The military significance of the atomic bomb was clear: it wouldn't be aimed at the military. Nuclear weapons would be used to destroy an enemy's morale, and the [sic] some of the best targets were "cities of especial sentimental significance." (Schlosser 81–82)

The essential military posture of both the US and the Soviet Union depended on nuclear deterrence, the balance of power, and mutual assured destruction. It had already embraced the bomb essentially as a terror weapon, a means of coercion to be used in the exploration of political and diplomatic routes of negotiation. As the ultimate blunt instrument, wielding it would be hardly any less problematic than being the one against it would be wielded. Obviously, this was a fact that nuclear disarmament campaigners would never tire to emphasize. If, consequently, the use of such weapons by the US would have to be stripped of their unsavory connotations of state terrorism, cinematic narratives would have to find ways to suppress this unsettling knowledge as well. In order to understand science fiction films of the period, it is useful to spend some time looking at what else is going on in American cinema that has to do with war and, especially, nuclear war.[23]

Films which, against all representational odds, decide to visualize an atomic attack produce images that confirm the Derridean theory about the breakdown of signification under the impact of nuclear technology. In the television production *Atomic Attack* (Ralph Nelson, 1954), the bright light from outside a basement window of the suburban stage set, the shaking of the camera, and the hapless tossing around of housewife Gladys Mitchell (Phyllis Thaxter) fall woefully short of the dramatic impact that the rest of the narrative develops when it tracks the long-term effects of the blast. In the mockumentary *The War Game* (1965), also produced for (British) television, director Peter Watkins prints a few frames of the film as negatives at the moment when the bomb explodes; the device hyperbolically marks the flash of the explosion yet also sanitizes it by rendering it oddly abstract. In *The Bedford Incident* (1965), director James B. Harris arrests the flow of the film at the moment of explosion, a device reminiscent of the final montage sequence in Sidney Lumet's *Fail Safe* (1964). Harris also manipulates each arrested frame in a manner reminiscent of the projector's beam burning through, warping, and blacking the celluloid. The visual imagery in Watkins's and Harris's film respectively plays on the self-conscious realization that cinema itself, its technical apparatus, must capitulate when confronted with the challenge of capturing the unimaginable. It is easy to see in these strategies the visual and cinematic equivalent of Derrida's argument about the limits of linguistic signification within nuclear culture.

Whenever atomic blasts are not aesthetically framed, they tend to occur off-screen. We see this curious omission especially in the cycle of post-nuclear survival films that take their cue from earlier apocalyptic narratives (H. G. Wells's *War of the Worlds* [1898], M. P. Shiel's *The Purple Cloud* [1901], etc.) and then refashion the source material to fit the new nuclear reality. Literary bestsellers like Philip Wylie's *Tomorrow* (1954) or Pat Frank's *Alas, Babylon* (1960) would pave the way for films like Ray Milland's *Panic in the Year Zero* (1962), Arch Oboler's *Five* (1951), and Ranald MacDougall's *The World, the Flesh and the Devil* (1959). While writers like Wylie spend considerable time laying out in gruesome detail the nuclear attack on the US—much like Wells and Shiel, who revel in surreal hyperbolic scenarios of mass destruction—film and television productions by and large spare the viewer the actual moment of attack. For the most part, nuclear war tends to occur in a severely muted and visually neutered form (*The World, the Flesh, and the Devil*), or outside the frame (*Panic in the Year Zero*), or it has already concluded before the start of the narrative (*Five*), which then allows the films to focus entirely on the ingenuity of the survivors and their struggle to recover America's former glory.

While *Panic in the Year Zero* and *Five* are small, independent productions, the same representational reluctance is particularly striking in films more famous for taking an anti-nuclear stance. Stanley Kramer's *On the Beach* (1959) traces the long aftermath of nuclear war and the inevitable march toward death for all of the major characters in the story, including the film's central cast of stars (Ava Gardner, Gregory Peck, Fred Astaire, and Anthony Perkins). The nuclear war itself is long over before the film even starts, and thus remains outside the frame of representation altogether. Locations affected by the war and its deadly radioactive consequences are depopulated but otherwise mercifully unchanged. A sequence taking place in San Francisco shows the city fully intact when it is observed through a telescope from a submarine off shore. Though one crewman is clearly doomed to die from radiation when he goes AWOL and rows ashore, his death is communicated by a series of radio transmissions. And even these reports cease when the first physical symptoms of his imminent demise begin to materialize. Kramer follows a similar strategy with another member of the submarine crew. With the fatal diagnosis of having received a terminal dose of radiation, the sailor looks completely unchanged as long as he appears on camera. He then conveniently exits the narrative as soon as his conditions is reported to have deteriorated. Though the film is undoubtedly powerful in its melancholic evocation of humanity's slow, inevitable march toward self-destruction—Jerome Shapiro calls it "the 1950s classroom instructional film gone arty" (*Atomic Bomb Cinema* 92)—it has repeatedly come under criticism for this reluctance to visualize what its actual subject matter is supposed to be.

Sidney Lumet's *Fail Safe* (1964), another classic of anti-nuclear cinema, also keeps the bomb consistently off-stage. Inspired by the uneasy recollection of the Cuban Missile Crisis, the film is decidedly theatrical. Nearly all of its characters are locked into closed rooms where they communicate with each other and with the material world through the same technology that separates them from it. The film culminates in a nuclear exchange in which Moscow is destroyed by nuclear weapons, a tragic accident that then forces the American president to order the destruction of New York as a token of good faith. As melting telephones in both cities emit a high-pitched whine when the bombs annihilate the two cities, the film gives us reaction shots of various characters in extreme close-up. It also keeps the bomb off-screen. In order to dramatize the bomb being dropped on New York, Lumet resorts to a tightly edited montage of documentary shots of urban street life. He then rewinds that sequence, in a series of accelerating, staggered cuts, until the screen goes black for the closing credits. Again, as in *On the Beach*, the visual devices mobilized to represent the bomb are creative, impressive, and, without doubt, dramatically effective. But their ultimate function is the visual elision of the bomb and its effects.[24]

Complementing Lumet's *Fail Safe*, a film about the bomb without the bomb, Stanley Kubrick's *Dr. Strangelove* ironically fills in what Lumet had left out. Released the same year as *Fail Safe* (1964), Kubrick's film ends with a sequence in which a series of nuclear explosions, made up of stock footage of nuclear tests in the American Southwest and the Pacific, is lovingly put together over the song "We'll Meet Again." Kubrick drives the excess of visibility in this montage sequence of nuclear explosions to the point of deliberate repetitiveness. At first glance, this nonchalant overabundance clearly goes against the scarcity of adequate representations that runs through so much nuclear cinema. But on closer inspection, the film merely signals at visual excess—it does not actually deliver it. The use of the mushroom cloud, photographed from a safe distance, again leaves out what might be most crucial about the bomb: its material effects at and around the point of detonation. Ubiquitous as the mushroom cloud had become as an icon of nuclear weapons during the 1950s, it is ultimately a visual signifier that depends on the observer's physical distance. It is too vast to be seen up close, and who would want to be up close to ground zero anyway? Kubrick's lavish display of the iconic image, therefore, has a tendency to nudge the representational moment toward a lack of emotional engagement. In effect, the film strips the image of its direct human consequences.[25]

Not only did the bomb come with restrictions in regard to its visual representation, it also created problems for the process of storytelling. War films during the 1950s, unless they transpose their subject matter to a different historical period or a science fictional scenario, must go in search of dramatic ways to evoke the suspense and dynamic spectacle of combat. War films are still being made, but they face the central fact of the Cold War: the absence of conventional military conflict, of the traditional battlefield, and of bodies in action. Consequently, some films about the 1950s come with a World War II setting, while films with the 1950s as their historical setting move uncomfortably between the war film and other genres. This becomes especially visible in films about the air force, the US' primary delivery system for its nuclear arsenal during the early years of the Cold War. Fox's *Twelve O'Clock High* (Henry King, 1949) deals with this problem by projecting the World War II experience onto the postwar situation; Paramount's *Strategic Air Command* (Anthony Mann, 1955) and Warner Bros.' *Bombers B-52* (Gordon Douglas, 1957) look directly at the 1950s but must work hard to make this direct approach interesting. As Joyce Evans points out, neither one of the three films managed to establish themselves beyond their obvious political function: "Almost formulaic in their characterization and emphasis, these films were labelled Cold War propaganda tracts because of their glorification of the competence of the military as an organization and their portrayal of individual military heroes" (47). Despite their propagandistic thrust, however, they also illustrate the search for a new narrative, a new source of dramatic conflict, and a new validation of conventional heroism in this new type of war.[26]

Twelve O'Clock High tells the story of General Frank Savage (Gregory Peck), who, having been ordered to whip into shape a US Air Force bomber squadron stationed in Britain, rises to the challenge by endangering his own mental health in the process. A brief opening frame locates one of the central characters in the historical present, some time after the war, when he visits the abandoned airfield where the film's long central flashback begins. Unsure about the goal of their bombing missions, the men are unmotivated, unfocused, and undisciplined. Repeatedly, the film tells us that the goal is to train the men in daytime precision bombing, and part of that training is to prove the value of this military strategy and, in turn, justify the casualties incurred in the course of its pursuit.[27] In order to emphasize the men's lack of focus, the film refrains for an unusually long period from actually showing aerial combat. Instead, the narrative runs through the bureaucratic, administrative, psychological, and sociological transformations General Savage imposes on the squadron. Significantly enough, a large map in his office, a key location the film returns to time and again, depicts a graphic of the unit's organizational structure. The abstract hierarchy is humanized by individual personal photographs. Oddly enough, there is no map of German territory, a fact remedied eventually in the latter half of the film. As if to reward the audience for the long wait, the film's second half then provides the aerial combat that in retrospect legitimizes all the harsh authoritarian measures Savage implemented against his men. Beautifully assembled from documentary footage, the final battle scene is not the film's narrative climax. In accord with the thematic emphasis on military legitimacy, it ends with yet another crucial bombing run, albeit one in which Savage himself does not participate. Cracking under the mental strain, he suffers a breakdown before takeoff, which has him excluded from the final aerial battle. Together with Savage, the audience gets to follow the battle on the radio. By closing with a climactic scene that denies us visual and experiential access to the battlefield in the sky, the film deviates dramatically from the conventions of war films made during World War II. In the strict sense, its ending is anticlimactic. But in terms of thematic consistency, it reiterates the military's Cold War ideology. Recruitment, preparation and training, constant preparedness, and institutional efficiency are values to be respected even (or especially?) under historical conditions that may perpetually strip them of their practical application.

Setting their stories in the postwar years, films about the air force made and released after 1945 have to overcome even more dramaturgical obstacles in validating military expenditure and expansion without the prospect of imminent combat. *Bombers B-52* is a good example of what those obstacles look like and how they might be overcome. The film features Master Sergeant Chuck Brennan (Karl Malden) as the line chief of a ground crew servicing the film's eponymous bomber.[28] While Anthony Mann's earlier film *Strategic Air Command* (1955) highlights the hardships imposed upon the heteronormative couple as it transforms itself into a nuclear family, seen mostly through the eyes of the wife, Douglas focuses on the generational conflict between Chuck Brennan and his daughter, Lois. Incidentally, Brennan's daughter is played by young Natalie Wood, who is clearly reprising her role in *Rebel Without a Cause* (1955) as a good but troubled girl with father issues. Her function in the film, made explicit in the final scene, is to attract a younger demographic—to the film as much as to the air force.[29] The conflicts between father and daughter revolve around the daughter opposing her father's lack of social ambition when he is offered a lucrative, upwardly mobile position in a private company. The generational theme is played out in the professional and personal conflict between Brennan and the slightly younger Colonel Jim Herlihy (Efrem Zimbalist Jr.), a skilled pilot whom Brennan initially rejects as his daughter's suitor.[30]

Whenever the B-52 bomber appears in the film—courtesy of the US Air Force, which granted the film crew virtually unlimited access to the planes—Douglas shoots it in ways that demand audience identification with Brennan's technophilic excitement. Any explanation of the bomber's actual purpose is conspicuously absent; with all the family drama, who would want to contemplate the delivery of its nuclear payload to civilian targets belonging to the Cold War enemy? When the film finally does deliver a political rationale for its depoliticized technophilia, this rationale works against the incessant emphasis on the B-52's failings and shortcomings. During the first test flight, part of the landing gear fails to extend properly. Later, a computerized part of the machinery fails, setting the plane on fire and requiring the crew to parachute out. As counterintuitive as the repeated highlighting of the B-52's technical flaws might appear in a political context, they are nonetheless of great dramatic importance. Much like *Strategic Air Command*, *Bombers B-52* is a war film in search of a war.

The audience might be unsure of what to think about a statement delivered during the briefing of the B-52 flight crew: that "for centuries, it has been the job of a successful general to win wars; but in this nuclear age, it is the job of a successful general to prevent wars." But in terms of its political or even military validity, the statement describes perfectly the filmmaker's dilemma in creating a suspenseful narrative without the rousing spectacle of combat. While, structurally, the film's two dangerous test flights fulfill the function of battle scenes in a war film, the film's efforts to make these moments appear genuinely dangerous is transparent, perhaps even a little desperate. It is easy to imagine that air force script control would have insisted that, in neither mission, the plane is actually allowed to crash. So the film is left with an oxymoronic *straining toward* and *avoidance of* danger, which marks the absence of real conflict and, unfortunately, the absence of gripping cinematic thrills.[31]

Incidentally, both *Twelve O'Clock High* and *Bombers B-52* end on an ambiguous note when it comes to the historical continuity that links the "old air force" with the new one. When Chuck Brennan finds himself alive but immobilized in a hospital bed at the end of *Bombers B-52*, he looks out his window and sees his daughter and crack pilot Jim Herlihy drive off together. They make a romantic couple, ensuring biological and ideological reproduction; you can almost see the flock of army brats in their future. Noisily, bomber squadrons of the new B-52 fly overhead as a new generation of recruits is being whipped into shape by a gnarly veteran. As the respective wars of the old generation and the new generation blend into each other, all is right with the world. Meanwhile, at the end of *Twelve O'Clock High*, General Savage is just about to emerge from the catatonic stupor after his mental breakdown. As the film returns the audience to the frame narrative in the postwar present, Savage's former executive officer, Major Harvey Stovall (Dean Jagger), ends his trip down memory lane. Demonstratively he turns his back on the World War II airstrip, that space of nostalgic reminiscences, and cycles away. The airstrip may be abandoned and overgrown, just as the question remains unanswered whether General Savage ever made a full recovery and returned to active duty. But it is clear that the bucolic idyll of the British countryside is a product of the heroic sacrifices made by Savage and his fellow pilots. In both films, the old authority figures are not removed, but their authority is suspended, as if to keep them available if needed. Still, the films' shared closing gesture is ambiguous. The break in historical continuity is in the foreground, reiterated time and again by Cold War culture's insistence that the postwar world is a new, unprecedented one. Yet the return to World War II as a cultural, historical, and military reference point ensures that the war lives on and with it, its most notable creation: the military-industrial complex. If Christian Appy is right and Cold War America would habitually return to World War II "as a site of fantasy and nostalgia as much as stress" ("Sentimental Militarism," 95), then the effects of this stress deserve closer scrutiny. If World War II was such a comforting and reassuring memory, how could remembering it be simultaneously so stressful?

The Unresolved Trauma of World War II

As I said before, thanks to the technology itself, the past and projected future use of nuclear weapons by the US posed representational problems. These problems were exacerbated by the control of public information through the emergent security state and the ideological constraints surrounding information as a result of domestic and global anti-communism. Public debate during the postwar years would have to accommodate all that which could not be said or was not allowed to be said. If these complex constraints produced gaps in the conversation, those gaps would have to be filled with other content, or else the public would notice the odd, uncomfortable silences. This content would most likely not be germane to the Cold War itself; it would have to come from elsewhere. For genres as deeply invested in the military-industrial complex as science fiction, this meant that the present would be overwritten by references to a collective historical experience still fresh in almost everyone's mind by the 1950s: World War II and, by extension, the Korean War. Each in its own way might have been a traumatic caesura in American history, but at least they did not come with new incomprehensible, terrifying, and unspeakable weapons. But would the familiarity of World War II and the Korean War be reassuring enough to make Americans forget their traumatic impact?

For anyone writing in the aftermath of September 11, 2001, the term "trauma" comes with its very own historical baggage. One of the many critics writing about post-9/11 cinema, Stephen Prince has provided a useful comprehensive overview of the term's recent rise in popularity and its various uses within cultural studies. Among these uses, the one that is perhaps the least problematic is its direct application to an individual suffering the impact of an event so painful that it threatens to exceed the individual's ability to process it—an event with the power to fracture the integrity and dissolve the boundaries of the self. More germane to a vast historical event like World War II and to its subsequent cinematic representation are forms of trauma that Prince, in reference to E. Ann Kaplan's work, describes as "mediated" or "vicarious" (11). Prince is skeptical regarding theories that assume the media transfer of trauma from direct experience to that recreated through media, which is why he points out crucial differences between personal and mediated trauma (e.g., "movie narratives achieve closure; traumatic memories remain frozen" [12]). Eventually, though, he comes to agree with Wulf Kansteiner that cinema produces "a form of social knowledge about trauma" (13). What Kansteiner and Prince mean is a constructed individual experience that, by structural analogy, recreates trauma as a secondary psychological experience, an experience which—unlike the real thing—can be shared with others, discussed, negotiated, and deployed to various social and ideological ends. For the purpose of using the term "trauma" in the discussion to come, I would also add to Prince's cogent summary that trauma, as "a form of social knowledge," announces itself as a formal set of conventions within the cinematic medium in which it is expressed. A film can communicate to its audience that "trauma" is its subject matter, regardless of whether that audience actually experiences the film or parts of it as a secondary, mediated, collective trauma. Cinema audiences, in other words, can recognize and "know" trauma in their encounter with a film without experiencing it.[32]

Against this theoretical backdrop, the trauma of World War II varies from one individual and one group to another, depending on their relative distance from the battlefields of the war. Hence, it is difficult to argue whether World War II could be said to constitute a collective trauma to the US. On the one hand, its battlefields were elsewhere (as they always have been since the Civil War). Despite massive mobilization, the largest part of the population remained personally unaffected. Even the largest part of those drafted into the military never actually saw combat. Finally, the US emerged victorious from the conflict. While the US entered a period of unprecedented wealth and power, the war had effectively destroyed Europe and Japan and weakened the global system of nineteenth-century imperialism to which the US would become the primary twentieth-century heir. Compared to the vast destruction in Europe and Asia, as well as the enormous losses of life on the part of the Soviet Union and the nuclear and conventional devastation inflicted upon Japan, relatively few Americans could claim to be traumatized by the war as a matter of direct personal experience.

On the other hand, the US war effort geared toward the creation of what Chomsky has called a "quasi-totalitarian wartime command economy" (1991: 21) would affect more Americans than any other military conflict in the nation's history. Obviously, there were all those killed or wounded in action, their spouses, children, extended families, and friends. But even for those who remained unaffected by personal loss, civilian life changed. World War II constituted a radical caesura in the lives of large parts of the population: from the large displacements due to military enlistment and deployment, to labor migrations and the resulting demographic shifts in the racial composition of entire regions. More as volunteers than draftees, the Hollywood studios participated in this mobilization. Quoting the Government Information Manual issued by the Office of Wartime Information (OWI) on the subject of "The Home Front," Rick Worland lists among the propagandistic goals of Hollywood filmmaking that of "keeping up the spirits and the drive of the great body of civilians whose activities are not directly involved in war production or some other phase of the struggle" (56). What the Office of Wartime Information wanted was to see people "'cheerfully making small sacrifices for the war: buying bonds, donating blood, working for the Red Cross [. . .] serving as air raid wardens. People cooperating in food rationing and mileage rationing [. . .] Obviously well-to-do people using street cars and other public transportation rather than wear out their tires. People do these things because they want to, not because they are forced to'" (qtd. in Worland 56). To some extent, this list can be read as an indictment of behaviors and attitudes that are actually prevalent in American life—i.e., as a list of behavioral adjustments to "normal" American behaviors which remain, as yet, unaccomplished. More than that, though, the list illustrates the comprehensive nature of the effort of the wartime economy to include as much of the population as possible. Deciding whether these restrictive measures constitute, in the proper sense of the term, a collective trauma—most of them read more like inconveniences than actual sacrifices—is not the goal of this book. What is important is to recognize that, in order to legitimize their imposition and symbolically reward widespread public compliance, these measures are understood as personal sacrifices. And in the larger framework of mobilization, a personal sacrifice might register as traumatic.

In order to read 1950s American culture, and especially science fiction films from the period, as a response to the trauma of World War II and the Korean War, it is useful to look at an approach modeled by critical discussions about cinema and popular culture in other contexts. W. G. Sebald's

Luftkrieg und Literatur (translated as *On the Natural History of Destruction*, 1999) famously made the case that the curious avoidance of the World War II experience of strategic bombing in postwar German literature is a symptom of the traumatic impact this experience had made on the culture at large. According to Sebald, the most striking correspondence between postwar Germany and postwar America would be the strong forward orientation of both cultures away from the traumatic past. Fred Kaplan diagnoses exactly this same collective pull away from the past and into the future in his book on 1950s America. Triggered by the launch of the Soviet Union's Lunik 1 space capsule, US media wallowed in fantasies of "'the jet age,' 'the space age,' the world of the future,' 'the countdown to tomorrow'" (2). Kaplan reads this as a massive mobilization of cultural forces in the interest of historical amnesia. Anton Kaes's book *Shell Shock Cinema: Weimar Culture and the Wounds of War* (2011) harkens back to the impact of World War I on German cinema in the interwar years. Kaes argues that the unresolved trauma of the war "became Weimar's historical unconscious," haunting, troubling, and complicating the success story that was to be German resurgence between the end of the war and the start of the Great Depression (2).[33] Focusing such an approach specifically on the horror film, books by Linnie Blake (*The Wounds of Nations: Horror Cinema, Historical Trauma, and National Identity* [2008]), by Adam Lowenstein (*Shocking Representations: Historical Trauma, National Cinema, and the Modern Horror Film* [2005]), and by Kevin Wetmore (*Post-9/11 Horror in American Cinema* [2012]) have made the case that the horror film is particularly adept at capturing national trauma in allegorical form. Horror films, all three scholars agree, make it possible to discuss experiences too painful, sensitive, or shocking to be discussed as part of the public debate.

When American culture "remembers past battles," Elisabeth Bronfen muses, it does so not only because these past battles constitute an unresolved individual trauma or an unresolved national burden. Past trauma also remains relevant "because the collective act of recalling a national past of violent conflict has proved to be a particularly compelling way of addressing and negotiating anxieties and desires besetting the current cultural moment" (111). It is through this intersection of past and present, of unresolved trauma superimposed upon present anxieties, that 1950s science fiction films acquire topical relevance within their historical context. Just as Anton Kaes's analysis recognizes Weimar cinema as a belated response to World War I projected onto the unsettling experience of the Weimar years, I am arguing that science fiction films from the 1950s are a belated response to the national trauma of World War II and the Korean War projected onto the unsettling experience of the Cold War. With much of the critical work on the Cold War aspects of the films already delivered by other scholars, this book will weigh in on the side of the argument that has, as yet, remained critically neglected—the side of past trauma: on World War II and the Korean War, and their troubling legacy in the first decade of the American Century.

Chapter Overview

Each one of the following four chapters selects one thematic aspect that relates to the military and examines it in the context of one particular science fiction film. Each film also takes on one distinct subcategory of the 1950s cycle, from films about massive military engagements to alien invasion films, giant creature film, and films about American travelers stranded in exotic locations. The first chapter focuses on the recruitment of the audience into the "military metaphysics" C. Wright Mills decries as a symptom of America's Cold War mentality. More specifically, the chapter reads attempts at recruitment made by science fiction films of the period through the use of military stock footage. Pilfering the public domain for footage to be inserted into one's own film was a standard device of inexpensive filmmaking that found one of its most extreme expressions in Alfred E. Green's *Invasion U.S.A.* (1952). Generally dismissed as a hack job and mercilessly lampooned by *Mystery Science Theater 3000*, *Invasion U.S.A.* is a prime example of a politically engaged film using one of the common stylistic devices of 1950s low-budget filmmaking, which deserves thorough critical assessment exactly for its politics and cinematic style.

In the second chapter, the traumatized war veteran and the repressed memory of World War II take center stage. The key text of this chapter is Gene Fowler Jr.'s *I Married a Monster from Outer Space* (1958), a film produced at a slightly higher budget than *Invasion U.S.A.* yet still clearly a B-movie at heart. Fowler's film is a particularly apt starting point for such a discussion because it imagines the monstrous invader as an alien creature masquerading in human form. Underneath the perfect human surface is the grotesquely malformed alien creature—a potent visual metaphor that captures the complexity of the veteran's traumatization, especially when the injury is both psychological and physical in nature. The alien impostors in the other two films discussed in this chapter—William Cameron Menzies's *Invaders from Mars* (1953) and Don Siegel's *Invasion of the Body Snatchers* (1956)—do not come with physical disfigurements concealed beneath a deceptive surface yet they are no less bent on conquest. Casting women and children as alien impostors, these films address the larger impact of the male veteran's presence in the peaceful postwar community. The chapter will track the disturbance caused by the veteran as it spreads from romantic couples to families and to entire towns and the nation at large.

The third chapter switches the focus from iconic characters to iconic spaces, following the demographic changes brought about by World War II and the expansion of the domestic infrastructure during the Eisenhower administration. The emphasis here is on the ways in which the military encouraged certain ways of perceiving and experiencing cities, suburbs, and small towns in the transition from World War II to the Cold War. More specifically, the chapter takes on the desert landscape of the American Southwest and tracks its occupation by the military. Closely associated with the development and testing of the US nuclear arsenal, but also with the world of the American frontier and the Western, the southwestern desert appears, in turn, deeply familiar and eerily strange to 1950s American culture. Science fiction films like Jack Arnold's *It Came from Outer Space* (1953) and Gordon Douglas's *Them!* (1954) unfold as the Cold War overwrites the traditional connotations of the landscape.

The fourth and final chapter will examine the issue of Cold War decolonization as it appears in films that chose the global sphere as their setting. Films like Richard Fleischer's *20,000 Leagues Under the Sea* (1954), Irwin Allen's *The Lost World* (1960), and Ib Melchior's *The Time Travelers* (1964) testify to the science fiction film's interest in placing American travelers in postcolonial locations. Starting in the late 1950s and gaining momentum in the early 1960s, this trend was infused with new eagerness by the Kennedy administration's foreign initiatives (from the space program to the Peace Corps). Superficially, these films demonstrate that US intervention in the Third World is called for and legitimate whenever Soviet influence appears as a rival or counterforce to American attempts to gain allies or secure markets. However, upon closer inspection, some of these films also make room for an alternative reading of Cold War history. They acknowledge that the US must sometimes confront a danger more insidious than Soviet communism—political non-alignment driven by "economic nationalism." George Pal's beloved adaptation of H. G. Wells's *The Time Machine* (1960) provides a surprising insight into variants of, and alternatives to, conventional American "containment" politics. Following this fourth and final chapter is a brief conclusion which returns to Eisenhower's concept of the military-industrial complex and outlines the concept's extended afterlife, especially in regard to the so-called "war on terror" after September 11, 2001. A final consideration of what 1950s science fiction films can tell us about the US in the present day—their impact on later films and their continued relevance to the culture—concludes the book.

Chapter One
Military Stock Footage

Cinematic Recruitment: How to Mobilize an Audience

In order to tell the story of how 1950s science fiction films helped to mobilize public opinion in favor of the military-industrial complex, it makes sense to look at the beginning of the collaboration between Hollywood and the military. The origins of this collaboration, which are to be found in the propaganda efforts that accompanied World War II, are not interesting because they provide a logistical or economic blueprint upon which postwar film production would be modeled. On the contrary, what they help to show is how postwar efforts would *differ* from those organized during the war. It stands to reason that patterns and procedures of economics and politics would change as the nation moved from war to peacetime. Nonetheless, it is crucial to elaborate on these differences. To the degree that they help to shed light upon the peculiar, idiosyncratic features of postwar film production, they help to dispel any notions that the dynamic interactions between science fiction film production and the military-industrial complex during the 1950s would have been some sinister conspiratorial plot to bend the nation's democratic system into service to a ruthless, self-serving economic agenda. As often as Eisenhower's famous neologism might have been appropriated to paranoid fantasies of one type or another, the differences between film production during and after World War II illustrate that direct governmental influence on artistic creation and industrial production is as much or as little a symptom of the military-industrial complex at work as its absence. So let's begin the discussion by looking at the production of science fiction and horror films during World War II.

Since science fiction as a clearly defined cinematic genre had not played a significant role on American movie screens before the 1950s, its intersection with the horror film provides the best insight into the prehistory of both genres' convergence in the 1950s. And as film historian Rick Worland puts it, the horror film had been going through "a dismal decade" during the 1940s (47). Still, World War II had marked a high point in the cooperation between the US military and Hollywood. Created on June 13, 1942, in the wake of America's entry into the war after Pearl Harbor, the government's Office of War Information (OWI), aided by its Bureau of Motion Pictures' Domestic Operations Branch, set out to "'undertake campaigns to enhance understanding of the war at home and abroad; to coordinate government information activities; and to handle liaison with the press, radio, and motion pictures'" (50). Though the agency had no censorship power, its guidelines stipulated the cinematic explication of America's engagement in the war. It also managed the politically sensitive handling of nations considered essential allies to the US cause as well as of domestic racial policy and reality (what one might call racial equality under pre-civil rights conditions). All of this was handled by actively encouraging the pursuit of certain themes and storylines. The office's general power to assess and evaluate whether a film was suitable for foreign distribution carried significant economic clout helpful in enforcing its assessments. Still, "the Bureau of Motion Pictures was never automatically hostile to or particularly worried about the negative propaganda impact of horror films per se" (51). While the British government had instituted a ban on horror films in 1942, no "BMP reviews of horror films decry their violence or morbidity or claim any deleterious effects on civilian morale arising from movie terrors" (51). Regardless of genre, the overriding concern was a film's adaption to the parameters of mass recruitment to the war effort, both at home and abroad.[1] With victory in the Pacific theater, the Office of Wartime Information was dissolved on September 15, 1945. "Hollywood's extensive cooperation with the federal government in the creation of propaganda messages during World War II," Rick Worland concludes, "remains historically unique and largely anomalous" (61). In other words, as horror and science fiction films were heading toward the hybrid model typical of the 1950s cycle, direct governmental influence on themes and storylines was already a thing of the past.

If horror film production under the critical eye of the OWI during the war was largely geared toward controlling content rather than actively aiding in production, horror films, with their gothic trappings, inherited largely from the prewar cycle, made few demands on studio budgets.[2] Not just in the case of the horror film, budgetary considerations of wartime expediency in the allocation of resources would have been a constraining factor. Even when these budgetary constraints were removed after the end of the war, most horror films did not receive an upgrade to A-picture status. Only with the amalgamation of science fiction with the horror film during the early 1950s did the budgetary demands of the newly hybridized genre increase. This might have been an effect primarily of science fiction, as the genre would demand more ambitious visual special effects.[3] Meanwhile, horror films made and released during the war could be aligned with the agenda of wartime propaganda without making explicit references to the war or the military; in fact, Worland cites examples of OWI concerns about the escapist frivolity of horror films clashing with the seriousness of the war and the military as potential backdrops to dramatic storytelling. Only after the war had ended did the presence of war and the military become an essential element in the hybrid genres of horror and science fiction. In order to bring this essential generic element convincingly and, even better, spectacularly to the screen, and to do this in times when governmental support would no longer be easily forthcoming, filmmakers would have to appeal to the military directly. Practically speaking, they would have to ask not for permission but for personnel and material to be lent out and used as extras and props. If World War II had set an example for the cooperation between a state political agenda and the ideological orientation of commercial filmmaking in the US, then the Cold War would reconfigure and bring into focus this cooperation as a facet of what Eisenhower would come to refer to as the military-industrial complex—creating out of necessity an aesthetic that would, in and of itself, carry the power to convince audiences to buy into the Cold War's perpetual state of crisis.[4]

Buying into the Cold War: Interpellation Fifties' Style

Once World War II would be no longer available as an immediate and obvious reason for the military mobilization of American society, recruitment into a postwar political consensus that accepted not only the continuation but the entrenchment and expansion of the military-industrial complex would be of tantamount importance. This recruitment would have to invalidate all prior assurances that, once America's enemies had been vanquished, a "peace dividend" would await its citizens. Seeing these efforts of recruitment as a form of "interpellation"—a term I am borrowing from Louis Althusser, describing how individuals are made to accept and conform to ideology in general—requires a specific application of the Althusserian framework. Interpellation, as Althusser puts it, is the process of ideology "hailing" an individual, and thus transforming the individual into a subject; it is a "recruitment" into ideology, a body of ideas which "represents the

The American Empire: Calling on the Postwar Generation

imaginary relationship of individuals to their real conditions of existence" (Althusser, "Ideology").

This application would focus the term specifically on the creation of an individual subjectivity, as well as of a broader cultural consensus, characteristic of America after the end of World War II and in the buildup to the Cold War. First of all, there are specific conditions that apply broadly to bourgeois industrial capitalism. But there are also conditions that apply specifically to the unique configuration of the military-industrial complex and American historical messianism as it was expressed, for example, by Henry Luce's idea of the "American Century," the Truman Doctrine, and the Eisenhower Doctrine.[5] As the historical reality and its ideological reframing are bound to veer away from each other from time to time, cultural discourses are not only hiding and smoothing over the resulting gaps— a function perhaps most easily associated with ideology. Advertently or inadvertently, they also reveal and draw attention to them, and thus to the fact that the official narrative is essentially an ideological construct. Popular culture at large is engaged in this ideological labor in both functions. It tells the official story, and it undermines that story by revealing its gaps and fractures. Since most science fiction films of the 1950s are keenly aware of themselves as political statements, they signal their topical relevance to their audience. These films, in other words, work hard to make their viewers care—to make them recognize an issue *as an issue* and apply it as relevant to their own lives. This means that the films ask the audience to pay attention to their grand life-and-death issues, to take them seriously, no matter how preposterous their operating metaphors of alien invaders, fifty-foot women, and giant creatures may be. However egregious their creative overreach, these films are, at their core, deeply serious. In order to be taken seriously, they take great pains to interpellate, to use Althusser's term, their audience. The more forceful, assertive, persistent, or even desperate their gestures of interpellation, the more fractured the relationship they attempt to construct between the real world and the "imaginary relationships" their audience has with it.[6]

Many science fiction films from the 1950s are associated with B-movie production, and so audience interpellation is largely a matter of strategies and gestures that must work without the benefit of strong production values and against the limitations and inadequacies of the films themselves. In fact, many of these films are loud, garish, and sensational. Whether it is the exclamation mark in a title like *Them!* (Gordon Douglas, 1954), or the iconic opening titles for *It Came from Outer Space* (which has a flaming meteor heading directly toward the viewer and crashing, presumably, into the camera lens) and *The Thing from Another World* (in which the lines of the title are burning themselves through the surface of the title card), or William Castle's personal appearance at the beginning of *The Tingler*, the assertive grab for the audience's attention is an indispensable feature of the genres' aesthetic repertoire.[6] Writing with special emphasis on 1950s films about hypnotism, Kevin Heffernan has pointed out that Castle's personal appearance and direct address to the audience in the opening of *The Tingler* (1959) serves as an example of directors delivering—and physically embodying— interpellative gestures. Instructing and guiding the audience, Castle makes a personal appearance before *The Tingler* gets under way. Together with "Caligari-like figures" like "psychiatrists, carnival barkers, warlocks, and hypnotists," the director himself, as Heffernan argues, "can be seen as [an emblem] of the forces that mediate between, on the one hand, the horror

Attention-Grabbers: The Exclamation Point's Emphatic Urgency

Exploding off the Screen: The Opening Credits of *It Came from Outer Space*

William Castle in *The Tingler*: Cinema Between the Carnival Tent and the Emergency Broadcast System

The Opening Credits of *The Thing from Another World*: Burning Itself into Your Retina

genre's eruptions of shock and spectacle, and on the other, the efforts of the narrative both to impel and contain those eruptions" (2000: 61). What Heffernan reads specifically as a regulating function in regard to cinematic genres, I would see as one device in a larger array of strategies aimed at interpellating an audience into a larger ideological system. In this system, cinema serves as a vehicle of delivery for content so important, and yet so complex or ambiguous, that the audience's proper response cannot be left to chance. Containing and contextualizing "the horror genre's eruptions of shock and spectacle" is an important function, but more is at stake in that act of containment.

How ubiquitous such gestures of interpellation are for science fiction films of the 1950s also becomes visible in some of the period's iconic catch-phrases and lines of dialogue. The call to caution and vigilance at the end of Christian Nyby's *The Thing from Another World* (1951) speaks to the sense of 1950s Cold War paranoia geared toward xenophobic fantasies of invasion and subversion by some hostile alien force. The eponymous Thing has been defeated, and now one of the civilian members of the team broadcasts the news to the world. The important task falls to the journalist who had been prevented from notifying the world of the alien creature below the Arctic ice because of the military's information lockdown. Surrounded by the rest of the team, he is speaking urgently into a microphone. At the other end of the line is a larger world easily imaginable as the mirror image of the group behind the broadcaster. His words carry such urgency that the details of the dramatic events may be postponed; the warning needs to come first: "Keep watching the skies!" *Invasion of the Body Snatchers* (1956) ends on a similar note. When hard evidence corroborates Miles Bennel's story about alien invasion, Dr. Hill, the psychiatrist, decides to mobilize the authorities. As in *The Thing from Another World*, explanations are hardly necessary at this point. As demonstrated by the film's final shot, a medium close-up of Miles Bennel's face, concerted official action comes as a relief to the tension of prolonged collective ignorance and apathy.

Many of the films in the 1950s sub-cycle of giant creature films also end on a similar note. A strong influence on the US cycle, Ishiro Honda's *Gojiro* (1954) assembles in the final scene the military-industrial team that has succeeded in killing off the creature in Tokyo Bay with a weapon even more powerful and terrifying than the nuclear bombs that had awakened it and endowed it with some of its characteristic features. The outstanding senior scientist, Prof. Yamane (Takashi Shimura), having watched his scientific successor sacrifice himself with the deployment of the Oxygen Destroyer, looks into the deep and muses: "I can't believe that Godzilla was the only surviving member of its species. But if we keep on conducting nuclear tests, it's possible that another Godzilla might appear somewhere in the world again." The resonance of this scene is obvious when looking at Gordon Douglas's *Them!* (1954), in which a similar figure of scientific authority (Edmund Gwenn) closes the film with the brief monologue. As police officers, soldiers, and scientists incinerate a nest of giant mutated ants in the sewers underneath Los Angeles, Dr. Medford is asked, "If these monsters are the result of the first atomic bomb in 1945, what about all the others that have been exploded since then?" He muses: "Nobody knows, Robert. When man entered the atomic age, he opened a door into a new world. What we'll eventually find in that new world, nobody can predict." Considering that the film, right at this moment, cuts to the image of the conflagration below, Douglas seems very much willing to make predictions—and dire ones, at that.

In their blunt directness, these endings clearly perform a rhetorical gesture that functions at various levels. In *Gojira*, it is obvious that Prof. Yamane's words anticipate the string of sequels that would make up the franchise in decades to come. In *Them!*, the final monologue brings the audience into the debate about nuclear testing, this while keeping it visually enthralled to the far more potent scenario of nuclear war. More broadly, however, all those endings, from the ones in giant creature films to the ones in alien invasion films, interpellate the audience into attitudes that seem spontaneous but need constant refreshment and training. Invariably, these are attitudes of permanent vigilance and allegiance to an institutional system of surveillance. It is obvious that behind this system is the 1950s paranoia triggered by fears of an external nuclear attack and internal communist subversion. To the degree that an inflated sense of self-importance, coupled with a lack of self-confidence, and hyper-vigilance are recurring symptoms of this paranoid state of mind, the Cold War explanation captures the hyperbolic intensity of these endings perfectly well. Where the interpretation needs to be amended is in regard to the origins of interpellation in the political rhetoric and propaganda of World War II. Science fiction films in the 1950s extend this rhetoric to the Cold War. Thus, they both create and meet the demand for militarization by insisting on the normalization of the military-industrial complex as part of the postwar American way of life.

What is remarkable about these endings is that they testify to a concern on the part of filmmakers and/or studios that the defeat of the monster or the alien invaders alone will prove insufficient for re-establishing narrative equilibrium. Obviously, stronger measures are needed to achieve such final closure. Some of these measures even violate the fourth wall of conventional Hollywood storytelling; the monologue at the end of *The Thing from Another World*, for example, seems to be more addressed to the audience in the movie theater than whoever is at the other end of that microphone. True, none of the patriarchal authority figures in these films look directly at the camera as they deliver their interpellative addresses. But it would take but a small step to move from a dramatic monologue to a propagandistic exhortation of the audience. Both the importance of interpellation, and the anxiety over ineffective or insufficient interpellation, surface in these endings, evoking a larger critical debate about "containment" to which I will return later.

The same anxious, somewhat self-doubting drive toward audience interpellation is also at work in the frequent use of framing devices and narrative and expositional prologues. The ending of *Invasion of the Body Snatchers* is only the second half of a narrative frame which had opened the film with Miles Bennel (Kevin McCarthy) returning to his hometown of Santa Mira. This return to the frame gives Bennel the opportunity to address Dr. Hill (Whit Bissell), leading into the extended flashback that makes up the full narrative of the film. An ingenious twist on this framing device occurs in William Cameron Menzies's *Invaders from Mars*. The film closes with a repetition of the opening sequence when the main character, little David McLean (Jimmy Hunt), wakes up from the extended main narrative of alien invasion to find that it has all been a dream. Immediately, however, he discovers that events are about to replay themselves, this time presumably in the real world. This strange transfer of events between objective reality and subjective perception follows Miles Bennel's appeal to Dr. Hill. A deranged Miles Bennel argues for the veracity of events by way of their transfer from the internal, subjective, and presumably pathological to the external and "real." The process is demonstrated so emphatically that the film justifies its inherent interpellative function in its claim to empirical veracity. The crazy outsider turns out to be right every time.

A brief moment from the end of *Invaders from Mars*, following David McLean's realization that his dream is about to come true, also includes another common feature, this one tying it back to the film's opening sequence. Dissolving from a medium shot of David staring at a landing alien ship from his bedroom window, Menzies cuts to a backward tracking shot through the same miniature mock-up of outer space used in the film's beginning. This shot echoes, albeit in reverse, the opening sequence in which the camera tracks forward through outer space (not unlike the opening credit sequence of *Star Trek*). It also features an expositional voiceover connecting the idea of space exploration and alien life, with David McLean as an amateur astronomer as the camera moves in on David's bedroom window. The forward tracking shot, which is as expansive and aggressive as it is inquisitive, also undercuts each text's claim to peaceful exploration based on a disinterested scientific curiosity in one case, and military mobilization as a purely defensive measure against external aggression in the other. Explicitly counting David among the "scientists of all ages," the authoritative voiceover establishes David's vigilance as a prerequisite for his later usefulness to the military effort in defeating the alien invasion. To the extent that the film's (first) ending reveals the invasion to have been merely a figment of David's imagination, however, it is the closing reference to David as an astronomer that underwrites and confirms the connection between individual vigilance and military mobilization in a gesture of interpellation.

The interpellative gesture performed by the narrative frame in *Invaders from Mars* is complex enough to fulfill some other functions as well. On one level, it raises the issue of audience demographics, which comes up in connection with the character of David McLean being a child. Some viewers might read the narrative frame as an indictment of the immaturity and childishness of science fiction. They might also see in it the affinity that this childish—or, rather, boyish—imagination has toward military mobilization. After all, in his militarized dream David casts himself as the central character who repeatedly saves the day. Nonetheless, this extended power fantasy also functions as an (over-) compensation for the powerlessness David experiences during the first half of the narrative. But, then, given the logic of the frame narrative, David's initial powerlessness is also a childish fantasy. This fantasy, in turn, may be concocted in response to conditions that are not identified in the narrative, but may have something to do with Freud's remarks about all children imagining their parents not being their parents. Clearly, David is a character capable of serving as the focus of identification for all audience members, regardless of age. Hence, his interpellation engages the audience both in its masochistic enjoyment of powerlessness (the victimization and alienation by the alien conspiracy) and its sadistic overcoming in a climactic scene of retaliatory violence against the aliens (the power fantasy of being central to military mobilization). What all this suggests is that the double-sided psychic mechanism the film appeals to in the audience might be installed during childhood but persists into adulthood.

To the extent that David as a character is read specifically as a child, interpellation by way of the narrative frame also points to 1950s audience demographics. Amidst the range of possible viewers, some would have likely been children or teenagers themselves, like David McLean himself; others might have seen the film as adults, an audience to which the film's closing moments appeal when it asks for a dissociation from, and critical re-evaluation of, David McLean. While David might be this film's central character, most of the canonical films of the period—from *Them!* and *Tarantula* to *Creature from the Black Lagoon* and *Invasion of the Body Snatchers*—are centered on adult characters with adult problems. Generally speaking, characters serving as points of identification for the audience do not have to correspond to that audience's dominant demographic features. Given the predominance of adult characters in 1950s science fiction films, we might very well imagine an audience of older children and teenagers interpellated via identification with adult characters into patriarchal structures of authority. Obviously, while children and teenagers may have made up a sizable, and increasing, chunk of the target audience, they were not the writers, producers, directors, and actors bringing this material to the screen. In fact, in the later period of the 1950s cycle, films would be specifically tailored to the youth demographic (*I Was a Teenage Werewolf* [1957], *I Was a Teenage Frankenstein* [1957], *How to Make a Monster* [1958], *The Blob* [1958], *The Space Children* [1958], *Teenagers from Space* [1959]). The segregation of these films as a special subcategory of the genre indicates, by contrast, how "adult" in conception and execution most science fiction films of the 1950s really were. Television during the 1960s would pick up on the by-then sizable teenage market, taking its cue from the more specialized films of the previous decade. Stepping into the shoes of George Pal, producers like Irwin Allen would build television series for teenagers based on films they were likely to have grown up with as children (*Voyage to the Bottom of the Sea*, *Land of the Giants*, *Time Tunnel*). Inevitably, this would include characters in ensemble casts that would serve to interpellate specific demographics (e.g., *Lost in Space* with its demographically parsed family cast—more a precursor of *The Partridge Family* than a close relative of *Voyage to the Bottom of the Sea*). *Invaders from Mars*, however, demonstrates that early and mid-1950s films are far more interested in examining the roles of children and teenagers, at times quite critically, than in merely pandering to their rising power as consumers.

Although interpellation in a film like *Invaders from Mars* is tied to military mobilization, the film does not in the strict sense qualify as propaganda. Much like the World War II films that conform to this label—one might think of films like the ones in the *Why We Fight* series, commissioned by the War Department and intended to be shown to incoming recruits—1950s science fiction films are undoubtedly patriotic and embrace militarization as an inevitable aspect of life during the Cold War. At the same time, their commitment to mobilization remains suspended within a larger ideological framework that requires far more political finesse than World War II propaganda ever had to muster. To the extent that the films do engage consistently with the military-industrial complex, however, they do contribute to the normalization of the military as part of American life. One fact they must contend with is that the Cold War lacked precisely the clarity and immediacy that made World War II a politically more convenient excuse for demanding broad militarization. This is, I believe, the crucial historical difference complicating the politics that operate behind the films' insistent interpellative gestures. This is the source of anxiety for films like *Invaders from Mars*, the cause for their relative failure, the strange inadequacy, the lack of ideological thrust, which diminishes their status as propaganda films. What the Cold War failed to provide to bolster the propagandistic effectiveness of these films, World War II would have surely delivered. So how did 1950s science fiction films import World War II into the Cold War? If you had a competent editor at hand, the answer would be cheap and easy.

Military Stock Footage: Persistently Awkward, Unwittingly Hilarious

In light of the propagandistic agenda of 1950s science fiction film, any discussion of the link between cinema and the military-industrial complex is likely to arrive, sooner or later, at their use of military stock footage. Science fiction films would cull these images from film studio newsreels, from wartime propaganda films produced at the incentive of and with the aid of the US government, and from various other, albeit minor, documentary sources. In fact, it is this cinematic cycle more than any other before or after which adopted the practice with such frequency that it became one of its trademark features. Though virtually all studios availed themselves of the cheap and easy practice, Warren Luciano estimates that "Columbia Pictures, through the ingenuity of its producer Sam Katzman, must hold some kind of record among studios for incorporating footage from previous films into its later productions" (70). Giving Columbia a run for its money, "Republic Pictures [even] released two films in 1958 that are constructed of nothing but library footage [i.e., *Satan's Satellites* and *Missile Monsters*]." Somewhere in these films, there is always a scene in which the army rolls out the tanks against an alien invasion, or jet planes launch rockets at a giant creature. And every time the footage, obviously and embarrassingly, comes from elsewhere. *Plan 9 from Outer Space* (1959), one of the most egregious examples of this practice, features a scene in which the US military tries to shoot down flying saucers cruising over the Hollywood hills, while, in the background, spectators gather to rubberneck—spectators that are easily recognizable as Korean villagers. Kurt Neuman's *Rocketship X-M* (1950) visualizes an American lunar expedition getting under way by slipping in footage of a German V-2 rocket. To an audience in the 1950s, the rocket's unique black-and-white chessboard markings are clearly and unmistakably visible. No doubt, these moments made the films look "cheap"—a term referring literally to economics, and figuratively to aesthetics and its ability to signal cultural capital. It is this cheapness, in every sense of the word, that has stood in the way of genuine critical appreciation ever since.

Discussing the war film throughout the 1950s, Peter Biskind puts his finger on the convergence of economic, ideological, and aesthetic factors in commercial cinema, which also explains the use of military stock footage in horror and science fiction. "Although all films are subject to conflicting ideological pressures," Biskind points out,

> war films are particularly vulnerable, because they often depend on the armed forces for expensive props: planes, ships, tanks, and so on. The army's military aid to Hollywood had strings attached, and the Department of Defense's Motion Picture Production Branch existed to pull them [. . .] Department of Defense guidelines for Hollywood films mandated a "true interpretation of military life," and "compliance with accepted standards of dignity and propriety in the industry." Support was forthcoming only for scripts that satisfied the army's interpretation of these requirements. (83n)

Jean-Michel Valantin places Biskind's observation into an even broader context, referring to it as "national security cinema," a "giant system where political force, military might and the power of film pervade one another and are closely inscribed in the history of American strategy, largely defining its uniqueness" (ix). To the extent that horror and science fiction films of the '50s required images of military hardware and personnel—i.e., to the degree that they were permeated by what C. Wright Mills referred to as "the military metaphysics" pervading the 1950s—they found themselves in the same subservient position to the Pentagon as war films. The war film, despite the fluctuations of its popularity in the postwar years, may have been able to parlay its way into support with a modicum of cultural capital. Science fiction films, however, remained suspicious or altogether beneath the Pentagon's contempt.

Gauging the Pentagon's take on supporting science fiction films is difficult since decisions were obviously made on an individual basis. Given the genre's association with escapist entertainment and preposterous subject matter unpacked in its idiosyncratic 1950s subgenres (giant/shrinking humans, alien invasions, giant creatures, etc.), Pentagon support would not be as readily forthcoming as for the war film. Sometimes, though, the propagandistic potential of the genre, especially in its appeal to child and teenage audiences, produced exactly the opposite effect. The Disney studio's 20,000 *Leagues Under the Sea*, for example, "managed to obtain fairly significant Navy cooperation in the filming of both the feature and the documentary, as one scene included in both was shot from a U.S. Navy submarine, the *Redfish*" (Telotte 2010, 73).[7] "High quality films"—i.e., mid-budget films produced by major studios, like *The Thing* and *The Day the Earth Stood Still*—"used [not only] authentic scientific equipment borrowed from universities [but also had] tanks and machine guns on loan from the National Guard" (O'Donnell 171). However, the case of *The Day the Earth Stood Still* complicates the issue further since support from the National Guard had to be solicited after the army refused cooperation, perhaps because of the less-than-flattering portrait of the military in the film.[8] Meanwhile, studio projects at the B-level or projects produced on poverty row would find themselves completely locked out from such sources of support and authenticity, no matter how hawkish their political inclinations might have been and how favorable they would be in their portrait of "military life."[9]

Besides the cultural and political validation films could claim if they were produced with active Pentagon support, the economics of genre filmmaking dictated that an inexpensive solution to the representational problems of showing the military in action would have to be found.[10] This was true even at the low end of the budgetary scale where science fiction had wedded itself just as firmly to "the use of spectacle," as Victoria O'Donnell puts it, as it did at the high-budget end (171). Low budgets ruled out large casts of extras and expensive sets. Miniatures and mattes ("Some studios hired famous science fiction illustrators to do the scenic backdrops") provided a *relatively* inexpensive solution. But since there was an abundance of military stock footage after World War II and the Korean War, this material more than anything else provided *the* low-budget solution to the problem. Produced by the US government, stock footage was in the public domain, available not only at *low* but at *no* cost. Military spectacle, "though generally simplistic" (171), thus became available at any budgetary level.

Within a cinema that depended on "the use of spectacle," prestige would have been the price filmmakers had to pay in exchange for the savings that the use of stock footage allowed. Though the practice of using stock footage in general was neither limited to science fiction films, nor to B-movies and poverty-row productions, its status remained closely associated with an economics of desperation. It was also associated with a problematic aesthetics—deservedly or not—of technical incompetence, tearing open the smooth realistic surface of the classic Hollywood style and exposing the gaps, rifts, and incompatibilities of a text assembled from various disparate sources. Stock footage of locations or mundane activities, also commonly used in Hollywood filmmaking (e.g., a wide shot of a street scene that precedes the cut to a soundstage interior with principle actors), draws little attention to itself. These images are commonly limited to transitional moments, establishing shots, or cutaways.[11] But the desire of 1950s science fiction cinema to stage the display of the military within an aesthetic of spectacle inevitably draws attention to the moments when films' aesthetic and technical reach exceeds their grasp most egregiously. Some critics still see positive potential in the practice. Luciano, for example, argues that the "very fact that [newsreel footage] is easily recognizable as library footage—its poor quality contrasting sharply with the staged action—[makes] it a constant reminder that [a science fiction film] is an extrapolation from the known world" (71). This is an attempt at redeeming the practice which, simultaneously, acknowledges the "poor quality" of external materials and their integration into the film.

In the end, it is the economics of filmmaking that nudges a film toward the use of stock footage. This admission of low production value then places a film in a precarious position within a symbolic economy of conspicuous consumption—i.e., a sense of filmmaking in which large budgets are seen as "giving the audience something for their money." The inherent prejudices construed by this alignment of real and symbolic value, or the lack thereof, tend to obscure two important facts. First, the use of stock footage is a practice common in all Hollywood filmmaking. Like editing, which serves as its primary technical vehicle, it is essentially a non-mimetic device in service of mimetic ends, a practice that creates realism by the most artificial of means. Second, as a way of fabricating meaningful images, it is so prevalent in this specific cycle of films that it is one of *the* trademark elements of 1950s science fiction films. To consider it purely as a budgetary indicator fails to consider its meaning and function in the films themselves. It deserves critical consideration as a technology, a practice, a formal element with the power to tell a story. In other words, the question "Why are they all doing it" is a less important one than "What does it mean?" Having addressed the former question, I would like to move on to the latter one.

The focus in 1950s science fiction film on, specifically, *military* stock footage is obviously linked to the genre's thematic proximity to the military-industrial complex. Anyone conscious of the ubiquity of the military in these films, regardless of any individual film's political and ideological stance, will wonder how closely science fiction and the war film are operating in relation to each other. Which films, we might ask, were produced with the consent or even support of the Pentagon? What were the procedures by which the Pentagon could respond to a film, support it, criticize, or even suppress it? Besides these questions about the production end of things, we might also raise questions about cinematic aesthetics in service to ideology. In order to address these questions, I will first try to establish a baseline, an average, of cinematic techniques and aesthetic models by discussing specific examples from a variety of films. I will then move on to one film, Alfred E. Green's *Invasion U.S.A.* (1952), that comes closest to that category Luciano describes as being "constructed of nothing but library footage" (70). True, the claim of a film that is "pure" stock footage does not apply to *Invasion U.S.A.*—in fact, as the discussion will show, the parts that frame the imported footage serve an important function, minuscule as their standing might be in the film's complete running time. Yet the film still provides a fascinating example of B-grade filmmaking that eventually arrives at a self-reflexive critical stance toward its own material. Many critics read this type of self-reflexive stance as a form of camp, a radical form of self-deconstruction that highlights the artificiality and thus primarily the self-referentiality of the aesthetic form. In this film, however, I will emphasize how self-reflexivity can be read as a politically subversive gesture, a deconstruction of unquestioned ideological assumptions.

How to Splice and Dice: Some Distinctive Features

For a closer look at the use of military stock footage, let me return to the scene from *Plan 9 from Outer Space*. The sequence begins, as the voiceover narration tells us, with "three flying saucers over Hollywood Boulevard." Famously (or infamously), these flying saucers are represented by crude miniatures superimposed upon an urban backdrop shot out of the window of a driving car. The first stock footage is that of newspapers rolling off the printing presses, which are then picked up by a pair of anonymous hands that unfold the paper to reveal a headline that reiterates the visual information: flying saucers over Hollywood. The same newspaper appears in several different contexts leading into an extended montage sequence that returns repeatedly to the issue of incredulity (e.g., a drunk unable to believe his own eyes). Only then does Wood cut to stock footage of an airplane flying over the Pentagon, a rotating radar dish, a convoy of Jeeps driving along a country road, and rocket

Military Stock Footage 63

Splicing and Dicing: Bargain-Basement Aesthetics in *Plan 9 from Outer Space*

Flying Saucers over Hollywood—with Korean Villagers: *Plan 9 from Outer Space* (Ed Wood, 1959)

launchers setting up in front of that Korean village. As the battery opens fire, Wood stitches that image to a static shot of an actor dressed as a colonel watching the skies through a pair of binoculars. The sequence is expanded by cutting from the colonel as an observer, to the miniatures of the flying saucers being hit by the barrage, and on to the stock footage of the artillery pieces on the ground. While the first two are shots lacking movement and depth, the stock footage opens a view into a wide landscape. Because it is grainier and higher in contrast than the original footage, it draws attention to the mismatch of the two disparately sourced materials.

To the extent that *Plan 9 from Outer Space* is fairly representative of its time, Wood articulates themes not limited to his own unique vision. The figure of the observer, for example, who is spliced into the sequence by way of reverse-angle or POV shots, appears in other films whenever military stock footage is imported. Robert Day's *First Man into Space* (1959) features a scene in which actor Marshall Thompson, playing a military officer, witnesses the fueling and test-firing of a jet engine on the ground. A long shot in the stock footage includes a man in military uniform with his back turned to the camera sticking his fingers in his ears as he watches the revving engine. A reverse angle close-up shot of Marshall matches the gesture, inserts the actor into the stock footage, and legitimizes Marshall's function as observer. Though both scenes use the actor as a means of establishing continuity between the indigenous and the imported footage, it is crucial that the character in both cases is explicitly coded as an observer. As a literal eyewitness, he stands in for the audience's own visual experience, someone whose visual apperception of the military technology is established as a theme in its own right.

At times, 1950s science fiction films vary these basic techniques. In Fred F. Sears's *Earth vs. the Flying Saucers* (1956), military stock footage is not only spliced into scenes with narrative continuity, it is also used in rear-projection sequences. In one sequence, an artillery battery opens up on a flying saucer, not unlike the scene in *Plan 9 from Outer Space*. The impact of the shell registers on the flying saucer as it passes in front of the Washington Memorial, which is added in rear projection. A moment later, the saucer will actually crash into the memorial, now represented by a miniature. In another scene, we see a flying saucer pass in front of an airplane; rear projection is framed by the windows of the cockpit. The next shot features footage of a World War II bomber going up in flames and rolling over in mid-flight before it goes into a steep downward dive—all this while a model of the flying saucer passes in front of the rear-projected stock footage.

Military Stock Footage   65

Military Stock Footage in Rear Projection: *Earth vs. the Flying Saucers* (Fred F. Sears, 1956)

The second characteristic feature worth noting in the use of military stock footage is that it is frequently deployed in montage sequences dealing with scenes of military mobilization. Apart from the liftoff sequence in Kurt Neuman's *Rocketship X-M* (1950), which cuts back and forth between different participants in the launch, there is also Spencer Gordon Bennet's *The Atomic Submarine* (1959), which splices together images of US nuclear submarines with shots of an actor making entries into a log, adding close-ups of that log with the hand entering the frame in the act of writing.[12] Cutting back and forth between different images of the naval vessel and the log, the sequence compresses the long duration of the journey by briefly suspending narrative progression. Both in regard to naval technology and to the representational space of the log's page, the scene's scope is panoramic. It attempts a conceptual inventory of military technology and geographic space, aligning the two with each other within a cinematic register of actual and virtual mapping (i.e., the actor's writing hand versus the documentary camera).

The third recurring feature is that military stock footage used in these and other films almost always shows the conventional arsenal of the US in action. Even though the term "atomic" might be *the* catchword of 1950s science fiction (note its presence in the title of *The Atomic Submarine*), conventional weapons far outweigh their nuclear counterparts. Again, this is hardly surprising considering the treasure trove of cinematic material from World War II and the Korean War available in the public domain. The preoccupation with conventional weapons may also have been a result of the relative novelty of America's nuclear arsenal. The secrecy surrounding this new arsenal, which made access to visual material difficult, weighs in on the situation as well. Images of deployment would have had to come either from the two explosions over Hiroshima and Nagasaki—but, then, no original photography exists of the Hiroshima blast. They might also have come from subsequent atomic testing, leaving editors with the difficult task of endowing the relatively static images of nuclear tests with the dramatic tension one would have expected from the same weapons deployed in actual combat. Clearly, science fiction films helped to enshrine the mushroom cloud as *the* iconic image of the decade. Then again, even though the mushroom cloud symbolized "the awesome power of American scientific and military know-how," and even though it "was promoted by various administrations to generate support for an arms race designed to win the Cold War and save the free world" (Titus 105), the icon's high degree of conceptual abstraction made it problematic for dramatic use within heroic narratives. By contrast,

The Top of the Low-Budget Heap: Alfred E. Green's *Invasion U.S.A* (1952)

images of America's conventional arsenal did not come with such limitations. This arsenal did see plenty of action in World War II and the Korean War, action which also happened to be prodigiously documented on film.

Invasion U.S.A. (Alfred E. Green, 1952)

If Warren Luciano is right, the poverty-row studio Republic Pictures may have catapulted itself to the top of the low-budget heap (or, rather, the bottom) when it "released two films in 1958 that are constructed of nothing but library footage [i.e., *Satan's Satellites* and *Missile Monsters*]" (70). But it was American Pictures' production of Alfred E. Green's *Invasion U.S.A.* (1952) that helped to establish the model half a decade earlier. There is more to the film than its substantial, perhaps even excessive use of stock footage—almost all military in origin and subject matter. Yet it is the fact that Green's film pushes the envelope when it comes to the quantity of external material that a film can accommodate, and the qualitative uses to which this material is assigned, for which the film deserves a closer look. The fact that the balance between external and indigenous material in *Invasion U.S.A.* is so skewed toward the material that, in more conventional films, is supposed to function merely as supplemental, undercuts some of the film's basic claims. When it comes to genre, for example, Tony Shaw and Denise Youngblood do not consider its basic premise—that of an all-out invasion of the US by the Soviet Union—as extrapolative in the sense that Luciano does ("a constant reminder that [a science fiction film] is an extrapolation from the known world" [71]). They see it as an American version of "agit-prop," the "Soviet Union's highly politicized, often clumsy style of mass persuasion" (21), which entertains a precarious, politically charged flirtation with the truth claims and cognitive expertise of documentary filmmaking. Even if Shaw and Youngblood are right and the film does work primarily as a piece of "agit-prop," its idiosyncratic stylistic excesses promise insights into the use of military stock footage as a tool of interpellation.

The film's story is quickly told. In a New York bar, a group of strangers gather. Among them are the owner of a tractor factory, an Arizona cattle rancher, a businessman and what in the polite parlance of sexual innuendo of the 1950s would have been called a "female companion," a television journalist, the bartender, and a mysterious stranger. The journalist begins, as preparation for next week's broadcast, to interview the patrons, querying them whether they are for or against the universal draft (". . . and by that I mean everything, soldiers for the army, factories for war work, labor for factories, the whole business . . . ?"). The ensuing conversation eventually reaches the mysterious stranger at the end of the bar. Once he has given his opinion, the television news, playing all the while in the background with the sound turned low, announces that an attack on the US across the Bering Strait has begun. The patrons immediately begin to leave the bar, to return home to San Francisco or Arizona, or to return to their respective jobs. From there, each character's narrative outlines one particular set of events and experiences during the progress of the war. As the Soviet invaders overwhelm first the West Coast, then the East Coast, and finally establish control over the entire nation, one character after another meets a violent end. The owner of the tractor factory is gunned down when he refuses to switch production to military hardware for the enemy. The cattle rancher and his family drown in a deluge after the Soviets bomb a dam. The bartender dies in the rubble of a collapsing building when the Soviets drop a nuclear bomb on New York City. And the television journalist is shot when he tries to protect the young woman he met as the industrialist's "companion" in the bar; the two had become an item at the onset of the war. When she flings herself out the window rather than be raped by one of the boorish Soviet soldiers who have stormed into her apartment, her falling body is suddenly superimposed onto the brandy glass held by the mysterious stranger in the bar. This odd transition returns characters and audience to the opening scene. The stranger turns out to be a hypnotist and the war merely a collective (and apparently shared) illusion he induced in the patrons. The final scene mixes relief with warning; the war might have been a fiction, but one so instructive and persuasive that all characters go off on their separate paths with an enlightened, shared sense of patriotic fervor.

A few select details from the narrative should suffice to substantiate Shaw and Youngblood's claim that *Invasion U.S.A.* is basically a propaganda film, and a blunt and at times clumsy one at that. Though the Soviets are never identified by name as the enemy, when they do appear, they speak with the stereotypical accent one would expect. One of the two soldiers that invade the young woman's apartment is played by a somewhat diminutive actor, the other by a large, brutal-looking one. As a complementary pairing, one has his masculinity impaired by too little testosterone, the other by too much. Inevitably, the runt murders the journalist, while the brute's threat of rape sends the girlfriend hurtling out the window as the only escape from a fate worse than death. Even more insidious is a factory employee who, before the invasion, is shown as a lazy, disgruntled union supporter. Once the troops have arrived, he is revealed as a fifth columnist who, taking over the factory, backhands the owner and takes his cigar (as a signal that behind Soviet assurances about workers' rights is a thinly concealed upper-class urge to rule). To the extent that these story elements are part of an interpellative effort, the anti-Soviet propaganda is so blunt, so crass as to be almost laughable. But, then, this propagandistic aspect of the film as a whole resides exclusively in the material shot and directed by Green, which frames and contextualizes the embedded stock footage. It is the quantity, the handling, and the instrumentalization of this stock footage that determines the film's idiosyncratic style and grounds its relation to the military-industrial complex.

Embedded in the frame narrative that takes place in the New York bar are the scenes of warfare that make up the bulk of the film. These are the scenes that are clearly intended as the spectacle promised by the film's title. To a large extent, the film's aesthetics develop out of the editing practices required to assemble substantial military stock footage into sequences with narrative coherence. Some of these scenes depict the invasion with its various battles, first in the air, then at sea, and finally by ground troops moving, marching, and in combat. Repeated sequences show US pilots being called up, exiting barracks, running to planes, and hoisting themselves into cockpits. Aerial combat scenes feature both bombers, single and in formation, dropping bombs, and engaging in dramatic dogfights. Frequently these dramatic duels end with planes being hit and spiraling down to the ground. The less successful ones among these extended montage sequences rely on the repetition of material from one scene to another, and often require diegetic observers edited into the sequence so lengthy that they would otherwise lose narrative cohesion. Whenever it is successful, the editing accomplishes narrative cohesion and produces startling moments. One such moment takes place when a fighter plane heads for the camera within a stock footage sequence. Since the footage is placed in rear projection behind a glass window—a technique we have already seen in *Earth vs. the Flying Saucers*—the glass shatters when the plane opens fire right before pulling up above the top of the frame.

Also effective are two scenes in which stock footage is used to depict the dropping of nuclear bombs. In the first scene, the bomb is used against a military air field; in the second scene, the explosion takes place above midtown Manhattan, New York City. Each respective moment is prepared by high-angle footage shot of the location itself, a perspective reminiscent of the aerial mapping of bombing sites.[13] A hard cut then moves us to footage of an atomic testing blast. Then, literally a split second later, it cuts to a lengthy upward tilt of a mushroom cloud rising up. While the brevity of the footage showing the actual blast hides the mismatch between locations, the lingering tilt of the cloud reinforces the visual continuity of the sequence, from the location to the explosion and on to aftermath. The second nuclear attack in the film, this one against New York City, supplements the sequence with a wide shot taken from one of the city's high-rise observation platforms. Panoramically captured from this location, the cityscape is overlaid in a double exposure with a smudgy black shading that suggests the rubble of flattened city blocks, from which smoke rises in various isolated spots. In both cases, the visuals are surprisingly efficient in their evocation of massive devastation (or what one might imagine the aftermath of a nuclear attack might actually look like—a sight not seen since Hiroshima and Nagasaki).

Where such efficiency is lacking is in the mismatched material in its historical configuration. Like the Korean villagers watching the artillery barrage against the alien spaceships over Hollywood in *Plan 9 from Outer Space*, many of the aerial combat scenes over America take place over agricultural spaces that look more like Korean rice paddies than the wheat or corn fields of Washington State where they are ostensibly taking place. Although enemy airplanes are repeatedly described in dialogue and expository radio traffic as having "characteristically swept-back wings"—presumably those of Russian MIG fighters—the actual airplanes shown throughout the film tend to vary. In order to make up for these deficiencies, the film substitutes American jet planes, some vaguely resembling their enemy counterpart, others fairly easy to spot. In many of the scenes, fast editing conceals the US Hawker Hunters, F-86A Sabre, and F-J2 Furies inserted to represent enemy planes. Whenever actual MIGS are used, they tend to be shown flying in formation. Invariably their orderly flight patterns are shot in perfectly steady tracking shots without the shaking and overcompensation accompanying actual combat footage. This strongly suggests that the material was culled from air shows, which means that, properly speaking, it is actually Soviet propaganda footage. What remains absent from the film are sequences in which these exact planes are seen in actual aerial combat. The wild mixture of jet and propeller planes also suggests that Green went back as far as World War II to gather exciting sequences.

Since similar problems with the limited availability of actual Soviet military hardware in action also plague the sequences of the film that show naval and ground combat, Green came up with an ingenious plot contrivance to cover up and narratively legitimize what otherwise would appear to rupture the film's claims to documentary realism. Repeated throughout the film is the message that the invading Soviet troops are disguised in US military uniforms. The message is clear—enemy action is often concealed behind dishonest and treacherous mimicry. Once this idea has been planted in the audience's mind, the film can proceed with presenting material selected for spectacular impact rather than historical plausibility. Combat sequences feature US soldiers in action on assorted battlefields in Europe during World War II and the Korean War.

Stylistically, the rapidity of editing used in both scenes of conventional and nuclear warfare is a double-edged sword. On the one hand, the increased speed of editing that is necessary to conceal or distract from mismatches in the material would contribute to the documentary claim of entire sequences. A shaky camera, the overshooting and overcompensating in pans and zooms, the graininess of footage (especially footage shot under less-than-ideal lighting conditions), and lens flares: all of this would register as signals that the material is authentic.[14] Similarly, the hasty and rough editing at high speeds would likely be perceived as another sign of verity and mimetic accuracy. On the other hand, if mismatches in the material would demand that editing speed be increased to a degree that its function as a corrective would become apparent, the increasingly frenzied editing pace would actually draw attention to itself. At least to some portion of the audience, the technical efficiency of the editing would actually undermine its claim to enhance authenticity. In other words, a magician waving one hand around a little too enthusiastically will actually raise suspicions about what is happening in the other hand rather than distract from it.

Based on the propagandistic efficiency of images of military mobilization and might, Warren Luciano comes to this general conclusion about the function of stock footage:

> Newsreel footage helps give the alien invasion film its sense of reality. This footage, coupled with special effects footage, creates a kind of dialectic between reality and illusion. With live performers functioning as drama, special effects footage functioning as illusion, and newsreel footage functioning as an identifiable reality, the films offer not reality itself but its semblance. (71)

Invasion U.S.A. happens to be somewhat lacking in special effects sequences; the miniatures used in the nuclear attack on New York City are virtually the only ones that stand out. Still, the "dialectic between reality and illusion" Luciano describes is also at play here. I would argue that it serves as an address to the audience. It interpellates viewers by way of their expertise in recognizing differences between conventions of the feature film and the documentary. By the mid-1950s, the adult members of the audience would still recall wartime propaganda in the form of newsreels. They would recognize the material's claim to factual accuracy, a claim asserted with striking and compelling simplicity in the voiceover line accompanying John Huston's propaganda film about the Battle of Midway: "Yes, this really happened" (*Battle of Midway*, 1942). Dissected and recontextualized, fragments of these newsreels might have lost their absolute claim to authenticity. But in dialectic relationship with other textual elements, they would nonetheless still evoke their original ontological status and thus import a version thereof into a feature film. In this sense, *Invasion U.S.A.* would simply be a political propaganda film mobilizing the US population for an impending war against the Soviet Union, calling the nation to militarize preemptively.

In some aspects, however, Luciano's description fails to capture *Invasion U.S.A.*; he is, after all, discussing primarily alien invasion films in which the aliens literally *are* aliens. This is especially true for the excess of military stock footage that Green embeds into the film. While Green faithfully executes Luciano's ideological model in its surface aesthetic, he is also ratcheting up the quantitative excess that characterizes the film's aesthetic. Can we still speak of an aesthetic, and thus cognitive, "dialectic" if the balance of indigenous and imported material is so skewed toward the latter? What if military stock footage makes up the bulk of the film? What if it spills over from the transitional and supplemental functions that most other films tend to assign to it? What if the film, in effect, reverses the principle by which a good fictional story requires a few stock images, and, instead, presents a film in which the story seems a mere afterthought to the rich tapestry of what used to be mere filler? It is in this subversive stance toward its own compositional principle that I would like to read the film as—unwittingly or not—a deconstruction of the political propaganda which, simultaneously, it delivers with such conviction and spirit.

The first seams that begin to unravel under close scrutiny are the ones that hold together the fiction of a mighty and aggressive enemy opposing US military power. The Soviet Union undoubtedly mobilized a considerable military machinery as part of its own imperialist agenda during the Cold War years, but visual evidence of this military machinery seems scarce in *Invasion U.S.A.* It is, in fact, so scarce that the film needs to compensate for the resulting gaps in its narrative by substituting American military might that has been thinly, almost perfunctorily disguised. Judging by the film's own visual evidence, the Soviet Union would put its arsenal on display under controlled circumstances, such as air shows and military parades, but it had barely produced images under battlefield conditions—at least as far as the availability of such images in the public realm to American filmmakers was concerned. Unlike the German Luftwaffe and the Imperial Japanese Air Force during World War II, which had been formidable enemies for at least part of the war, the Korean War produced little imagery of equal dramatic impact. Presumably US air superiority had been so crushing that actual air battles would remain an exception in the daily progression of hostilities (what testifies to this fact is that the extensive strategic bombing of North Korea from the end of 1951 to the end of the war, by and large uninterrupted by North Korean, Chinese, or Soviet interference except from the ground). As a result, *Invasion U.S.A.* actually undercuts its claim regarding the danger posed by the Soviet Union every time it resorts to using military stock footage from World War II and the Korean War. Cynical viewers might go so far as to point out that, as a propaganda film, the film's visuals support a message diametrically opposed to its surface narration. Particularly in regard to the Korean War and to air superiority, the film inadvertently announces the first of many instances of asymmetrical warfare in which the US was going to engage in the course of the Cold War (more about that in Chapter 4).

This self-defeating visual logic also applies to the exceptional status nuclear weapons enjoy among the military technologies *Invasion U.S.A.* puts on display. The two nuclear attacks featured in the film—one on an air force base, the other on New York City—are constructed out of footage of nuclear tests conducted, obviously, by the US. More is made of nuclear weapons in the film's expository dialogue. The audience learns, for example, that American forces have used nuclear weapons against many targets within the Soviet Union, carrying the war to the enemy's homeland and giving as good as they got. But these actions remain resolutely off-screen for a number of reasons. For one, the film delivers a cautionary tale about America's lack of military preparedness. Therefore, it needs to be as dire in its depiction of American casualties as possible in order to achieve the rousing effect it is aiming for. On a more practical level, repeated scenes of nuclear explosions would have had to be constructed out of re-edited versions of the same limited amount of stock footage. The result might have been a little too transparent, even for Green and his team. And, finally, the film invites the audience's masochistic enjoyment of victimization; once it has shown the devastation of New York City with casualties on the ground, the visual evocation of corresponding casualties among the enemy is likely to undercut vengeful enthusiasm for retributive violence among the audience. Within the military imagination of its time, the film's two scenes of nuclear deployment underwrite the idea of the tactical nuke, a reductive application of military strategy derived from conventional weapons to nuclear ones.

Hence, World War III, as *Invasion U.S.A.* imagines it, is essentially a conventional war, despite the nuclear bombs that are dropped on- and off-screen. The bulk of its mobilization and combat scenes follow the drawn-out maneuvering of conventional armies claiming and occupying territory. Its primary agents are airplanes, tanks, battle ships, and platoons of marching GIs and descending paratroopers—a vision sharply contrasting with competing and far more persuasive projections of World War III as a violent spasm, a rapid, unheroic, high-tech "fifteen minute war" that crops up in literary science fiction of the period.[15] This commitment to a vision of conventional war also extends to the use of nuclear weapons in the film. Any mention of nuclear fallout, of the devastating long-term effects of radiation poisoning on those surviving in the vicinity of the various ground zero locations throughout the film, is resolutely suppressed. Life in New York City after the atomic blast is allowed to march on to its grim conclusion—invasion, occupation, enforced collaboration, murder, and rape—with no one's health visibly affected. Unwilling or unable to confront the technological idiosyncrasies of nuclear war, the film reverts back to heroic, nostalgic visions of World War II and the Korean War and commits to these visions as its political model.

All of these inconsistencies and disruptions within the film's visual fabric call for the story to come to the film's rescue. Only a safe, officially sanctioned narrative can contain the visual chaos. Interpellation, if it is to proceed smoothly and accurately, must be shored up against the textual flaws. This worked for *Invaders from Mars*, which frames its spectacular alien invasion narrative as the colorful fantasy of a little boy; it is, the film tells us, merely a visual embodiment of the infantile "illusion of central position" and "omnipotence of thought" Freud talks about in his discussion of the uncanny. *Invasion U.S.A.* also resorts to a frame narrative, this one presenting Soviet aggression as a cautionary fable conjured up by the mysterious stranger in the bar for the education of the other patrons. Again, on a superficial level, the use of military stock footage delivers an easily accessible message of political propaganda. As Luciano puts it, the sight "of the massive military hardware marching against the invaders is a rallying point not only for the cinematic characters but also for the spectator [who] knew all too well the firepower of America's military might" (72). But something else is going on here as well. The propaganda message in *Invasion U.S.A.* is framed as a consensual fantasy; the television journalist and the young woman recognize their shared romantic subplot as soon as they have been woken up to reality, just as everyone in the group appears to be cognizant of everyone else's fate, even if they were not present for parts of their storylines. With this recognition, the film comments upon itself. More specifically, it presents a meta-commentary on the embedded narrative as an ideological fiction and as a piece of politically partisan cinema.

For one, there is the failure of the film to produce that enemy with its visual strategy of supplying embedded stock footage as documentary evidence. Without the Soviet Union as a viable enemy, the essential part of the film's ideological construct is called into question. This would be the idea that the film actually mobilizes for an all-out war against the Soviet Union. True, the suspenseful and ultimately unsuccessful struggle of the US against the alien invader is the threat on which the narrative as a cautionary tale hinges. Had the US been better prepared militarily, had the nation been more suspicious, more committed to decisive action, the enemy would have never been emboldened to attack, or never been successful in vanquishing America. This narrative logic is spelled out in a title card used during the closing credits, which shows a quote by George Washington superimposed upon a regal portrait of its author: "To be prepared for war is one of the most effectual means of preserving peace." However, the repeated pronouncement of the film's nameless fictional president that the Soviet Union's attack of the US constitutes "another day of infamy" links the attack to Pearl Harbor (not surprisingly, this president is vaguely reminiscent of Eisenhower, yet, inexplicably, he is only shot from behind in a half-glimpsed profile shot).

This may be the last time that the film has the opportunity to allude to World War II, a historical referent that had already been insistently underscored by the film's use of World War II stock footage. But, then, World War II has already played an important role in the frame narrative itself. In the opening scene, before the characters are put under hypnosis by the mysterious stranger, the television journalist Vince Potter (Gerald Mohr) polls the patrons of the bar on the question whether they are for or against a universal draft. While the question sounds like it concerns matters of military preparedness—a Cold War concern if there ever is one—the qualifying comment following directly afterward reroutes the question's main thrust from military to economic and political matters: ". . . and by that I mean everything, soldiers for the army, factories for war work, labor for factories, the whole business . . . ?" In response, the cattle rancher complains that "there is too much government in business already." He does not like the government imposing market and price controls on his business and weighing him down with high income taxes. At this point, the mysterious stranger jumps into the conversation, commenting that, if the rancher is paying high taxes, then he surely must be making good money. "I do all right," he replies modestly and a little smugly, but still raises his glass to the toast, "Down with taxes!" Next on the journalist's roster is George Sylvester (Robert Bice), the tractor manufacturer, who replies, "Draft factories? Well, that's communism." He goes on to tell about an army major who was sent into his plant a week earlier. This is an episode the film recounts in a brief flashback. The major is asking for the plant to halt or slow down civilian production to meet army demands for new tanks. Refusing cooperation, Sylvester insists on the importance of his private profits and on the profits of his distributors who depend on him. He gets quite irate when the major points out that a future national emergency might very well lead to a mandatory seizing of his plant by the federal government. Sylvester's female companion, Carla Sanford (Peggy Castle), recounts how she quit her job in a munitions factory during World War II because it ruined her hands. At this point, the congressman having a drink at the other end of the bar, Arthur Harroway (Wade Crosby), steps in and delivers an impassioned speech about his constituents not liking communists, war, and high taxes. This is an agenda of mutually exclusive priorities he seems all too comfortable to gloss over in the spirit of bureaucratic inefficiency and spinelessness typical of a slightly oily professional politician. Tim the bartender (Tom Kennedy) eventually gets a chance to chime in with a blithely apolitical opinion: he will mix and serve drinks regardless of who is in charge of the country.[16] In the end, all characters are eventually either punished (the bartender dies in the nuclear attack on New York, the cattle rancher and his family drown after the bombing of a dam, and the tractor plant owner is gunned down when he refuses collaboration with the communist invaders), or they are converted to the film's explicit message (Carla Sanford, the female companion, volunteers as a Red Cross nurse, and Vince Potter, the television journalist, tries repeatedly to enlist; all this earns them only a few moments of romantic bliss before both become casualties of the new cruel masters as well). It is hard to miss where the film's political sympathies lie.[17]

Within the political logic of the film, the issues at stake are clearly prioritized: military defeat is a result of insufficient preparedness, which, in turn, is a result of civic irresponsibility and selfishness. Within this logic, perpetual vigilance and preparedness are clearly linked to the civilian population's readiness to make sacrifices. These commendable attitudes are, in turn, linked primarily to economic matters, from the ratio between corporate profits to federal taxes to the degree of governmental control over private enterprise. There is also a collective historical narrative implied in this prioritized thematic and political agenda: from a period in which the population was willing to make such sacrifices—World War II—to the period in which the necessity for the continuation of the sacrifice was seen as being less obvious or even altogether lacking. What the film has in mind here is the transition from the immediate postwar period to the mid-1950s, which it posits as the resurgence of that old spirit of national sacrifice. Carla Sanford's story is exemplary in this respect; she went from the World War II munitions factory to a life of leisure and then returns, triggered by the film's fictitious invasion, to quasi-military duty. It is exactly this remilitarization the film ultimately advocates, a return to the spirit of World War II. And, as the film's visual vocabulary has it, World War III will be exactly like World War II, from the "day of infamy" with which it begins to the conventional arsenal with which it will be fought and, more important, won.

The Shifting Consensus

There is a strong sense of urgency with which a film like *Invasion U.S.A.*—and, by extension, the signifying power of embedded military stock footage in general—advocates the nation's return to the ideological consensus of World War II. Given this urgency, it is useful to point out where and by how much the film's ideological agenda diverges from what is commonly regarded as the culture of containment typical of 1950s Cold War America. In reference to Paul Boyer's book *By the Bomb's Early Light*, Alan Nadel has summarized this cultural consensus brilliantly by drawing attention to what he calls "a whole language of awe and terror, apocalypse and utopia, internationalism and xenophobia emerging specifically around atomic weaponry and generally about atomic power" (14). Emerging from this condition, Nadel sees "a national narrative developed to control the fear and responsibility endemic to possessing atomic power" (14). Together with Boyer and many others, Nadel reads "the central motif of that narrative [as] 'containment,'" a strategy or posture "in which insecurity was absorbed by internal security, internationalism by global strategy, apocalypse and utopia by a Christian theological mandate, and xenophobia—the fear of the Other—by courtship [. . .]" (14). It is fairly obvious that the critical emphasis on containment as a key theme in US Cold War culture underwrites readings of 1950s horror and science fiction films that focus on their anti-communist stance and their nuclear rhetoric. In the film's nervousness about the enemy's nuclear arsenal and the covert activities of fifth columnists, the propagandistic surface text of *Invasion U.S.A.* expresses the xenophobia and the apocalyptic ambivalences surrounding nuclear weapons Nadel sees as main concerns of containment culture. The imperatives of containment as a form of collective reassurance against "insecurity," a blueprint for a "national narrative developed to control [. . .] fear," would explain how someone likes Luciano reads the "sight of the massive military hardware marching against the invaders [as] a rallying point not only for the cinematic characters but also for the spectator [who] knew all too well the firepower of America's military might" (Luciano 72).

What Nadel calls "the trauma caused by witnessing a Great Depression, a Second World War, an ascent to atomic power, and a fantasy-like economic boom in less than one generation" (*Containment Culture* xi) makes it necessary to construct a new ideological and political agenda. This new agenda serves as a bulwark against bad historical memories. Especially after World War II, it also links this sanitized version of the past to fears about the future. Nadel's backward glance, from the 1930s to the '50s, is particularly revealing in regard to the use of military stock footage. After all, the practice extended the visual presence of World War II into the postwar period, allowing 1950s films to demand a return to World War II values and practices by positing historical continuity. This reframing of the World War II experience by way of military stock footage did not only perform the cultural labor of manufacturing or reconfirming collective memories that contravened the trauma of that war; it also integrated a new military conflict fought with a conventional arsenal—i.e., the Korean War—into the same overarching narrative. It is noteworthy that the Korean War halted and reversed the massive demobilization of the conventional arsenal the US had undergone subsequent to World War II. It was the Korean War which, in Howard Zinn's words, "mobilized liberal opinion behind the war and the President [and] created the kind of coalition that was needed to sustain a policy of intervention abroad, militarization of the economy at home" (Zinn, *People's History* 420). This ideological continuity comes with the military continuities between World War II and the Korean War—two wars fought by conventional forces, with Hiroshima and Nagasaki as *military anomalies* within World War II. It also comes with strategic deliberations to deploy nuclear weapons in Korea as a minority opinion. Fortunately for all involved, this opinion never gained actionable support within the Eisenhower administration. Given the strong predilection for the conventional arsenal within military stock footage, 1950s horror and science fiction films reassert these continuities. They do this not only to the retrospective benefit of World War II, but also to the benefit of the American experience on the Korean peninsula. What appears as a historically indiscriminate amalgamation of imagery from different conflicts provides visual evidence of the essential sameness of these conflicts. It thus extends, by implication, the triumphalist discourse on World War II to the Korean War as well—an invaluable benefit for a war as barely understood and as badly conceptualized and legitimized. Not only did the historical superimposition underscore and extend post-World War II triumphalism, but it also absorbed, or at least contained, the ambivalence most Americans felt about the outcome of the Korean War—i.e., the ceasefire agreement signed after both warring factions had withdrawn (permanently, as it turned out) to the territorial border from which they had originally started. While the Korean War may have helped to set in motion a new cycle of war films, science fiction films still relied on complex mechanisms of displacement and projection in amalgamating historically disparate conflicts into one and the same legitimizing discourse.[18] In this regard, they participated in a larger cultural effort to lower the profile of the Korean War and thus erase its more troubling implications from historical memory.

While *Invasion U.S.A.* fits into this general pattern, it also sheds light, more specifically, on the role that the military-industrial complex plays in this narrative of historical continuity. In an odd twist, the film goes against the prevalent use of frame narrative. Conventionally, frame narratives tend to "contain" the subversive potential within their embedded narratives (one might think of the endings of films like *The Cabinet of Dr. Caligari* or even *Invasion of the Body Snatchers*). In contrast, the subversive potential in *Invasion U.S.A.* actually emerges from the frame narrative itself. I am referring to the television journalist's daily poll questions about the introduction of a universal draft (or, to be more precise, the reversal of the abolishment of the universal draft that came at the end of World War II). The agenda behind this poll question is strongly reminiscent of Alan Nadel's catalogue of historical trauma—"a Great Depression, a Second World War, an ascent to atomic power, and a fantasy-like economic boom in less than one generation" (*Containment Culture* xi). This may be a list of traumatic events that affected ordinary Americans, but it is also a list of grievances on the part of the military-industrial complex. From this perspective, the economic distress in the run-up to World War II might be caused or at least exacerbated by US hesitation to intervene militarily in Europe and react militarily to Japanese imperialist expansion. It would also be the equivalent of the economic slump that came with massive demobilization and labor unrest in the immediate postwar years. The lessons from these booms and busts of American economic history are clear: war is good for the nation, which is why the US should operate as a permanent war economy.

If World War II was to be the model for this permanent war economy, the question arises whether that war lived up to the full significance—part nostalgia, part actual history—with which 1950s discourse seems to invest it. "By certain evidence," Howard Zinn argues, "it was the most popular war the United States had ever fought. Never had a greater proportion of the country participated in a war: 18 million served in the armed forces, 10 million overseas; 25 million workers gave of their pay envelope regularly for war bonds" (*People's History* 398). Though Zinn wonders to what degree support for the war was "manufactured," he must also concede that "almost all Americans were [. . .] in agreement—capitalists, Communists, Democrats, Republicans, poor, rich, and middle class" (398). This is a list in which particularly the American left, including labor unions and the Communist Party, stands out as the epitome of a broad consensus. Coming from a historian on the political left like Zinn, this characterization of World War II seems to confirm the high level of significance which *Invasion U.S.A.*, and, to various degrees, many other science fiction films that use military stock footage, assign to it. As far as national unity is concerned, World War II would be an exemplary precedent for rallying the nation around the agenda of the military-industrial complex.

If the war did indeed provide the crisis that helped to assemble this broad consensus, it imparted a useful historical lesson. If the Cold War was predicated on the threat of a perpetually imminent crisis that would never reach the tipping point, how would one demand sacrifices from all for a common good? In a historical situation that did not exactly meet the conditions of war, the urgency of a genuine crisis had to be manufactured in order to justify extending wartime measures. As *Invasion U.S.A.* itself argues, large parts of the population—from industrialists to the man or woman in the street—are unwilling to make sacrifices as long as no compelling reason exists. *Invasion U.S.A.* is limited by its propagandistic bluntness to deal with these widespread reservations in any other forms than to condemn them as individual character flaws. Some people, the film argues, are lazy and selfish. They are limited by narcissistic inability to see beyond their own personal satisfaction and well-being. In the film, these are signs of a lack of political education, or symptoms of a social malaise in which civil virtues have yielded to the softening influences of affluence and comfort. To rouse such an audience from its stupor, a didactic shock must be administered. The film's grimness makes sense when measured against this intention; seeing the US lose an imaginary war against a Soviet invasion might very well be that shock.

Considering how blunt and persistent the propagandistic overtones of *Invasion U.S.A.* are, one cannot help but wonder what resistance the film was gearing itself up to overcome. If Green deemed such aggressive interpellation necessary, he must have been convinced that there was considerable resistance to the military-industrial complex entrenching itself as a permanent way of life. In his examination of World War II as "the people's war," Zinn points out the fractures in the nostalgic historiographic fiction of national unity during the war. The grains of sand in the nostalgic machinery included the racial segregation of the armed forces (406), the internment of Japanese Americans (407), and the large numbers of conscientious objectors (409). More important, he also reminds readers of the "fourteen thousand strikes, involving 6,770,000 workers, more than in any comparable period in American history" (408) that plagued the nation during the war. Despite "the overwhelming atmosphere of patriotism and total dedication to winning the war, despite the no-strike pledges of the AFL and CIO" (408), labor and capital remained in enemy camps.[19] These forms of protest would continue after the war, confronting the Truman administration with a variety of challenges to domestic, racial, social, and economic policy. Despite its ultra-conservative leanings, *Invasion U.S.A.* ultimately testifies to this political resistance against both World War II and the Cold War no matter how much, superficially, it appears to confirm the myth of the 1950s as a period of conformity and complacency fostered by universal affluence and broad social consensus.

In the final instance, it is important to remember that the propagandistic effects of military stock footage in 1950s science fiction films are achieved entirely without the cooperation of the US military. In fact, films would resort to military stock footage in response to budgetary limitations and in pursuit of political subject matter precisely *because* the Pentagon denied them cooperation and approval. One would suspect that the vast array of Hollywood productions that were, in contrast, actively endorsed and supported by the military-industrial complex (war films, historical epics, etc.) would have had to undergo far more scrutiny by the Pentagon. Exacerbated by the studios' unwillingness to jeopardize material support and thus endanger profits, these films were likely to come with an ideological agenda far more supportive of American postwar militarization. And yet this is exactly my point about postwar American militarization and the impact of the military-industrial complex: that science fiction films of the period contributed to, and participated in, a system larger than the nexus of cinema and the military, or cinema and politics. They served as a component of what C. Wright Mills called "the military metaphysics," a more pervasive and totalizing set of interactions and practices in which the military provided the subject matter, the methods and procedures, and the underlying ethos. Whatever *Invasion U.S.A.* unwittingly or unintentionally might reveal about national mythology, the makers of the film were actively in pursuit of an agenda that operated diametrically opposed to the more critical aspect of the film. In other words, no matter whether a film endorsed militarism yet failed to garner Pentagon support; no matter whether a film explicitly criticized militarism and failed to garner Pentagon support—the central significance of the military in the film itself would remain a constant. In judging the success of individual films as tools of recruiting an indifferent, ambivalent, or, in some cases, actively opposed population to this system, one might consider Howard Zinn's historical summary of the long 1950s.

> Around 1960, the fifteen-year effort since the end of World War II to break up the Communist-radical upsurge of the New Deal and wartime years seemed successful. The Communist party was in disarray—its leaders in jail, its membership shrunken, its influence in the trade union movement very small. The trade union movement itself had become more controlled, more conservative. The military budget was taking half of the national budget, but the public was accepting this. (*People's History* 433)

Fractured as the historical subtext in science fiction films from the 1950s might have been, Zinn's pessimistic overview of history suggests that surface rather than subtext would turn out to be a more accurate predictor of the larger political context with which a film would align itself. In fact, as an example of Cold War propaganda, *Invasion U.S.A.* can be counted as a success in legitimizing the Cold War consensus. This means that it can also be counted as a successful endorsement of the military-industrial complex, which seemed to have replaced the consensus established before and through World War II by the New Deal.

The extended and spectacular military fantasy in *Invasion U.S.A.* enshrines World War II as the ultimate historical touchstone of whatever the next war was going to be; it celebrates the hardware, the material abundance of weapons, and the dynamic spectacle of battle. And yet it does pay relatively little attention to the human agents of the conflict: the soldiers on the battlefield. The experiences of these soldiers upon their return from the battlefield would require a whole new set of metaphors to express and contain the horrors they had witnessed. How science fiction films provided a crucial metaphor for this cultural labor is the topic of the next chapter.

Chapter Two
Veterans

Perfect Copy, Poor Substitute: Scenes from a Postwar Marriage

One of the most striking depictions of a 1950s marriage in trouble is to be found not among the melodramatic "women's films" of the time. Though the film's sensational tabloid-style title, which seems to speak in a breathless and intimate female voice straight out of *True Confessions* magazine, links it exactly to those films, the film in question is one of the minor science fiction films of the 1950s cycle, Gene Fowler's *I Married a Monster from Outer Space* (Paramount, 1958).[1] In a key scene of the film, the newly married husband and wife, early on during their wedding night, are toasting each other in a romantic restaurant. What we know that blushing bride Marge (Gloria Talbott) does not is that husband Bill Farrell (Tom Tryon) has been replaced by an alien impostor. While the real Bill is kept in suspended animation on a concealed spaceship in the woods, the alien will engage with Marge in a somewhat conflicted and ultimately unsuccessful attempt to procreate. As Marge and the fake Bill face each other across the table in profile, another couple is reflected in a window between them as if to provide a visual double that represents the particular nature of compromised authenticity of the one in the foreground. As the couple retires to their hotel room for what the film leaves very little doubt will be the first-ever consummation of the marriage, a thunderstorm breaks outside. Thunder and lightning provide the suitably gothic backdrop for Marge standing on the balcony as Bill comes up behind her. Both confess their sexual inexperience to each other: "Maybe you've guessed," Marge admits, "but I've never been on a honeymoon before," to which Bill replies, "Neither have I." Bill only tells Marge that he loves her after she compels him to say it; she knows it, and so does the audience. Bill's sexual reluctance is as strange as his apparent lack of comprehension that the sound from across the ocean outside is that of thunder. It is not clear whether the romantic kiss Marge then demands proves satisfactory to her or not, but Marge's announcement that she will "go inside" is more of a sexual invitation than a sign of

Suppressed Male Menace in the Postwar American Marriage: *I Married a Monster from Outer Space*

disappointment. She is undeterred, ready and willing to have a go even if her husband is not quite living up to the active role she has a right to expect from him. Obviously, she will need to do all the work. As she walks away, the camera stays on Bill, who continues to stare out into empty space in an odd mixture of blankness and emotional intensity. He then moves into a tighter close-up so that, as lightning illuminates the frame, we can see, in a flickering double-exposure, a hideously swollen, convoluted fleshy substratum below his handsome face. A cut to the inside of the room shows Marge, both unaware of her husband's real face, as Bill's back is turned to her in that brief moment of truth, and framed by a wall mirror which shows, in reverse reflection, the waiting marriage bed (or, rather, two separate beds, in accordance with the Production Code). Again, she needs to call him by name to bring him into the room, an address that reminds him of his connubial duties. To the degree that gender roles are ideologically determined, this is what Louis Althusser would call an act of interpellation, demanding from Bill that he does what society demands of him. A second kiss follows, clearly more passionate for Marge than for Bill. Yet the scene does not end in mid-kiss, as one might expect. After the kiss has ended, both cling to each other in a rather ambiguous pose that suggests both union and separation, desire and coldness, sexual intimacy and a deep mutual unease with just that intimacy. Though the final fade-to-black omits the ensuing sexual encounter, body language in these last few seconds suggests that most likely, there will have been none when the night is over. And how could there be when Bill is an alien from outer space?

What Marge cannot know is that her husband—or, rather, the alien impersonating him—is a familiar figure throughout 1950s science fiction films. Whenever popular cinema at the time does not imagine alien invasion as a full-scale military assault on humanity, the invaders tend to come disguised as human beings, a bodily incarnation of the other visually indistinguishable from the self. Alien invasion then becomes a matter of creeping, silent infiltration, of internal subversion and corruption, a paranoid nightmare of fifth-column activities, secrecy, sabotage, and brainwashing. In the final instance, this silent subversion makes military might obsolete because it has already hollowed out the nation, robbed it of its identity, corrupted and alienated it from itself, and brought it to the verge of implosion. The figure of the alien invader—who looks and walks and talks like us, and is likely to appear as someone we know and love—comes in a variety of shapes and forms. In *It Came from Outer Space*, the aliens are taking over and inhabiting human bodies as a temporary measure, a metaphor that transforms the supernatural trope of demonic possession into a science fiction metaphor of corporeal takeover. True selves are returned to their matching bodies, both unharmed, after these bodies have served their purpose. In *Invaders from Mars*, humans are turned into aliens by being implanted with a small device, barely visible at the nape of their necks, which renders them pliant to alien commands; removal of the device comes with catastrophic consequences for the host. *Invasion of the Body Snatchers* imagines the entire human body being replaced by an alien seed pod that develops into a perfect copy of the original, which is then discarded as a lifeless husk.[2] The result of each one of these substitutions is what appears to be a human being who is a mere shadow of its former self. The product is an entity acting just peculiar enough to draw attention to itself, or one so perfectly normal that, to the properly paranoid observer, this very normality becomes a warning sign that something is not quite right. After all, the fact that the fake Uncle Ira in *Invasion of the Body Snatchers* has a scar exactly where the real one does is the reason why his niece Wilma is convinced that *this* Uncle Ira is not *her* Uncle Ira (King, *Danse Macabre* 312).

Subtle as the differences among these films might be, the alien impostor has a distinct shape and form created by the performance of actors and actresses, some of whom are asked to play a character both before and after he or she has been transformed into an alien impostor. The shape and form of the alien impostor are also determined by a cinematic style that tends to frame his or her appearance and performance in a manner that accretes particular stylistic elements to that particular figure. And, finally, there is an apparatus of cinematic props and special effects, from the bodily mark of the alien implant to subtly transformed bodily features, which helps to create this figure. At one end of the spectrum, we find alien impostors whose bodies and actions are clearly marked as odd or conspicuous when measured against the impostor's attempt to pass him- or herself off as human. Their actions tend to be stiff and mechanical; their gaze is tightly focused yet without object; their entire demeanor is uneasy, self-conscious, and stiff. Often, this unnatural demeanor if accompanied by bodily marks which give away their bearer's true identity. To the extent that these marks are subtle (the stiff pinkie in *The Invaders*, the mark on the neck in *Invaders from Mars*, the ability to see in the dark in *I Married a Monster from Outer Space*), the alien impostor acts with an uneasy self-consciousness and sensitivity matched only by the amplified attentiveness to such giveaways induced in the audience.

Attentiveness is also a feature of the cinematic style. Close-ups of the alien impostor's face often reveal a suspicious action or a blank stare to the audience, while characters in the film are denied this visual information. The camera tends to linger on the alien impostor, more suspiciously than curiously, regardless of narrative expediency, almost as if to catch the character at a moment of slippage. This attentiveness is at its peak with films on the other end of the spectrum. In these films, the alien's mimicry is so perfect that the lack of slippage, the absence of symptoms of otherness beneath the deceptive surface, becomes itself a symptom of the impostor's otherness. Films at this end of the spectrum do not feature blankly staring, robotically shuffling creatures barely able to conceal their true nature. Instead, they give us characters so emphatically normal that their very normality appears vaguely alarming. Paranoia reigns supreme, since the answer to the question of who is and who isn't an alien impostor is often withheld from the audience for long periods of time. *Invasion of the Body Snatchers* never leaves much doubt about whether one of the central characters has been "turned" or not. But among its cast of minor characters, it is anyone's guess as to who is and who isn't an alien impostor (quite yet). The alien seed pod and the discarded body of the human being replaced by an alien impostor also shift the revealing bodily marks away from the suspicious body and project them onto two separate objects. While these objects are kept in concealment, the alien impostor's body itself is free from any suspicious marks that betray his monstrous otherness.

Though it begins with the individual human body, the specter of a deadly quiet and inconspicuous alien infiltration that hangs over 1950s American popular culture ultimately envisions a final scenario in which the entire nation has been brought under alien control. A vast network of secret agents, disguised as human beings of all walks of life, will reveal itself to be in charge of the institutions of power. From the romantic couple as the smallest unit of social organization to the nuclear family, and from there to the American small town, alien invasion will radiate out to the rest of the nation. Films from the period, when read together as an overarching text, track this spread of subversion: Gene Fowler's *I Married a Monster from Outer Space* concentrates on the romantic couple, following its internal subversion when the husband-to-be is replaced by an alien impostor; William Cameron Menzies's *Invaders from Mars* begins with a similar substitution but examines the consequences within the realm of the nuclear family through the eyes of a child that is looking at its parents; and Don Siegel's *Invasion of the Body Snatchers*, after going through both of these earlier, more intimate stages, expands the view to the scale of the American small town, with an eye on the spread of the invasion to the rest of the nation. In none of these three films are the boundaries clearly drawn; Fowler's film does end in the same small town in which it begins. It is a town not unlike Santa Mira in *Invasion of the Body Snatchers*, which, once taken over by alien impostors, becomes a beachhead for a vaster onslaught on the nation and, presumably, the world. Taking matters one step further, *Invaders from Mars* keeps a watchful eye on the alien invasion spreading quickly from the nuclear family to the centers of political, economic, and military power out there in the larger world. Still, in each one of the three films one spatial dimension, linked to a unit of social organization, is given particular attention, establishing a thematic dominant that my own critical discussion is going to follow. Let me begin, then, with the smallest unit of social organization: the romantic couple.

Broken Husbands: The Romantic Couple's Failure to Reproduce

Taking some detours on its interpretive path to the heart of the romantic couple, scholarship on 1950s cinema began by focusing on larger historical contexts. Given widespread cultural concerns about social conformity and corporate dehumanization, the first wave of criticism read the aliens as allegorical representations of the threat of communism, stealthily invading and subverting the US, its social structures, and its institutions. In a complementary move, which retained emphasis on conformity and dehumanization but flipped the historical connotations of "self versus other," a second wave of criticism saw in the alien impostors the united, mindless, and intolerant forces of anti-communism. To these critics, the aliens were not the dreaded fifth columnists haunting the nightmares of McCarthy and HUAC, but McCarthy and HUAC themselves, silencing opponents and ensuring the uniformity of the American way of life. As an adjunct to this reading, some critics pointed out that corporate America, in the age of the man in the grey flannel suit, seemed to foster similar attitudes in the reorganization of the nation's economic life during the 1950s.[3] The third wave of criticism was to draw attention away from the compelling yet rigidly literal-minded application of the Cold War dichotomy to the films and their tropes. Here, the focus would be on the reflections of domestic policy and social life, the changing relations of the sexes, of generations, and of social classes, and the social and organizational paradigms that were to hold America together throughout these internal transformations.

The metaphor of the alien impostor proves flexible even beyond the boundaries of the fundamental Cold War polarity. This becomes apparent in two other interpretations of the film with which I started this chapter and to which I will return: *I Married a Monster from Outer Space*. David Seed, for example, reads the alien impostor in the film as a "compensatory fantasy" in response to "revelations in the mid-1950s of American POWS collaborating with their Korean captors, sometimes under brainwashing" (133). An immediate precursor to Richard Condon's bestselling novel *The Manchurian Candidate* (1959, adapted by John Frankenheimer in 1962), Fowler's film ties in to public shock and bafflement at footage of American soldiers admitting to crimes against humanity and refusing to return to the US upon release from North Korean and Chinese captivity. By assigning an explanation to this incomprehensible behavior—couched in the paranoid, xenophobic genre terms of the alien impostor—the film would provide its audience with what Seed considers "a compensatory fantasy for Korea" (133).[4] Not only would it remove all troubling ambiguities from the destabilizing behavior, it would also redeem the culprits, who, in the film, are released from their temporary suspension and returned to their true selves when a posse of men storms the alien ship and forces it to attempt an emergency takeoff.

Another critic, Robert Genter, reiterates Seed's assessment of the cultural impact of the Korean War POWs and the concern about Soviet and Chinese brainwashing techniques. Genter points to a medical rather than military context within American culture defined by a widespread interest in hypnotism. The phenomenon starts with the 1954 reports in the *Denver*

Post, written by William Barker, about "the strange experience of 33-year-old Colorado housewife Virginia Tighe, who, under hypnosis, had transformed into the personality of a long-deceased Irish woman from Cork [named Bridey Murphy]" (154). Following these reports, hypnotism would become a ubiquitous psychological technique linking a number of urgent cultural issues with each other. For one, there would be the rising popularity of Freudian psychoanalysis, which would feed into the recognition of psychological trauma of veterans returning from the Korean War (and, in turn, revisiting the same yet still largely unresolved issue in the context of World War II). In civil life, there would also be the rise of a burgeoning culture of self-help and therapeutic intervention (from the rise in popularity of Alcoholics Anonymous, after World War II, to the science fiction writer L. Ron Hubbard's creation of Scientology in the early 1950s). A parallel though not entirely unrelated concern was the rising awareness of and anxiety over the advertising industry. Especially in regard to its increasingly sophisticated techniques of customer research and manipulation, books like Vance Packard's *The Hidden Persuaders* (1957) and, less directly, Erving Goffman in *The Presentation of Self in Everyday Life* (1959) would become successful bestsellers.[5] Clandestine CIA research into psychopharmacological mind alteration and the manipulation of memory as a key to personality, as noted by Ken Hollings, must be added to this mix as well. The composite figure that emerges from all these hot-button issues of the time is the glassy-eyed, robotic, and externally directed character in science fiction films—the one I am describing as the alien impostor. In all its ambiguity, it embodies a complex allegory of various social obsessions and anxieties of the period.

Looking at the sexual politics of 1950s America, Harry Benshoff has discovered another important dimension of *I Married a Monster from Outer Space*. Benshoff traces the film's unease about the alien husband and his opaque sexuality back to the cultural afterlife of Alfred Kinsey's two reports on male (1948) and female (1953) sexuality (123–32). Since public discourse at the time habitually linked the medical deviance of homosexuality with the political deviance of communism (130), the insufficiently resolved tension created by Bill Farrell's odd sexual reluctance, uncomfortably on display in the wedding night scene, not only points to his political otherness, but it also complicates the Cold War requirement of sexual normality, of clear-cut gender roles, and of stable marriages. While Bill's sexual inexperience is somewhat curious for a young man so attractive, it might not in itself raise questions about his heterosexual commitment. However, the film goes on to complicate this sexual inexperience even further. First, it shows Bill repeatedly in situations of relaxed camaraderie with a group of men who are equally asexual or, if married, openly dismissive or even contemptuous of women altogether. It also shows Bill's sexual reluctance turning into a frightening sexual aggressiveness. Coupled with the frequent nightly visits with his male friends to the woods adjacent to the town, this adds up to a substantial challenge of his reliability as a "real man" devoted to a "real woman." Like "many of the 1950s films with communist infiltration subtexts," *I Married a Monster from Outer Space* "can also be read an [an allegory] about the invisible homosexual," Benshoff concludes. It is, after all, the story in which "a newly-wed husband [. . .], secretly a monster queer, finds it preferable to meet other strange men in the public park rather than stay at home with his wife" (130–31). Given Kinsey's discovery that Americans, beneath the surface, were far less sexually conformist with public morality than they would claim in public, Benshoff is not far off suspecting more than a touch of queer panic in *I Married a Monster from Outer Space*. In the light of this sudden uncertainty about sexual mores, the film might tell the story of a wife's discovery of her husband's closeted homosexuality at a time when divorce would, at best, be a shameful way out of this even more shameful conundrum.

What exactly does or does not occur in the bedroom, at least for the first half of the story, is left tantalizingly ambiguous, even though queer panic continues to linger over the entire film. On the one hand, the film offers a scene in which Marge consults her physician, who assures her that there is nothing physically wrong with her that would explain why, after one year of marriage, she has not conceived yet. This suggests that the couple is in fact sexually active, despite the fact that no conception has taken place. This would mean that Bill is either impotent or sterile. On the other hand, there is a scene preceding the wedding night in which Bill and his circle of friends—nearly all of them alien impostors like himself—gather at a roadside bar to celebrate his bachelor's party. As the camera travels through the room to settle eventually on the table of men, it stays briefly on two young women sitting at the bar. One of them complains to the other that, although they themselves are no less attractive than the men across the room, none of the men have paid them any attention whatsoever. This heterosexual disinterest on the part of the men sets the stage for the wedding night and the ensuring year of childlessness by suggesting Bill's sexual dysfunction to be a lack of interest rather than an inability to foster a child. He's just not that into Marge.

Linking the young bride's horrible suspicion that her husband might be a closeted homosexual back to that group of male friends at the roadside bar, the film provides another possible context for the group's social and, potentially sexual, cohesiveness. This would be a context that links the group loosely to a military background. *I Married a Monster from Outer Space* is one of those rare exceptions among 1950s science fiction films from which the military is conspicuously absent; the alien invaders are not beaten back by full-scale military mobilization, but by a posse of male townies armed with shotguns and aided by dogs. Still, the invaders themselves are, upon closer inspection, members of a military commando unit dropped behind enemy lines to prepare for a larger invasion. Their camaraderie is shown both as an easy, comfortable sense of togetherness and as a slightly more strained sense of boredom, dissatisfaction, and stress. It reflects this experience of hardship conditions, as does their shared dislike, distrust, or open hostility toward women, which serves as an additional theme of their social bonding. Even the single member of the group who admits to liking women, or at least to finding them interesting, does so in a manner that suggests an attitude of misogynist exploitation rather than genuine affection. To the film's late 1950s audience, the social and sexual dynamics of the group would be immediately recognizable as that of a military unit. This recognition might be based on personal experience if they themselves had been veterans of World War II or the Korean War, or on exposure to Hollywood films and television rehashing the imagery of non-sexual male bonding (what Eve Kosofsky has called "homocial" in distinction to "homosexual") in war films or other forms of male melodrama.

Benshoff does not explicitly link the film's queer anxiety to this underplayed military theme. But it is tempting to speculate to which degree postwar American culture might have been plagued by a suspicion that the boundary between acceptable homosocial bonding and homosexual attraction among soldiers would be more permeable and flexible than mainstream culture would ever be willing to admit. After all, war demanded that men would be spending extended periods away not only from their wives and girlfriends but from women altogether. They might be sharing hardship, loss, and traumatic experiences with other men—an experience from which women would be categorically excluded. Historian John Bodnar also suggests that for many young men, the military provided a space that was explicitly marked as exempt from the parental and communal surveillance in service of narrow prescriptive gender roles and behaviors. "During the early 1940s," Bodnar argues, "soldiers could enter into all kinds of sexual relationships—including homosexual ones—that would not have been tolerated had they remained under the close scrutiny of their families and hometowns. In fact, the lenient nature of wartime life and the mobility of the population actually precipitated the flourishing of gay and lesbian communities in many areas" (66). While the emphasis in Bodnar's description is clearly more on heterosexual behaviors (such as the age of first sexual contact, changing sexual partners, social commitments associated with sex, etc.), the larger loosening of social strictures would also have included changes in the tolerance toward homosexuality. However, this new freedom and its resulting queer panic did not quite come with the same urgency for female members of the military services, as Elaine Tyler May points out. "Although enlisted women could be dismissed for lesbianism, few were. The armed services were reluctant to enforce such policies because they did not want to acknowledge that military life fostered the development of lesbian relationships and communities" (72).

Given women's absence from actual combat duties, policing gender boundaries was determined by the cultural nexus between masculinity and violence. As John Bodnar puts it, the postwar "crusade against communism sought to purge not only communist sympathizers from American public life but also gay men, who were now considered too feeble to join the fight against America's enemies and infected with a proclivity for traitorous behavior" (66). For those on the home front, repressing or disavowing awareness of homosexuality in the military might even go so far as to produce evidence of a person's heterosexual credentials. The common occurrence of prostitution surrounding military bases at home and abroad or the acknowledgment of illegitimate children fathered during a tour of duty might have been distasteful, but they did meet expectations of traditional masculinity (Sloan Wilson's novel *The Man in the Grey Flannel Suit* revolves around just this occurrence).[6] That not everything that had happened in Guadalcanal would stay in Guadalcanal would only become an issue when veterans were returning home. Here, they would be expected to modify and adjust the homosocial bonds forged in the heat of battle or the ennui of its anticipation and to submit more properly to the heterosexual imperative of mainstream civilian life. Even, or *especially*, in cases where homosexuality played absolutely no role at all, the veterans' homosocial bonds must have appeared suspicious, if not alarming to those women who were categorically excluded from the circumstances under which these bonds had been forged. To the degree that Fowler's film remains firmly wedded to Marge's perspective during its first half, her lack of understanding for her husband's odd behavior registers as unease bordering on panic. It is in this moment of nervous backlash to wartime leniency that *I Married a Monster from Outer Space* locates the sexual suspiciousness of Bill and the military camaraderie of the group of male alien impostors.

While *I Married a Monster from Outer Space* keeps our point of view steadily aligned with Marge's subjective experience, the sexual dynamic of her relationship with her husband begins to reverse itself halfway through the film. By the way, it is important to remember that for the most part, we are dealing with the alien impostor impersonating Marge's husband; the real Bill Farrell only appears briefly in the beginning and even more briefly at the very end of the film. While the wedding night scene reveals a lamentable lack of sexual interest on the part of Bill, the alien impostor, in his beautiful and willing bride—a sexual disinterest confirmed by the couple's persistent childlessness—the time period that follows is characterized by the opposite state of affairs. As Marge discovers the true nature of her husband, and as her husband slowly learns to appreciate the possibilities of sexual pleasure granted to him when he assumed this male human body, he suddenly develops a sexual interest in Marge. Meanwhile, she has lost all sexual interest in him. Knowing that he is an alien, she is appalled; understanding what it means to be male (which the film equates with being human), he, in turn, suddenly begins to desire her. The problem of not enough sex in their first year of marriage leads to the problem of too much sex thereafter. As Marge recoils from Bill, the specter hanging over their marriage now is that of rape. As Bill enters Marge's bedroom and loiters suggestively and, increasingly so, menacingly, he has gone from a sexual nonentity to being a heterosexual aggressor. A scene in which Bill, in a moment of sexual frustration, crushes a metal ashtray further emphasizes that, from now on, the threat of violence, and not just sexual violence, will be part of this marriage.

There is also one other facet to Bill's sexual pathology that is important to consider. As the plot unfolds, the film makes it clear that the alien impostors have suffered defeat long before the posse of "real men" have rounded them up and beaten back the invasion. The fact that the aliens are "a dying race"—a trope repeated with almost obsessive regularity throughout 1950s films—has doomed them to extinction at the moment of sexual failure in the bedroom. The objective of their invasion is the impregnation of human females, and thus the continuation of their race. Yet the persistent sexual disjunction between Bill and Marge—first through his inability to perform, then through her unwillingness to let him perform—has dealt a crushing blow to whatever Bill represents in the film. Unable to sustain himself as an individual (like his fellow aliens, he cannot breathe oxygen), and unable to sustain himself as a member of his race, Bill and his kind will ultimately fade away, even if they are not actively defeated right away. The bedroom is the battleground where the invasion fails.

In search of the roots of Bill's sexual pathology, especially in regard to Benshoff's reading of the film's queer panic, one must wonder about the place, the location, the space where Bill was transformed from the perfect husband he promised to be into the sexual neurotic he turns out to be. Fowler spends very little time with the real Bill; and yet the character exercises a hold on the film's imagination as the standard of masculine normality throughout. Thus, the film's opening scenes, where we encounter the real Bill, are especially important. We see him on the eve of his wedding among a circle of friends, many of whom, we have reason to suspect, have already been replaced with alien impostors. The film follows him on the way home from this informal bachelor's party, on the country road as he is driving back, the place where is car is stopped and he is taken. The bar and the bachelor's party are clearly marked as male spaces. The two female barflies are poignantly excluded from the reigning spirit of male camaraderie. In fact, the sense of shared male bonding is very much achieved at the expense of, or by way of the deliberate exclusion of, these women. Many contemporaries, according to Elaine Tyler May, "feared that returning veterans would be unable to resume their positions as responsible citizens and family men [and thus] worried that a crisis in masculinity would lead to crime, 'perversion,' and homosexuality" (88). In the film, therefore, it is also the transitional space of the return, the homecoming journey along the open country road at night, which is marked as treacherous ground. If "the postwar years witnessed an increasing suspicion of single men as well as single women" (88), it is because of their dissociation from the home and their relegation to these transitional spaces. When Bill's drive home is concluded, and he has passed from the world of men, and through the transitional space of the road, he is the suspicious single man now awkwardly embedded in a failing marriage.[7]

Bill Farrell's Secret History: World War II Veterans in Postwar Cinema

Ever since Harry Benshoff's comments on the sexual subtext of *I Married a Monster from Outer Space*, the figure that has been insinuating itself into the conversation is that of the war veteran. If we take our cue from the one reference in the film to the military-the alien invaders as a forward unit trying to establish a beachhead on Earth—it is not too much of a stretch to see a larger pattern emerge in which Bill and his comrades in arms represent the experience that civilian society in the 1950s had when confronting the men who had returned from World War II and from the Korean War. The morphology of the alien impostor and the traumatized war veteran are remarkably similar, based on the perception that their shared underlying pathology is that of a traumatic experience that is shaping behavior and demeanor. In order to understand the character of Bill Farrell, and some of the other fictional characters to appear in the course of this chapter, I will pause for a moment and fill in some historical context.

Though America had entered the war in Europe relatively late, and had sustained casualties that remained far behind those of, for example, Germany and the Soviet Union, war casualties had been substantial. "By most estimates," Richard Lingeman writes, "405,000 American servicemen and –women died in World War II [. . .] There were also the 607,096 wounded, some of them permanently disabled, and more than 200,000 mentally scarred" (2). Responding to these figures, postwar care increased the extent of medical services substantially; in "1946, VA hospitals treated 37,000 former soldiers as inpatients. An additional million utilized outpatient services, including 144,000 who saw social workers for counseling—double the number in 1944. More than half these veterans were treated for neuropsychiatric conditions" (May 78). Citing John Appel's essay published in the *American Journal of Psychiatry* in 1945, Robert Genter points out that mental instability already registered during the war with the Selective Service System, which "weeded out roughly 12 % of the 15 million men examined for apparent psychiatric handicaps [. . .] The Neuropsychiatry Consultants Division of the Surgeon General's Office reported that between January 1, 1942, and June 1945 there were approximately one million hospital admissions from the Army for neuropsychiatric disorders, a rate of approximately forty-five admissions per 1,000 soldiers a year" (qtd. in Genter 156). Less than a decade later, the process would replay itself, albeit on a smaller scale, with men returning from the Korean War, a war that would prolong the relevance and urgency of the returning veterans' issue throughout the 1950s and into the early '60s, thereby keeping it alive for the science fiction film of the same period.

Returning veterans were considered a potential source of social destabilization for several reasons. Some reasons were connected to postwar fatigue with all things military, strongest among veterans. This was seen as a destabilizing influence by a military-industrial complex that would have been disadvantaged by "strong efforts in the late 1940s [replaced, in 1950, by the Korean War's revitalizing effect on remilitarization] to temper the obsession with national defense with an insistence that wartime sacrifices demanded a powerful effort to fashion a more democratic society in America" (Bodnar 69).[8] Other reasons reached back to the mistakes that had been made in the wake of World War I. "Over the return of the World War II soldier dead hung memories of World War I, when there were reports of disrespectful handling and coffins dumped without notice on grieving parents' doorsteps" (45). Processing returning veterans with efficiency and respect thus would be a matter of ensuring social peace. "Because of fears of postwar unemployment, many Congress members feared another veterans' march on Washington—like the Bonus March of the early thirties, only much bigger and angrier" (103). This disconcerting prospect was directly responsible for the passing of the 1944 GI Bill, which would facilitate the social enfranchisement of a large demographic—a group of unhappy American GIs who had already demonstrated, during the agonizingly slow process of military demobilization at military bases abroad, that they would riot and rebel to expedite their return to civilian life.

Added to these economic and social anxieties were concerns about the veterans' psychological state after exposure to the cruelties of combat and depravities of war. Indicative of these concerns is a print advertisement for Old Gold cigarettes, part of a larger campaign published in *Life* magazine (August 6, 1945, 77).[9] The ad shows a young man in uniform with a young woman on his lap. Both are sitting on a couch, behind which a little boy is crouching. The relationships depicted are somewhat unclear; the little boy could be the woman's kid brother, or perhaps the three are a family with the father just having finished his military service or being temporarily home on furlough. While the woman holds out a pack of Old Gold to the man, he is reaching behind the couch with one arm ready to slap the boy for his intrusion into the romantic moment. The caption reads: "Why be Irritated?" A further insert at the bottom of the page adds: "Light an Old Gold." Though this is clearly intended as light comedy, the underlying assumptions about the man in uniform are less humorous. First, he is on a short fuse, and second, he is about to take out his anger, presumably caused by sexual frustration, on the little boy. A small insert in the bottom left corner begins with the line, "There's uninterrupted pleasure in Old Gold . . ." The thematic link between male sexual frustration and imminent violence speaks volumes about the ubiquity of a problem that, in its sexual more so than its psychological dimension, would be difficult or impossible to acknowledge openly in a Hollywood film of the 1950s.[10] Though childlessness is the bane of the marriage of Bill and Marge Farrell in *I Married a Monster from Outer Space*, it is easy to recognize Bill as the man in the advertisement.

I Love a Man in a Uniform: (Dis)Trusting the American Veteran

Since, as Richard Lingeman reminds us, "the operative prefix of 1945–46 was "'re': reconversion (economy) readjustment (veterans to civilian life), [a process that] encouraged looking backward, not forward" (63), the triumphalist moment of the US emerging victorious from World War II would have to be staged at the expense of prolonged national introspection on the veterans' issue. Veterans were not a taboo topic, but they were a thorny, sensitive, and problematic one. A milestone in mainstream cinema in regard to this dynamic of earnest concern on the one hand, and impatience and repression on the other, was William Wyler's *The Best Years of Our Lives* (1946), a film that traced the problems of returning veterans with the help of three major characters at the most problematic early period of demobilization. The film garnered such critical and popular acclaim that it is worth dwelling on for a few moments. Notable about the film is that despite the problems all three major characters face, these problems are resolved toward the end of the film. Romantic and family relationships are mended, and meaningful jobs are procured for those who lost their old ones or were forced to reacquaint themselves with the one waiting for them upon their return.[11] The film's emphasis on the postwar trials and tribulations illustrates Richard Lingeman's characterization of "the veteran-return pictures" in general: that they "enacted a symbolic ordeal or test that the returned hero must undergo before he can be reintroduced into the tribe. He must also show that he has purged or cleansed himself of the aggression and violence that he needed as a warrior" (118).

Films made a few years after the war—e.g., the adaptation of Sloan Wilson's 1955 novel *The Man in the Grey Flannel Suit* (Nunnally Johnson, 1956)—tend to visualize the veteran's memories of combat and military life away from home and family. Hence, it is the absence of flashbacks in *The Best Years of Our Lives* that stands out. The story begins as all three characters meet during the return to the same hometown, and reaches its final conclusion when all loose ends are neatly tied up. The war is mentioned, remembered in dialogue, but it never appears on screen. The two brief exceptions from this strategy of visual omission are in themselves quite revealing; both are clearly motivated by the narrative's alignment with its characters' struggle in the present and orientation toward the future. Incidentally, both the present and the future are offered as reference points for the film's ambiguous title; the past—i.e., the war itself—hardly ever is. The closest the film ever comes to a flashback is the auditory hallucination experienced by one of the three protagonists. When Fred Derry (Dana Andrews) is sitting in the cockpit of a decommissioned bomber remembering the horrific mission during which some of his fellow crewmembers lost their lives, the complex soundtrack fills in the sound of the engines which, in the present, have been stripped from the junked bomber. The film reads the trauma on Fred's distraught face as the soundtrack goes non-diegetic with the roar of revving engines. As much as this scene evokes the site of trauma—spatially, by way of the cockpit, and temporally, by way of the auditory flashback—it also avoids and screens out this trauma by denying it visual representation. The fact that the plane is decommissioned, that it stands in a scrapyard, and that only minutes after Fred's dark midnight of the soul, the foreman of the scrapyard crew will offer Fred the job that will lead him out of his emotional and economic depression, all work in unison to neutralize the full force of this already affectively muted representation of the war trauma.

The second element in *The Best Years of Our Lives* that marks the permanence of the war trauma is the physical injury of Homer Parrish, played by an amateur actor named Harold Russell, who had lost both hands in an industrial accident during his navy service. Homer appears early on in the film, and so do his hands—or, rather, the hooks that replace his hands. He and his injury are an embodiment of the various casualties of the war. As a metaphor, he is all the more powerful because his injury is explicitly, even emphatically *not* being recreated by special effects. Time and again, the film carefully engages in visual tactics by which Homer's hands are alternatingly concealed and revealed. There is nothing sensationalistic about the display of Harold Russell's amputations; Wyler's approach is carefully and deliberately calibrated to distinguish itself from the fascinated lingering looks at the unconventional bodies in, for example, Tod Browning's *Freaks* (1932). Nonetheless, in trying to accomplish conventional narrative closure for Homer's storyline, the film works hard to contain the horror emblematically represented by Homer's hands. It is important to note that Wyler selected an amputee as a character—i.e., someone whose traumatic injury is quite literally marked by something invisible, the part that is missing from his body. By contrast, one of the many burn victims the war produced would have had the devastating traces of the war written on his body as a highly visible presence. Wyler's artistic choice, therefore, is designed to omit as much as to represent.

As in Wyler's attempt to summarize the diversity of veterans and their problems with the help of three representative storylines, science fiction films tend to treat returning or returned war veteran as a distinct demographic, a more or less visible social type, and a social problem. A film like *The Cult of the Cobra* (Francis D. Lyon, 1955), which comes down more on the side of supernatural horror than science fiction, traces the postwar lives of a group of army buddies first seen during the moment of demobilization somewhere in Asia. On a lark, they desecrate a snake cult's shrine and, in retribution, a deadly supernatural creature follows them back to the US. Like Wyler, Lyon approaches each character as a member of the military community, which, in its moment of disbanding, has left the individual adrift and in search of a social substitute. For long periods, the film is more interested in the minutiae of civilian life after demobilization than in the supernatural decimation of their numbers by the mysterious snake woman. And so it delves into the rearrangements of romantic relationships among the men, as a former girlfriend switches romantic attachments from one member of the group to another. It also explores the temporary postwar housing shortage that forces four of the men into roommate arrangements with each other. And it inventories the promises and frustrations of the postwar economy as some among the men embark on white-collar careers, while one of their friends is left behind; he ends up running the family business, a bowling alley.

Cult of the Cobra relies on its audience to recognize these elements of character and setting as familiar from their own everyday lives—not just among returning veterans themselves, but also among the larger population coming into contact with them every day. The war trauma itself seems almost incidental to the plot. Only when the female figure of retributive violence follows the men from Asia to America and begins picking them off one by one does the film engage with war trauma. The guilt of the men's transgression abroad manifests itself in the form of the supernatural avenger, who is taking on the shape of an attractive noir-ish femme fatale. As she begins to seduce the men and intrude upon their existing romantic relationships, the film begins to question postwar masculinities. To this end, it looks at the homosocial relationships that developed during the war and continued in its aftermath, and at the men's heteronormative relationships with more or less socially acceptable American women. The outcome of this examination is, at times, quite ambivalent. The masculine roommate arrangement, for example, offers opportunities for examining the strength of psychological, social, and even erotic bonds between men in contrast to those between men and women. The film also calls into question the full reorientation and commitment of returned veterans to the normative 1950s psychosexual regime of civilian life by showing how susceptible the men are to the charms of the exotic, dangerous female avenger

Since psychological damage is only one aspect of war trauma, 1950s science fiction films, with their interest in prosthetic and make-up effects, are poised to address the veteran's physical damage as well. They were, after all, referred to as "monster movies" at the time for a reason. Perhaps the urtext of 1950s science fiction in this regard is to be found in the remarkable work of British writer Nigel Kneale. With a series of television productions—later adapted by British Hammer Films for the big screen with larger budgets and in color, and revolving around the scientist Bernard Quatermass—Kneale created a blueprint for more than one of the larger

Richard Wordsworth as Victor Carroon in *The Quatermass Xperiment*: Not the Man He Used to Be

No Longer a Victor: Carroon's Fully Transformed Body and Post-Imperial Britain

themes running through science fiction both in Britain and the US. In the first of these films, *The Quatermass Experiment* (BBC, 1953, remade by Hammer as *The Quatermass Xperiment* [Val Guest, 1955]), a spaceship returns to Earth with two of its crew members missing and the third surviving crewman strangely transformed "into a fungoid-like creature" (Rolinson and Cooper 158). In the Hammer version, a remarkable performance by actor Richard Wordsworth has the surviving crew member Victor Carroon transforming into an increasingly grotesque monstrosity, gradually shedding human bodily characteristics until he is entirely inhuman by the end of the film. Though critics like Rolinson and Cooper have read Carroon's fate in a number of ways, many of them germane specifically to postwar Britain—as

Third Degree Burns: Richard Day's *First Man into Space* (1959)

a sign that "Britain has overreached itself (160); that he represents "the threat of the sublimation of the individual into the homogeneous mass"; or, more specifically, the "outsider suffering social alienation from a false community engendered by mass culture" (160)—his physical appearance suggests the appearance and demeanor of the veteran who has been both psychologically and physically traumatized. "Although Carroon returns home a public hero, the serial's narrative is shaped around the diagnosis of the hidden sicknesses of this celebrated 'Victor'" (159); sicknesses that are hardly hidden considering the grotesque deformities his experience in outer space has inflicted upon his body.[12]

Kneale's plot of the space traveler returning strangely altered also found its way into Richard Day's *First Man into Space* (1959), in which the same fate awaits air force pilot Dan Prescott. The make-up applied to actor Bill Edwards, playing the eponymous test pilot, is revealing. At the advanced stages of the transformation, he is covered in a prosthetic body suit that, with a raw, pebbled surface, simulates nothing so much as severe third-degree burns all over the surface of his skin. The burn metaphor is further enhanced by his labored breathing and stiff gait, symptoms, as many severely injured veterans and their caregivers had to learn, of the influence of extreme heat on the upper respiratory system and muscle control. More than the amputated limbs, which signify monstrosity largely by absence, lack, or bodily asymmetry—as in the case of Harold Russell playing Homer Parrish in *The Best Years of Our Lives*—these prosthetic and make-up effects rely upon full, spectacular visibility. By the standards of advancing special effects in the horror film, they may be relatively crude. But their reference

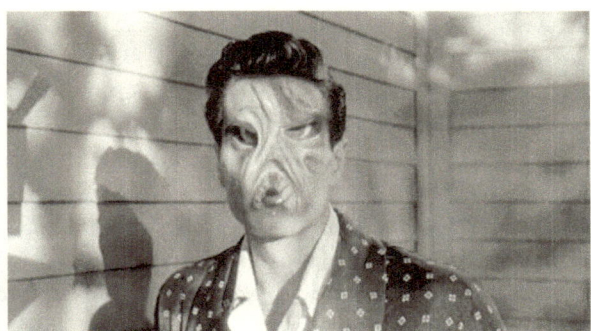

Frightening Thoughts Written on the Body: PTSD in *I Married a Monster from Outer Space*

to the consequences of traumatic bodily harm, as suffered in combat or through relatively new military technologies like napalm (developed in the early 1940s and used in strategic bombing raids against Germany and Japan), is difficult to miss.[13]

Bill Farrell, the main character in *I Married a Monster from Outer Space*, seems outwardly normal and unscathed. And yet there is a deeper layer to the character where his war trauma is represented. On that deeper layer, Bill Farrell is literally a mass of physical scarring, but it is a sight that is hidden from view. We, the audience, catch a glimpse in that rare unobserved moment during the wedding night, but Marge, his wife, never sees what Bill looks like "on the inside." What is visible about him, however, is his behavior—the sexual apprehension and aggression, the barely repressed rage, the emotional dissociation from all those around him. We have a choice: to read Bill's grotesque secret body as a literal reference to his physical wounds, or as a metaphor for his psychological wounding. Either way, though, Bill fits the profile for post-traumatic stress disorder, or PTSD, a contemporary term which, in the context of military life, has been variously referred to as shell shock or battle fatigue. According to the National Institutes of Health, the condition includes among its symptoms flashbacks to the traumatic event, nightmares, and "frightening thoughts" (NIMH, "PTSD"). Aside from these "re-experiencing symptoms," the list also includes "avoidance symptoms," among them emotional numbness, guilt, depression, and worry; being unable to remember the traumatic event is as common as re-experiencing it in flashbacks time and again. While these symptoms are more apparent to the sufferer than to bystanders, outward behavior apparent to everyone would include "being easily startled," "feeling tense or 'on edge,'" and "having difficulty sleeping and/or having angry outbursts" (NIMH, "PTSD"). The last three symptoms are listed in the category of "hyper-arousal symptoms," a category that stands in contrast to some of the symptoms in the "avoidance symptoms" category. Emotional excess, both in the positive and the negative, yokes both affectless and emotionally hyperbolic behaviors together within the same pathological profile.

The way the film contextualizes Bill's behavior further emphasizes the experience of World War II or Korea as a likely origin. His traumatization, as I have argued before, takes place in a remote location to which women do not have access. It is a location associated, both in its remoteness and the absence of women, with the homosocial camaraderie of the military unit behind enemy lines, a gendered milieu in which male bonding is often achieved by way of shared gynophobia and misogyny. Upon his return to the domestic sphere, Bill is outwardly unaltered; superficially, he is the same person. Underneath, however, he is no longer the same man. Alternatingly, he is hyperemotional and affectless, just as he is secretive and uncommunicative. As far as cinematic conventions of the alien impostor film are concerned, it is easy to see behavioral patterns of the PTSD sufferer enacted by Bill's affectless demeanor, just as his violent outbursts, as in the scene in which he crushes that metal ashtray in violent anguish, illuminate the emotionally hyperbolic aspect of the syndrome. Fowler's film also traces these affects in their impact on Bill's and Marge's sexual life as a newly married couple trying to—or expected to—conceive; what appears first as Bill's impotence and then transforms itself into the persistent threat of rape corresponds to an inner turmoil that appears to have been deeply familiar to many wives who saw their husbands return from military duty in Asia or Europe, as manifested in rising divorce rates throughout the 1950s.

Broken Fathers: Trapped Inside the Nuclear Family

As deeply as *I Married a Monster from Outer Space* is probing the psychological and sexual dynamics within the romantic couple during the 1950s, its take on the alien impostor as exclusively male makes it an exception among science fiction films of the period. In most alien invasion films, both men and women are being taken over and replaced. Since women were, by and large, not serving in the armed forces in positions where they were likely to be traumatized, my own reading of *I Married a Monster from Outer Space* as a reflection of the traumatized veteran may, therefore, not apply to other films. Thus, in order to broaden the scope of the reading, I would like to move on to a film in which both men and women are being replaced by alien impostors. This film, I will argue, still addresses anxieties surrounding the traumatized veteran, but this time in a manner that explicitly includes women as well. The film is William Cameron Menzies's *Invaders from Mars* (1953). Much like *I Married a Monster from Outer Space*, which told its story from the young wife's point of view, the narrative perspective in *Invaders from Mars* is also one dissociated from the male veteran himself. Here, it is aligned with the little boy, David MacLean (Jimmy Hunt). After spotting an alien craft landing in the woods behind his suburban house, David watches helplessly as first his father, then his mother, and eventually half the town are being taken over by the alien invaders. Like a young suburban housewife, his is a vulnerable position—a position that needs to recruit social support from authority figures and the rest of the community before it can assert itself as truthful and bring about military mobilization.

Having gone out to investigate his son David's claim about the alien landing the night before, George McLean (Leif Erickson) returns from his own backyard a changed man. He looks slightly disheveled, and has lost one of his slippers. But most of all, his behavior is markedly different from the easygoing, benevolent father and husband he used to be. An earlier scene in which David's parents send their son back to bed makes an explicit point of illustrating their "normal" behavior as cordial, friendly, and supportive. In an odd mixture of distractedness and tense concentration, irritation and determination, George McLean commands his wife Mary (Hillary Brooke) to bring him coffee and to stop interrogating him about his whereabouts. When David, standing behind him, spots a small wound on his father's neck, George McLean nervously hikes up his collar to hide the mark and offers an explanation that is patently false ("I caught it on a barbed wire fence"). When David questions the likelihood of this explanation, his father backhands him, a vicious slap that lands the boy on the floor, more surprised and bewildered than physically harmed. His mother's first response when she returns from the kitchen and finds David on the floor is surprise as well. Clearly this aggression, irritability, and furtiveness are atypical behaviors both toward herself and toward the child. Still, it only takes her seconds to snap back into the role of the wife, as she takes her husband's side, telling David to mind his father and do what he says.

From the removal of the male character to a remote location where something unspeakable happens to him to the sudden uncharacteristic outburst of domestic violence, the film follows the pattern at work in *I Married a Monster from Outer Space*. It is easy to read George MacLean as a traumatized veteran and the suburban home as a gothic space in which a male authority figure terrorizes his family. But when the alien invasion continues, it is Mary McLean who is next in line to be replaced; of course, this happens after her husband has taken her to the backyard. As with her husband's, her transformation has occurred off-screen. We see Mary as an alien impostor first when she enters the police station where her son has taken refuge from the alien conspiracy. She is now dressed in a tight black costume designed to conceal as much as it reveals her body. The outfit emphasizes décolletage and naked skin between sleeves and high tight gloves. Her upright posture, her rigidity even when she bows down, gives her a hard, unyielding look, which stands in stark contrast to the soft colors and contours that defined the character in the domestic setting of the previous scene. Clearly, her femininity has been re-written to fit a femme fatale straight out of a post-war film noir. She is all angles and stark, sharp outlines. This icy sexuality is underlined by a beautiful close-up of her face that indulges in the surface perfection of the Hollywood glamour shot rather than offering the kind of access to the character's emotional core that usually comes with a close-up. All this happens as she embraces her son, looking over his shoulder with that same mix of intense concentration and emotional detachment we have seen in David's father. The character's stark sexualization is all the more alarming because it is shown in her interaction with her own son. In her newly acquired sexual allure, she is not defined as David's mother so much as in relationship to her husband. Whatever mysterious transformation he has undergone, she shares her husband's symptoms. This alignment had already announced itself in her first response to seeing David physically abused by his father. Despite her being embraced by her son, it is George McLean whose imprint is on her, not David's.

In between these two moments—one showing George McLean's transformation, the other that of his wife Mary—are scenes in which David realizes that others have been similarly affected. The two police officers who come to the house have been "turned." So has a little girl from the neighborhood who then proceeds to set her parents' house on fire. While the emotional resonance is strongest within the affected nuclear families, these scenes establish a larger social environment in which the pathology first exhibited by David's father is increasingly becoming an acceptable social norm. Though the police officers show respect for the privacy of the nuclear family as they enter the McLeans' suburban home, their tacit acceptance of the obvious traces of parental and spousal abuse legitimizes George McLean's violent behavior. Similarly, the first response of David's mother, when he is struck by his father, suggests a type of complicity, or at least a predisposition toward complicity, that has already normalized abusive behavior before Mary McLean has been taken over by the aliens.

The domestic abuse, first at the hand of the father, then adopted as a behavioral pattern by the mother, also speaks to two issues pertinent to 1950s culture. On the one hand, the behavior is inconsistent with postwar attitudes toward physical punishment of children. George's treatment of his son prior to his conversion, as well as his interaction with Mary, show him to be a patriarch, but an enlightened, egalitarian, and open-minded one. Interactions among the family members are based on shared goals and mutual respect, just as parental authority is enforced not by coercion but by the child's consent after a decision has been explained to him. A return to physical violence as manifestation of patriarchal authority signals a developmental backsliding, from the ideals of enlightened child-rearing to the bad old times when parents would habitually slap their children. This is not to say that physical punishment vanished from 1950s America, but that it lost ground as a socially acceptable behavior.

One aspect of this anxiety over developmental backsliding comes with a class anxiety that might be specific to 1950s America. While physical punishment would remain more widespread among working-class parents, it was middle-class parenting that strove to abandon the practice. This was a period during which, thanks to postwar economic recovery and the GI Bill, the generational divide marked roughly by the war would also be a divide created by the children's upward social mobility. Thus, George McLean backhanding his son David comes with the disreputable social origins of such behavior, which a solidly middle-class family like the McLeans would probably prefer to suppress. With one strike, lower-class social origins suddenly erupt within the supposedly solid bourgeois space of the suburban home. To the extent that George McLean represents a traumatized veteran unable to control himself, the domestic abuse he inflicts on his wife and child undercuts the class pretensions of the entire family. In an instant, he drags his wife back with him to a developmental stage both of them believed they had superseded. Socially orphaned, his son begins to seek surrogate parents who conform more properly to bourgeois norms.

One other thing is notable about *Invaders from Mars*. Just like Bill Farrell's drive down a dark country road in *I Married a Monster from Outer Space*, both the McLeans and assorted other townspeople in *Invaders from Mars* must take a trip to the McLeans' backyard where the exchange takes place. Noted by many critics as one of the remarkable features of the film, this backyard is a stark expressionistic soundstage oddly alien in its suburban environment (comparable in essence, though not in style, with the woods in *I Married a Monster from Outer Space*). It features a sandpit that churns and sucks people down below ground, a blasted tree that intersects the frame in a jagged black diagonal, and the crooked banister of a fence that rises toward the ridge of the horizon like something out of *The Cabinet of Dr. Caligari*. As a realistic extension of suburban space, even at the outer edge of zoning and development, this space makes little sense. Rather, it is a nightmarish internal reality, a metaphor for a battlefield, a zone of combat, a space in which trauma occurs and which visually imparts trauma to the observer. This is the place from which, first among all victims of the alien invaders, David McLean's father returns a changed man; the place to which he demands his wife accompany him and from which she also returns as someone harsh, cold, distant, violent, and erratic. Later in the film, this space will literally become a battlefield. The military will move in and direct artillery fire into the sandpit in an attempt to blow the aliens out into the open and off the face of the Earth. But before any of this happens, this backyard is the space where trauma is communicated from the one person who has been directly affected to those drawn around him within the circle of the nuclear family. To the degree that David experiences his family as increasingly dysfunctional—for most of the film, he actually recruits a pair of more suitable substitute parents—Menzies's film traces the spread of the psychological and social disintegration back to a single origin: a traumatized veteran whose pathology spreads and affects the entire family.

Broken Communities: "They're already here!"

At first glance, Don Siegel's *Invasion of the Body Snatchers* (1956) stands out from the previous two alien impostor narratives because it tells its story not from the perspective of someone controlled by an adult white male— whether Marge Farrell, the suburban housewife living in fear of her husband, or David MacLean, an eight-year-old getting slapped by his father. Siegel's protagonist is the white male himself, Santa Mira's small-town physician Miles Bennell (Kevin McCarthy). The film also departs from the pattern suggested by the other two films by imagining the impostors gaining ground not among those close and dear to this central character; Miles is divorced, childless, and without extended family in town. Except for some casual friends, Miles does not actually have anyone who is close to him. Instead, Siegel suggests, and then confirms, that alien impostors exist within the larger community of the town and thus among Miles's patients and acquaintances. In fact, it takes almost the entire film until an alien impostor finally reveals herself close to him. This happens in a climactic and highly dramatic moment right before his escape from Santa Mira when Becky Driscoll (Dana Wynter), Miles's potential love interest, is finally "turned." Until then, the invasion takes place within a wider social circle surrounding the main character, allowing him to serve as an emotionally detached observer, a detective or sociologist of sorts. It takes more than half of the film until Miles becomes the focus of the alien conspiracy.

The fact that almost all of Santa Mira has been replaced with alien impostors brings about a peculiar reversal of perspectives. While the respective protagonists of *I Married a Monster from Outer Space* and *Invaders from Mars* eventually succeed in rallying around themselves a respectable counterforce to oppose the alien invasion, Miles Bennell grows increasingly isolated. In the end, he remains the only one still human in a community that has become entirely alien. Much like the protagonist of Richard Matheson's novel *I am Legend* (1954), Miles ends up being the outsider, a monstrous threat to the community, pointed out, isolated, and hounded out of town. Only out in the "real world," outside the bounds of Santa Mira, is he reluctantly granted credibility and comradeship (and that only in the film's final closing frame). In the course of Miles's increasing isolation, he has conversations in which the aliens, individually or collectively, speak to him about the pleasures of joining them. In a calm and measured tone, they advertise the relief it would bring to give up his unique sense of self and submit to the newly established collective. Siegel has his alien impostors act less mechanical, robotic, or weirdly focused/distracted than Fowler and Menzies in their respective films; this is one of the films in which the very absence of distinguishing marks is itself a distinguishing mark. The differences between them and their original human sources are minor; it is the fact that they are virtually indistinguishable that generates unease. As much as the audience shares Miles's point of view, their calm reasoning renders his impassioned refusal to submit irrational, even hysterical. Until the final few minutes of the film, his state of isolation, driven to its bitter extreme when Becky finally is "turned," provides a portrait of a man deeply out of sync with his own community.

As in the case of *Invaders from Mars*, there are already small signs announcing Miles Bennell's relative isolation from his hometown long before the alien invasion ever begins. Like Becky, he is a divorcee. Divorce is no longer the shameful stigma it used to be after the postwar spike in the statistics, but it still a mark of distinction that sets him aside from the rest of his social circle, his patients, and his married friends (notable among them is his receptionist Sally [Jean Willes], who, upon appearing for the first time in the film, is immediately linked to her husband and their baby). It is this outsider status that drives him toward Becky Driscoll, herself a recent divorcee. Considering how much Siegel keeps emphasizing the strong social bonds holding the community together, Miles Bennell is both a well-known and respected member of the town and yet stands oddly at its outer margins.

In a key scene of the film, Miles is confronted by his fellow townsfolk who have already been "turned" and now try to talk him into compliance. Though their numbers suggest the threat of violence should Miles refuse to cooperate, the film grants them a moment of expository monologue in which they lay out for him and Becky what life as an alien impostor would look like. On the surface, the film casts their vision of a life devoid of emotion as an inhuman nightmare—something that Miles gets to insist on angrily in response to their entreaties and on behalf of the film's audience. And yet his rejection of their proposal comes across as oddly hyperbolic, presumably because "passion" signals humanity within the narrative logic of the film. He still has Becky at his side, a witness to the authenticity of his own position. But the aliens' therapeutic gesture—their calmness and didactic rhetoric—represents a normality the audience would quickly recognize as the voice of the social consensus. Considering how deeply disturbed Miles is, how unhappy and isolated, and how disruptive a force he is within the well-functioning community, it is easy to imagine how the connotations of who is normal and who isn't would flip against Miles. One can see how easily the film has been read by later generations as either a fable about the dehumanizing danger of communism or the dehumanizing danger of strident anti-communism. The metaphor works either way.

It is also important to note that Miles begins to notice signs of change in Santa Mira after having been away from the town for a medical convention. The reason for his absence, if only for a few days, is quickly dismissed in the narrative. That medical convention he attended is more a plot contrivance, and thus not worthy of further discussion. It hardly registers as an essential element in the development of the film's theme. Miles's absence is also elided structurally. The film starts with the opening frame, in which Miles initiates the flashback. In this flashback, he tells a doctor outside of Santa Mira how he came to stumble through highway traffic yelling about the invasion in progress. This opening frame transitions directly into the flashback itself, which begins with his arrival back in town. While his voiceover tells us that "something evil had taken possession of the town," the images illustrating his return could not be any less conspicuous. Normal town life comes rushing up to him immediately as his receptionist Sally picks him up from the train station. There is no dwelling on where he has been and what he has done while he was away. Miles's experiences during his absence are unimportant, the film tells us; the only thing that matters is what happened in Santa Mira while he was gone. There is no reason to believe that the aliens waited for Miles to leave town so they could start invading, just as there is no doubt that the town is not what it was before he left. To the degree that we experience this shift into the strange and vaguely unfamiliar from Miles's point of view, the film insinuates that Miles, by virtue of his absence, has lost touch with the town. Ever since he came back, he has strayed onto a path divergent from the one the town has taken. Miles no longer belongs to what he experiences as the "new" or the "different" Santa Mira.

As the alien invasion begins to spread from Santa Mira, Miles and Becky watch from a window above the central intersection as the town goes about its business early on a Saturday morning. The two observers' elevated perspective permits Siegel a long shot of this central node where people, in response to an inaudible signal, flock in loose yet synchronized mass movements to the center of the intersection. The siren of a departing police cruiser, taking strangers out of town, precedes this siren sound. Meanwhile, almost simultaneously, the phone rings in the office where Becky and Miles are hiding. Unlike the signal down on the town square, the ringing phone remains unanswered. Miles will persist in his refusal to be recruited (or "interpellated") into this new community that wants him to come down and join in. Siegel alternates between the long shot of the plaza and a two-shot of Miles and Becky above—the community versus the romantic couple. This is the couple that, in the next plot twist, is going to be reduced further to the last remaining humans in the entire town. With this intense emphasis on the solitary state of the observers, the townspeople now really do act peculiarly as they begin to unload alien seed pods for export to other towns all over America. As a police officer with a bullhorn links deliveries with specific towns *by families,* Miles may comment on the events but is dissociated from communal life even further. All he can see is the "malignant disease spreading throughout the whole country." This is a country that will leave Miles behind; he will have no place in it. He is about to lose Becky as well. She will drift away and become one of "them,"

They're Here and You're Next: The Veteran as Crazy Loner in *Invasion of the Body Snatchers*

irretrievable and incomprehensible. Fittingly, the film ends with a return to that severely attenuated frame narrative from the beginning: Miles reeling through traffic on the interstate, crazily yelling that "they're here" and "you're next!" At this point in the narrative, he is a crazy loner, by turns either dangerous or pitiful: the crazed war veteran who has lost his wife, his friends, and his place in society.[14]

Conclusion: No Happy Endings

Considering the enduring popularity of *Invasion of the Body Snatchers*, viewers who would have seen the film years after its original release must have had little trouble recognizing the traumatized war veteran when they were watching Miles Bennell reeling through oncoming traffic. All elements of what was to become a popular iconography are present. Not only is Miles physically disheveled and in a state of neglect, and disoriented, deranged, and angry; he is also screaming in public about a preposterous conspiracy. Motorists passing by, with blank faces in the car windows staring at him, display the behavior one would expect from ordinary Americans instinctively shunning the outsider. Of course, they are afraid of him for the disruption he brings and the danger he poses to them and to himself. By the time of the Vietnam War, the cultural stereotype of the deranged veteran had settled in. One might only think of Travis Bickle (Robert De Niro) in *Taxi Driver* (Martin Scorsese, 1976) laying the groundwork for the ease with which the stereotype slides into place in a science fiction film like *Jacobs Ladder* (Adrian Lyne, 1990). While postwar culture did take on the plight of the veteran, "social problem films" like William Wyler's *The Best Days of Our Lives* are the exception to a rule that has the veteran appear largely in coded form. Postwar film noir and the Western are teeming with steely-eyed, cold-blooded killers whose murderous credentials have, most likely, been collected during their stint in the war. Nonetheless, films like Henry Hathaway's *Niagara* (1953), in which Joseph Cotten plays Marilyn Monroe's self-destructive, murderous husband, or John Ford's *The Searchers* (1956), in which John Wayne's character seems to have come by his mean-spiritedness by way of his war experience, are hardly remembered as films about veterans. Compared to the rather genteel representation of the veterans' fractured lives in Wyler's film, which largely omits the sexual consequences of war post-traumatic stress disorder, it is film noirs like *Niagara* and science fiction films like *I Married a Monster from Outer Space* that dare to take on the thornier sides of the issue. Perhaps they can operate more freely because the conventions of science fiction—especially the more preposterous tropes executed with B-movie budgets—allow makers and viewers to feign ignorance of what is hidden behind the movie monster mask. Compared to a well-intentioned, thematically well-balanced, and very literal-minded social problem film, science fiction comes with the hyperbole, the barely contained emotional excess, to express with a greater degree of urgency public anxiety over the veteran's destabilizing presence and the sense of the veterans' anguish and despair.

How deeply the thematic link between the traumatized veteran and the alien impostor had embedded itself in the generic vocabulary of science fiction becomes visible in the later stages of the cycle, especially in the adoption of cinematic tropes by television. The theme of the individual losing his or her footing in reality, articulated so well in *Invasion of the Body Snatchers*, is absolutely central to *The Twilight Zone* (1959–1964). In the show's opening episode, entitled "Where is Everybody?" (October 2, 1959), a man, who, in the final denouement, is revealed to be a pilot unknowingly undergoing a psychological endurance test for lengthy outer space missions, awakes within a small town entirely devoid of human beings. The test ultimately destroys him; his collapse is watched by the agents of the military-industrial complex, who nonetheless decide to continue the program with other test subjects. *The Twilight Zone* would return to this trope time and again. No matter if a lone individual ends up in the past or a parallel dimension; no matter if he is replaced by a doppelganger, unrecognizable to all who used to know him; no matter if he finds himself unable to return to his point of origin—the precariousness of social embeddedness would become one of the series' hallmark themes. With that theme, the series would challenge the reassurances of the uniformity and solidity of the 1950s social consensus. Of course, there is a more general concern in the series, and in the culture, with conformity and the cost of its maintenance and enforcement. This makes it suitable for the representation of various marginal social demographics (racial, sexual, political, and so on). But the trope also perfectly reflects the alienation and displacement of the traumatized veteran. The behavioral experiment conducted by scientists and generals in "Where is Everybody?" makes this thematic link explicit.[15]

A later episode of *The Twilight Zone*, "The Thirty-Fathom Grave" (January 10, 1963), takes on the plight of the traumatized veteran more directly. When a US Navy ship detects noises coming from a submarine sunk in battle during World War II, one member of its own crew, revealed to be the only survivor of that sinking, is compelled by visions of his dead crew mates to join them at the bottom of the ocean. Written by series creator Rod Serling himself, the episode's structure revolves around the open articulation of the crew man's war trauma. It becomes clear that his hitherto unspoken survivor's guilt disturbs the tight military discipline representing postwar American rationality and efficiency. While "Where is Everybody?" revolves around a similar moment of allegorical revelation, "The Thirty-Fathom Grave" arrives at a starker, less conciliatory conclusion. The military-industrial complex that has staged and observed the scientific experiment in isolation and disorientation ultimately learns from the sacrifice imposed upon its human test subject. In a move familiar from films like *First Man into Space*, the human damage is legitimized and sentimentalized as a heroic sacrifice and not as failure. In the final instance, it imposes on the experimenters the moral responsibility to continue undeterred. There is little such comfort in "The Thirty-Fathom Grave." Stricken by survivor's guilt, the crew member flings himself into the sea. The erasure of the character bearing the trauma is final. Not only is his body never recovered, but the captain also suggests that it would be best for everyone involved if the incident's true dimensions were covered up.

Among the successors to the 1950s cycle in cinema, *The Outer Limits* (1963–1965) would return the American television audience repeatedly to protagonists who, unmoored from their community by choice or accident, would face the marginalization and alienation of the traumatized veteran. Several episodes of *The Outer Limits* would even feature explicitly the representatives of the military-industrial complex. From research scientists to test pilots, these heroic figures provide dramatic illustrations of the

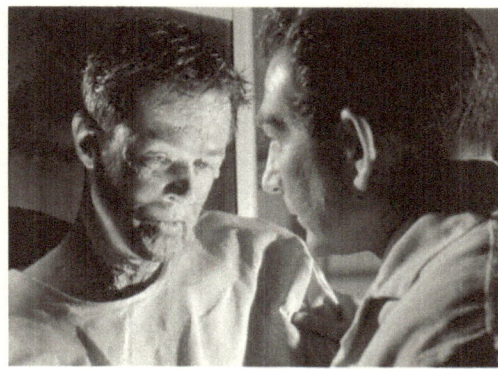

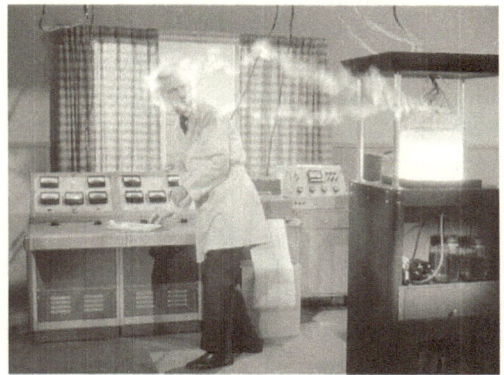

The Outer Limits: "The Architects of Fear" and "The Brain of Colonel Barham"

veteran's condition. In an episode entitled "The Architects of Fear" (September 30, 1963), for example, a scientist allows himself to be surgically transformed into an alien creature in order to help stimulate global peace and cooperation by triggering a unifying fear of an imminent alien invasion. Another episode, "The Brain of Colonel Barham" (January 2, 1965), has a scientist agreeing to the removal of his brain and its linkage to a computer. More focused than *The Twilight Zone* on the bodily rather than the psychological trauma that causes dislocation, episodes like these would place their protagonists in situations which antisocial aggression and self-destructiveness would follow the traumatic bodily alteration, placing them beyond the scope of the social consensus.

In order to move from the recognition of the theme of the alien impostor to an assessment of what these narratives actually try to accomplish within the larger discursive framework surrounding traumatized veterans during the 1950s, it is useful to look at the way in which most of these narratives achieve closure. In the two episodes of *The Outer Limits*, the protagonist's identity and trauma are finally revealed to those around him whose first response was merely to recoil in horror. In "The Architects of Fear," the scientist's wife eventually recognizes her husband beneath the monstrous transformations. Still, that recognition comes too late; the process is too far advanced and irreversible so that the only possible outcome is the man's death. This death is tragic, perhaps futile, but nonetheless seen as heroic because of his intentions to help bring about world peace. The eponymous Colonel Barham, in the other *Outer Limits* episode, also dies, and his death is reminiscent of the one that eliminates the traumatized World War II veteran from the narrative in the *Twilight Zone* episode, "The Thirty-Fathom Grave." Though the narratives flirt with the prospect of reintegrating these characters into the community, their fates as outsiders are sealed. In Westerns, they might have been allowed to leave the community and ride off into the sunset; this is how John Ford ends *The Searchers* (1956). In film noir, they might be taken in by the authorities and given psychological treatment; this is how Phil Karlson ends *Five Against the House* (1955). In science fiction films, their neutralization as a destabilizing influence inside the community invariably demands harsher measures. The unanimous resolve with which these narratives deny the characters reintegration into the community is accompanied by a gesture of their moral and social exoneration; they all attempted, or even succeeded at, something truly heroic. This, then, allows the audience to mourn their passing without having to accept their return. In turn, they are ostracized, celebrated, and eliminated.

The films I have been discussing earlier follow this pattern in their own way. In all three films, paranoid suspicions about alien impostors are verified. The invasion itself is subsequently foiled, the invaders are beaten back, and normality is restored. *Invasion of the Body Snatchers* ends with the prospect of military mobilization, while *I Married a Monster from Outer Space* has a group of true-blue American patriots fighting off the alien impostors. *Invaders from Mars* goes the furthest in showing military mobilization and actual combat with the aliens. It allows the military, which itself had become contaminated by alien impostors, to cleanse not only the nation but also itself in a cathartic battle. This retributive violence against the alien impostors is indicative of a complete and utter lack of sympathy with them. Nonetheless, it is an indifference or hostility which, within the framework of the traumatized veteran's narrative, is all the more troubling. *I Married a Monster from Outer Space* at least makes a gesture toward sympathy with the invaders. The second half of the film actually makes a concession to the veteran's subjective experience when the alien impersonating Bill Farrell gets to articulate the desperation of his doomed species. This happens when he discovers his affection for his wife; in the end, he even surrenders during the shoot-out with the lynch mob in order to end the fight. Nonetheless, the film reigns in this empathy as soon as it is extended. Instead of asking the audience to imagine a truce or peace with the invaders, the film transforms the audience's momentary empathy into the recognition that the inevitable demise of the species is a tragic event. With her husband's impostor eliminated, Marge embraces the true Bill with an intensity designed retroactively to erase all sympathy she or the audience might have mustered for the alien impostor. Of the three films, only *Invasion of the Body Snatchers* engages directly with the veteran's perspective, his subjective experience of alienation and displacement within normal postwar society.

Whereas "veteran-return pictures," as Richard Lingeman calls them, enact "a symbolic ordeal or test that the returned hero must undergo before he can be reintroduced into the tribe," and thus demand that he must "show that he has purged or cleansed himself of the aggression and violence that he needed as a warrior" (118), science fiction films take a grimmer route. By and large, this route fails to arrive at the successful reintegration of the veteran into civilian society. Having mobilized the generic inventory of science fiction in an effort to "other" the veteran, the films either deny the veteran reintegration altogether, or they demand a far more complex process of displacement before reintegration is allowed to take place. In return for such grim predictions, they do, however, accomplish two things that films like *The Best Years of Our Lives* or *The Man in the Gray Flannel Suit* do not. Instead of downplaying the full extent of the traumatic violence to which these men were exposed, they take a close look where other films avert their eyes. They reflect faithfully the full extent of the social panic that, for the 1950s audience, accompanies the issue of the returning veteran. Without an optimistic or conciliatory ending, they do justice to the social panic that was, after all, predicated on the sneaking suspicion that, despite all good intentions, many of these men would be too broken ever to leave the war completely behind. Their insistent demand for violent erasure of the troubling outsider might seem harsh and pessimistic, but the hysterical, hyperbolic pitch at which the demand is delivered speaks volumes about the intensity of the social panic following World War II and the Korean War.

Meanwhile, more conciliatory films with endings that promise the eventual reintegration of the veteran might speak to America's better self. They may have, therefore, found more resonance when later generations were to look back to the 1950s. But their containment of the true horrors of war might also have provided the conditions for the normalization of the military-industrial complex and the renewed mobilization for other wars further down the road. One might speculate whether the more controversial representations of traumatized veterans that were to emerge from American cinema in the wake of the Vietnam War were any more successful in highlighting the high human cost of military intervention than those that came after World War II and the Korean War. The violence with which 1950s science fiction films regularly eliminate the veteran from their narratives certainly does not speak to the nation's better self, but it does testify to warfare's human devastation. In his discussion of memorials erected in the wake of World War II and their retrospective patriotic framing of the war, Richard Lingeman reminds his readers that the "stony finality [of these monuments] contrasts with a body of dissent just after the war, the voices warning against the growing militarization of society" (52). It is exactly in the helpless violence with which the alien impostor films imagine the elimination of the traumatized veteran as a source of economic, political, social, and sexual destabilization that 1950s science fiction films capture a true sense of the sacrifices in physical and mental health demanded from Americans by the military-industrial complex.

Chapter Three
The Southwest

Imagining National Space: The Bigger Picture

Among the most striking images demonstrating how the early period of the Cold War altered public perceptions in the US not only of the world at large but of the familiar American landscape are those representing nuclear attacks. One such image can be found inserted as a double-page illustration in Philip Wylie's *Tomorrow* (1954), a novel that reflects its author's enthusiastic endorsement of civil defense as a national priority. *Tomorrow* demonstrates the ameliorating effects of civil defense measures after a Soviet nuclear attack on the two imaginary Midwestern cities of Green Prairie and River City. The novel also tracks the attack itself in gruesome detail, from the moment of impact to the long aftermath and the community's eventual recovery. The image is of a map which shows the geometric grid of, as the index tells us, "the central area" of both adjacent cities. Like most American cities, they are all right angles except for a few irregularities where the Green Prairie River cuts across downtown, bifurcates around Swan Island, and then rejoins itself before meandering off toward the southeast. Superimposed upon the urban grid, in which streets are marked by a thin double line, is a set of two concentric circles, marked in a broader black line; their center is identified as "Ground Zero" and is linked to a straight dotted line coming in from the northeast, identified as "Path of Guided Missile." The inner circle carries the indexical mark "2000 YARDS FROM GROUND ZERO—AVERAGE PERIMETER—TOTAL DESTRUCTION—FIRE STORM" while the outer one is identified as "SEVERE DAMAGE—APPROXIMATE OUTER LIMIT—FIRES ONLY LOCAL." To a 1950s audience with nuclear doom on its mind, the image speaks for itself.

This imaginary piece of cartography—one of many such images to be published in magazines and newspapers throughout the Cold War—encompasses most of the elements of the Cold War imagination. It manifests in concrete detail the vague dread of imminent nuclear attack. Seen from the victim's perspective, it confirms military concerns over the vulnerability of

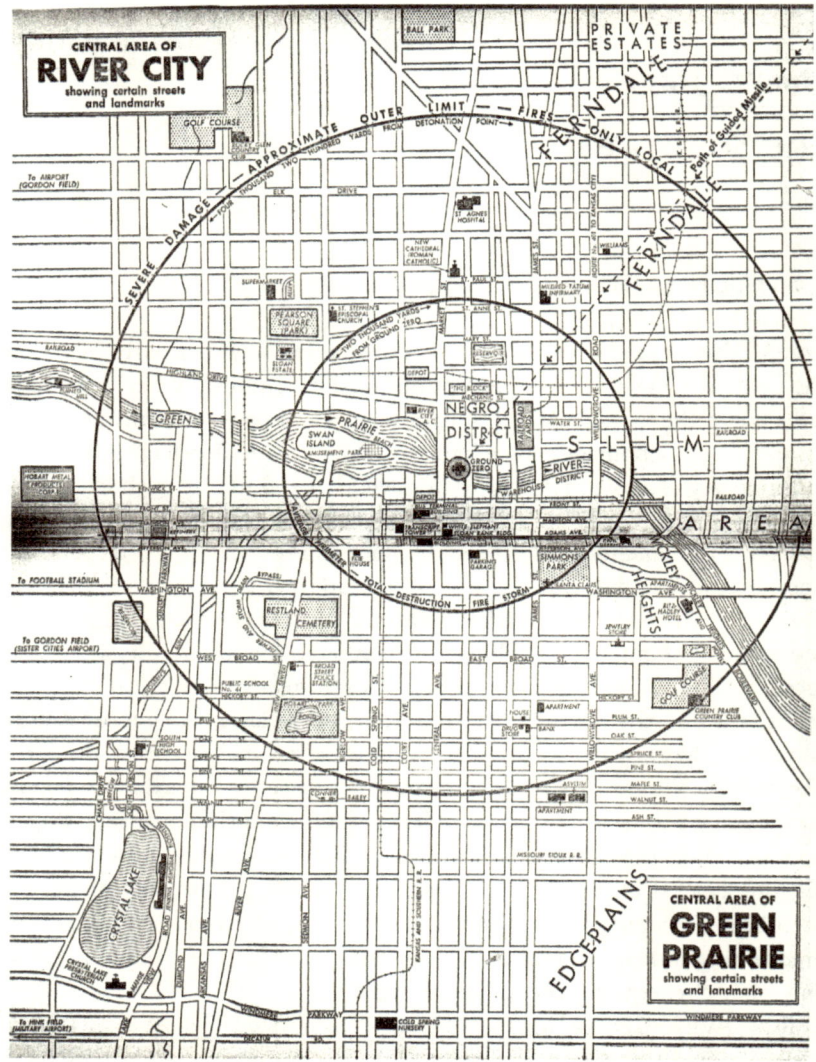

Ground Zero of the Nuclear Imagination: Philip Wylie's *Tomorrow* (1954)

American cities—hence, Wylie's advocacy of civil defense—as it lays out the city as an open target without defenses. Seen from the perspective of the one wielding nuclear weapons, it seems to imply military reassurances regarding the use of tactical nuclear weapons on a limited battlefield; the second concentric circle implies the presence of other circles further out, i.e., of a potentially unlimited battlefield in which the actual target is carefully chosen. Its cartographic perspective is that of someone looking down from above as if from the cockpit of the strategic bomber deploying the device (or, more precisely, through the vertical scope of the bombardier on that plane); clearly, it invites active, aggressive, perhaps even sadistic identification with the power of the pilot. The clinical, technocratic jargon used in the indexical language all over the map enhances this identification further. It emotionally dissociates the viewer from the details of carnage on the ground (something that Wylie's text more than makes up for—a compensatory overabundance of such details that ultimately calls into question the usefulness of civil defense). There is also a gendered subtext to the map as it superimposes the concentric circles of the blast onto the orderly rectangular grid of the city; within this double figure, the rational structure of the grid is subjected to a massive entropic shock that reduces everything in its range to shapeless abject rubble. In its various degrees of abstraction, the map is reminiscent of the mushroom cloud that hovers over so much of Cold War culture—a representational device that simultaneously expresses and represses, represents and distances, articulates and mutes the horrors of nuclear weapons. Though this particular bomb is delivered by missile, the perspective into which Wylie's map invites the viewer—a perspective that includes the missile's trajectory as a cartographic detail—evokes that branch of the United States military forces which is entrusted throughout the 1950s with the virtual monopoly of control over the nation's nuclear arsenal: the air force.

As much as Wylie's map is all about nuclear weapons and thus representative of the Cold War, it is its endorsement of a positive viewer identification with the sadistic position of the bomber pilot that harkens back to World War II. The US Air Force would come into its own during the strategic bombing campaigns against Germany and Japan, which constituted a significant part of the Allied war effort and was carried out predominantly by the US and Great Britain. A vast coordinated effort of advanced industrial warfare, strategic bombing during World War II would provide a model for the kind of warfare against civilian populations the Joint Chiefs of Staff were forced to contemplate in 1947 in their consideration of nuclear weapons (Schlosser 81–82). Before nuclear weapons would become available, strategic bombing was already aimed at weakening enemy infrastructure and terrorizing and killing civilian populations. However, since the ethical implications of causing, or at least tolerating, civilian casualties on the ground were just as uncomfortable to consider in the case of conventional weapons as in the projected use of nuclear weapons, public discourse during World War II, as well as during the Korean War, largely repressed such considerations.[1] The continuation of this imbalance in the public debate from the 1940s into the 1950s was made possible by extending the ideological justification of strategic bombing during World War II—from America's own righteous cause to the indictment of the enemy as absolutely evil or inhuman—toward the projected use of nuclear weapons during the Cold War.

This harking back to World War II also manifests itself in the fact that postwar American cinema, when entrusted with the task of celebrating the air force, had two choices. It could either engage in a depoliticized celebration of technology, as in *Strategic Air Command* and *Bombers B-52*, or it could tell stories about strategic bombing during World War II, rife with life-and-death drama and clearly coded enemies; these stories would then serve as thinly allegorized representations of Cold War politics. A postwar film like Henry King's *Twelve O'Clock High* (1949), for example, celebrates the air force only two years after it had been constituted as an independent branch of the armed forces with the passing of the National Security Act (1947). The film laments the lack of competent military personnel during the course of World War II—an issue of far greater importance for the air force during the war-weary aftermath of World War II than during the war itself. It also chronicles the mounting psychological stress for crews and commanding officers as the number of required missions keep increasing—an issue of equal concern to World War II crews (and thus the central conceit in Joseph Heller's *Catch 22* [1961]) and to the crews training for the delivery of nuclear payloads for the Strategic Air Command after the war. King's film clearly reaches back to outright war propaganda like William Wyler's *The Memphis Belle: A Story of a Flying Fortress* (1944) or films made during the war like Mervyn LeRoy's *Thirty Seconds Over Tokyo* (1944). As in *Twelve O'Clock High*, cinematic history throughout the 1950s would be written largely by superimposing the ideological certainties of World War II on the ambiguities and uncertainties of the Cold War. Much like the map used in Wylie's *Tomorrow*, the political and historical narrative would integrate circles and right angles, past and present, old and new enemies into a single geometric pattern. It would superimpose the shocking and as-of-yet indeterminate new history of the atomic age onto the reliably familiar history of military superiority and triumph in World War II and Korea, with the Midwestern twin cities of River City and Green Prairie providing the imaginary space in which this historical alignment is imagined and acted out.

Science fiction films of the 1950s participate in this reimagining of history and space, from urban settings to regional landscapes. They may be free from the constraints of representing both World War II and the Cold War realistically, but they are still tied to both conflicts as an allegorical subtext. Though many of these films would go on to imagine the nuclear attack that Wylie's map visualizes so well, their relative distance from Ground Zero, literally and figuratively, would allow them to direct attention very specifically to a number of space and locations 1950s American culture is interested in. The first wave of concern is about urban centers, the projected Ground Zero of a nuclear attack by the Soviet Union. Suburbanization promises to be the remedy for this ailment, scattering the population over a wider area and thus denying the bomb the maximum efficiency that would be the cause for its deployment. Science fiction of the period reflects this new anti-urbanism: from Clifford Simak and Ray Bradbury to Jack Finney, writers of Golden Age science fiction paint pictures of American cities abandoned by mass exodus.[2]

It would not take long, however, for the suburbs themselves to be overtaken with the fear of nuclear attack. Urban flight seemed to have carried that fear from the centers to the margins of American cities. With a little imagination, one might see in the ubiquitous suburban ranch-style houses, with their "low-pitched roofs, rough-hewn stone and timber, pronounced horizontal lines and deep eaves" (Boucher 17), an architectural figure huddling close to the ground, crouched in a defensive posture.[3] This contamination of the suburbs with earlier urban fears is explicitly linked to the expansion of the nation's road system with the passing of the Federal Aid Highway Act in 1956, during the Eisenhower administration. From the television adaptation of Judith Merrill's 1950 novel *Shadow on the Hearth* (*Atomic Attack*, 1954) to Ray Milland's *Panic in the Year Zero* (1962), films would express doubts about the success of urban evacuation and the social coherence, or lack thereof, within the suburban sprawl in case of a nuclear attack. In his book on the US highway system, Tom Lewis has characterized this nexus of infrastructure and public sentiment this way:

> Eisenhower's appointment of a general [i.e., Lucius Clay] to head the advisory committee [on the National Highway Program] made plain the connection between highways, national defense, and the fear Americans had about their security [. . .] Clearly, so the popular thinking went, the new roads would enable a mass evacuation. Given enough warning, citizens would be able to pack the family in the car and head out of town on one of the new superhighways. (*Divided Highways*, 107–108).

The Perils of Suburbia: *Panic in the Year Zero* (Ray Milland, 1962)

After the bomb drops on New York City, *Atomic Attack* has a somewhat truncated family and a few adopted outsiders huddle down in a suburban home as the suburbs around them turn into unfamiliar territory, populated by displaced persons and vaguely threatening strangers. Similarly, an episode of the *Twilight Zone*, "The Monsters are Due on Maple Street" (March 4, 1960), draws on the relative isolation of a suburban separation from the urban center, exploring the claustrophobic transition of community into lynch mob. Not surprisingly, two years later, *Panic in the Year Zero* would advocate preemptive escape from the suburbs as the most reasonable response to a nuclear war. As much as the expansion of the US highway system was conceived partly to serve as infrastructure for Cold War mobilization and evacuation, military considerations in science fiction films would follow a trend toward rising disenchantment with suburbanization in civil society. In the end, the suburbs would conjure up less the reassurance of safe population dispersal far removed from a potential Ground Zero at the urban center, and far more the alarm and insecurity over a lawless, underserved zone with neither the advantages of urban life nor the safety of its rural counterpart.

The spatial divide between urban centers and suburban accumulations often figures in the iconography of science fiction films in the 1950s, regardless of any specific region; both cities and suburbs often appear as visually bland, interchangeable default spaces across a variety of films. And yet the Cold War also begins to rewrite the American landscape in regard to more specific regions, affecting not only abstract, utilitarian, and politically defined "spaces," but also geographically and morphologically distinct, unique "places." While industrial modernity had been eroding regional differences for quite some time—a process exacerbated by the geographic mobility enforced first by the Great Depression and then mandated by World War II mobilization—there were still regions in the continental US which most of the population would consider remote and somewhat exotic.

"Wide open spaces" had always been an essential part of American frontier mythology; it is no coincidence that the Cole Porter song "Don't Fence Me In," which celebrated and romanticized geographic mobility in the vernacular of the cowboy song, would pop up in a military context throughout 1940s and '50s culture (e.g., in the war propaganda film *Hollywood Canteen* [1944] and in the war film *Hell and High Water* [1954]). The odd mixture of contradictions in the popular imagination—a regional landscape being both exotic and familiar, geographical mobility being both desirable and enforced—seemed to work best for the Southwest of the United States: from the southeastern part of California, through Nevada, Arizona, New Mexico, and Utah, as well as the eastern part of Texas and the southern part of Colorado. Traditionally associated with the Old West and thus the cultural heritage of the Western, these landscapes begin to take on new meanings in the 1950s. Like the concentric cycles radiating out from Ground Zero in Philip Wylie's map from *Tomorrow*, the science fiction film superimposes a new reality onto the traditional map of the "wide open spaces" in the American Southwest.

Lost in Space: The Girl in the Desert

Among the most quietly dramatic, eerie, and frightening moments in 1950s science fiction is the opening scene of Gordon Douglas's film *Them!* (1954). A little girl is walking through the desert; her stride is steady and she seems to know where she is going, but there is no discernable destination ahead of her. Wearing a bathrobe and slippers, she looks unharmed yet slightly disheveled. Her gaze is steady but empty, and she seems oblivious to the fact that in one arm she is holding a doll. As she walks along, a police squad car and a single-engine plane belonging to the New Mexico State Police are tracking her progress, exchanging information over the radio. The film cuts back and forth among these three focal points of action, looking up to the plane from the ground, or down at the girl from the plane, following the squad car from a position on the ground or tracking its progress from the air. Eventually, the squad car pulls up and one of the officers calls out to the girl. When she fails to respond, he runs over to her and halts her progress. She remains passive, catatonic, as her dead gaze goes out into the distance.

As it turns out, the little girl is the sole survivor of an attack upon her family's trailer, far out in the desert of New Mexico, by giant ants mutated as a result of atomic testing conducted in the course of the Manhattan

The Girl Wandering the Desert: *Them!* (Gordon Douglas, 1954)

Project. She alone has escaped, and later on she will be the one who, when woken from her catatonia, will utter the terrified scream that gives the film its title—"Them!" From the moment she is discovered wandering the desert, the film follows two consecutive processes. First, it is a detective story in which representatives of the law enforcement, the military, and the scientific community—i.e., representatives of the military-industrial complex—are trying to determine what happened to her and her parents, and thus discover the origin and the nature of the larger threat to which they fell victim. Once the inhuman murderer of the little girl's parents has been named, the rest of the film follows the attempts of this network of institutions to locate and eliminate the threat. Containment is an essential step in that process since the ants have begun to spread from their breeding grounds in New Mexico, with their queen having taken flight. The team finally succeeds when the queen's nest is discovered in the irrigation tunnels underneath Los Angeles. The film ends with the nest being incinerated while the audience ponders the ominous question posed by one of the main characters: "If these monsters are the result of the first atomic bomb in 1945, what about all the others that have been exploded since then?"

Despite the cautiously phrased critique of nuclear testing common in films of the period, critics have primarily read this narrative of detection and containment—in which the enemy is a robotic, emotionless, and endlessly self-perpetuating species intent on wresting control over the Earth from humanity—as an allegory of 1950s communist hysteria. Since *Them!* belongs to a generic sub-cycle of giant creature films—or, to be more precise, giant mutated insect films (together with, to name but a few, *The Beginning of the End* [Bert I. Gordon, 1957], *The Black Scorpion* [Edward Ludwig, 1957], and *Tarantula* [Jack Arnold, 1955])—it is fair to argue that the metaphoric link between insects and communists had quickly solidified into a standard trope. It is a convenient shorthand for conjuring up an iconography that, at its best, would merge fears of silent invasion (hence, the process of detection in which covert subversive activity must be uncovered) with fears of nuclear attack (containment and elimination invariably requires military mobilization and frequently features scenes of urban warfare and destruction). "Reviewers of *Them!* quickly recognized," Victoria O'Donnell argues, "that the ants were a projection of fear of atomic bombs [. . .] The ants could also have been a symbolic enemy, the Soviet Union, for in one scene the entomologist says that ants are 'savage, ruthless, and courageous fighters.' He also tells how ants use slave laborers in their colonies, evoking images of a totalitarian society" (186). To all those critics reading 1950s popular culture through the lens of the Cold War, such as the one reviewing *Them!* in the *Hollywood Reporter*, the film would obviously appear as a "natural exploitation piece that, from the viewpoint of timeliness, fits in perfectly with the current fears over possible effects of hydrogen bomb explosions'" (qtd. in O'Donnell 186).

In spite of such obvious topical urgency for the film's 1950s audience, the overall picture begins to change if films commonly assigned to the giant creature sub-cycle are rearranged into a different configuration. One divergent grouping would abandon the specific cinematic sub-cycle; though giant creature/insect films like *Them!* and *Tarantula* would still figure prominently, they could instead be read side by side with films like *The Monolith Monsters* (John Sherwood, 1957), a unique case of alien invasion narrative that features animated, self-replicating rocks from outer space, and a more conventional alien invasion film, with genuine alien invaders, like *It Came from Outer Space*.[4] What justifies the grouping is not so much a common sub-cycle; it would even be a difficult grouping since giant creature films would also have to include films in the wake of Ishiro Honda's *Gojira* (1954), such as *It Came from Beneath the Sea* (Robert Gordon, 1955) or *Twenty Million Miles to Earth* (Nathan Juran, 1957), neither one of which sustains the communist metaphor particularly well. Rather, what ties these films together is their use of the southwestern desert landscape as a setting. From *Them!* and *Tarantula* to *It Came from Outer Space* and *The Monolith Monsters*, this landscape figures not only as a dramatic backdrop but quite prominently as an object of considerable dramatic, visual, and thematic attention. This regrouping does not entirely invalidate the films' significance as commentary on nuclear anxieties and communist hysteria, but it does shift emphasis in a way that opens the films up for the kind of approach I would like to explore in the rest of this chapter. In order to map

130 The Southwest

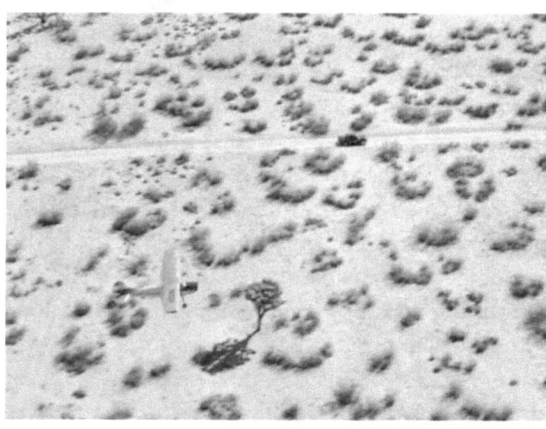

Mapping the Southwest Desert: *Them!* (Gordon Douglas, 1954)

out this approach, let's return to the little girl in the New Mexico desert in the opening scene of *Them!*

Aside from the narrative of detection and containment initiated by the dramatic opening of *Them!*, what is most striking about this scene is Douglas's use of setting and mise-en-scene. From the wide open vistas of the landscape and the bizarre flora intruding eerily into the frame, to the sense of loneliness, emptiness, and even desolation that permeates the frame, the landscape is haunting and evocative. In equal parts, this is a landscape the film discovers and represents, but also a space that the film produces, a cinematic construct of the highest caliber. The very first image of the scene, carried over from the opening credits, is shot against the outline of a Joshua tree, a bizarre, spiky plant that does not, in fact, grow in New Mexico. Botanical verisimilitude aside, though, the tree provides a stunning visual prop for a production designer and director in search of the unfamiliar and grotesque.

As the plane keeps looping overhead, the camera repeatedly tracks its movements with the Joshua tree in the foreground. Similarly, at the moment when the police officer catches up with the little girl, their coming together in a two-shot takes place in front of a Joshua tree, with a follow-up shot placing the trees at the margins of the frame and in the background, marking depth of space. It is exactly the biological and geographic discrepancy between the location and the Joshua tree—which, incidentally, appears in other science fiction films of the period, regardless of whether the story takes place in Nevada or Southern California—that suggests a mythic approach to the landscape and geographic location. The fast and easy handling of this visual motif is reminiscent of John Ford's use of Monument Valley, a location Ford famously returned to no matter which part of the West its idiosyncratic features were supposed to represent. New Mexico—home of the central research and production facilities of the Manhattan Project around Taos, and the first locations for testing at Trinity Site around White Sands and Alamogordo—has already been announced as the scene's setting by the markings on the police cruiser and plane. These markings send a clear signal that allows the audience to make the connection between landscape and nuclear weapons, or, more broadly speaking, between geographic space and the military-industrial complex. Specific as that signal may be as to the scene's location on the map, however, the landscape in its mythic dimension is flexible, malleable, and culturally overwritten, a product of national mythology reaching back to referents that predate the Cold War. Most of all, this landscape evokes the frontier, but this is not the frontier audiences might have come to expect from the Western. It is a frontier that has been gothicized, made strange, eerie, and unfamiliar, the archetypal setting of the Western overwritten by the military-industrial complex.

For those viewers hesitant to make the connection between giant mutated ants and the Western's frontier mythology, the little girl catatonically wandering through the desert makes the point more emphatically than the mythical landscape. The bathrobe, the pigtails, the doll—obviously, this is a latter-day version of the Indian Captivity narrative, the raid on the trailer out in the desert a version of the Indian raid. Tom Engelhardt sees behind it "the oldest hook in our cultural pantheon, the capture of white women by savages and their subsequent rescue. If it worked for Mary Rowlandson back in 1682, then why shouldn't it still work almost three centuries later?" (317). It is not difficult to see the line that extends from this frontier image to the stereotypical image that mixes horror with science fiction—the screaming (or fainting) woman carried off by the monster. Jerome Shapiro also notes other characters in the film as links between the Western and science fiction: "The storekeeper is described as the proverbial crafty old codger, the American/rugged individualist, who lived in the desert longer than anyone else and knew the danger" (103). Characters like him, however, are easy prey for the mutated ants. "The loner, the rugged individualist of the Old West, no longer has a place in the post-Hiroshima world of *Them!*" (104).[5]

Genre and Space: Overwriting the Landscape

If there was a cinematic genre that could rival science fiction's mass appeal during the 1950s, it would have to be the Western. "The Western genre," Peter Lev reminds his readers, "once the dependable mainstay of Hollywood film production, was by the late 1950s a mainstay of network television [. . .] Older Western films were also constantly appearing on television. Nevertheless, top-quality Westerns continued to be made in surprising numbers" (232). Some of them would come to update and redefine the genre politically (e.g., *High Noon*), sociologically (e.g., *Shane*), psychologically (e.g., *Winchester 73*), or formally (e.g., *The Far Country*). Having reached "a peak of popular appeal in the 1950s, when Hollywood production of A-Westerns was at an all-time high and series like *Wagon Train* and *Rawhide* dominated American evening television" (Kitses 2), the genre's capacity for articulating essential social and national themes made it a delivery vehicle for images of a very particular American region and landscape. The Western, Elaine Bapis argues,

> had long offered viewers a grammar and vocabulary for male identity in men's place [sic] in American history. Eastern journalists, artists, novelists, and others had portrayed two centuries of Western myth in writings, paintings, travelogues, and novels. The frontier West was an attractive myth for commodification in popular culture, politics, land, music, tourism, rodeo sport, and fashion because it brought action and strength together in a national identity. (100–101)

As the Western had matured into a form acutely attuned to the zeitgeist, it was also confronting the issues of the Cold War during the 1950s. Many Westerns of the period show a degree of moral ambiguity and a willingness to embrace the darker sides of life that would have been difficult to imagine in the previous decades. While "Westerns dealing with the Indian conflict have usually offered the most direct analogy with the contemporary diplomatic scene" (Lenihan 25), their historical setting tended to impose certain thematic limitations on the genre. Hoberman goes so far to argue that, even though "conventionally set in the twenty years following the Civil War, the Western could not help but address Cold War concerns, including the impact of advanced weapon technology (the Gatlin gun, cannon, and repeater rifle), mobilization, instrumentalized violence, and war against a racial enemy" (139). While any of these nineteenth-century technological innovations could very well function as an allegory of nuclear weapons, 1950s Westerns would have to make considerable efforts to endow them with the hyperbolically apocalyptic overtones nuclear weapons would carry at the time. As public awareness of the impact of nuclear fallout and radiation on the human body would increase throughout the 1950s and early '60s, the Western's metaphors for cutting-edge military technology would also be hard-pressed to accommodate these idiosyncratic qualities. If Hoberman's reading of the Western's ability to address America's new nuclear arsenal might be overly optimistic, his observations nonetheless do full justice to what is perhaps the most crucial fact about actual military deployment during the 1950s—that it was all about the mobilization of the US' conventional, *not* nuclear arsenal (as, for example, during the Korean War). As far as this reality was concerned, the Western was indeed particularly well equipped to capture the nature of military conflict. Like many science fiction films of the period, the Western also helped to superimpose the conventional warfare of World War II and Korea upon Cold War scenarios of nuclear confrontation, with the same political consequences—assuaging apocalyptic fears, projecting past military triumph on to uncertain future ones, and ensuring the continuity of the military-industrial complex.

When the Western finally began its decline as a popular genre in the 1970s, it was not because of its inability to allegorize nuclear war, but because of the broad sense of disenchantment and demoralization that yet another conventional war, the one in Vietnam, had cast over what Tom Engelhardt has broadly referred to as "victory culture." For "adults and children alike," Engelhardt writes,

> watching sheriffs, gunslingers, and cowboys walk an endless Main Street or patrol the savage frontiers of freedom on TV seemed a thrilling escape. Yet television proved a powerful motor for storylessness [. . .] the consoling world embodied in that war story barely lasted out the decade on television [. . .] As the new decade began, a young president would acknowledge a postwar loss of narrative. He would call upon other, even younger Americans, promising "new frontiers" at the far reaches of the earth. (89)

Engelhardt's historical narratives make it clear that if the Western, exhausted and politically discredited, would pass the torch to another genre, it would most likely be science fiction. Other critics concur; in trying "to come to grips with the apparent vanishing of America's oldest and heretofore most enduring of genres," Jim Kitses writes, "some critics [. . .] dissolved differences, suggesting that in fact science fiction is indeed the Western in futurist dress" (3).[6] If this is in fact the case, then science fiction films from the 1950s that chose as their setting the archetypical landscape of the Western may have had an exacerbating influence on this transition (even though they came to prominence at a time when the Western was still going strong).

For commercial filmmaking, the Western's indebtedness to the southwestern desert landscape may have had reasons that were more soberly pragmatic than mythological, and yet this still helped to determine crucially the genre's visual aesthetics. What is true for the 1950s science fiction films is true for the Western: "Hollywood budget needs usually dictate that the town be in the Arizona or California desert" whereas a larger budget "allows a much greater play back and forth among several model environments," including, of course, the modern American metropolis (Sontag, "Imagination of Disaster" 102).[7] Jack Arnold biographer Dana Reemes recounts that Arnold would shoot in the desert for the first time early in his career not while making a Western but while making *It Came from Outer Space* (1953). His subsequent output until 1955, which consisted of noir melodrama and science fiction films, does not return to the desert. This only happens with *Tarantula* (1955), in which the desert location is dictated primarily by the commercial success of the earlier Gordon Douglas film *Them!*, which Universal-International tried to cash in on with one of its own giant creature films. What is, in turn, notable among the use of desert locations in *Tarantula*, is that, right before directing the film, Arnold made *The Man from Bitter Ride*, "an action western" (80), and that, "just after the completion of *Tarantula!* [sic], Arnold directed another color Western, *Red Sundown*, released in January of 1956" (Reemes 82). In some ways, this steady alternation between Westerns and science fiction films with a desert location would be standard practice for the studio directors without auteurist ambitions. Jack Arnold and Gordon Douglas, who were responsible for making a fair number of the most well-remembered science fiction films of the period, are prime examples of this practice. To the degree that directors would go back and forth between both genres, the demands of industrial filmmaking suggest that visual style, mood, and atmosphere were not the exclusive property of one or the other genre, but that they would travel freely with the director from one genre to the other.[8] Hence, science fiction films would either share stylistic features in their treatment of landscape, or develop new and divergent ones. In the end, each genre would be able to do justice to its own set of specific themes and yet still express a unique ideological viewpoint.

For the Western, as many critics have argued, this viewpoint would largely be defined in moral terms; landscape would always and inevitably be a vehicle for the expression of a moral vision. Robert Warshow made the case in 1954 that the visual impact of the landscape—i.e., its specifically *cinematic* nature—reflects the moral simplicity of the Western as well as the "apparent moral clarity" of its protagonist. "Much of this apparent simplicity," Warshow argues, "arises directly from those 'cinematic' elements which have long been understood to give the Western theme its special appropriateness for the movies: the wide expanses of land, the free movement of men on horses" (109). Even when Westerns venture into more morally ambiguous territory, the link between landscape and morality remains intact. As Jane Tompkins would put it a few decades after Warshow: "All there is [in the beginning of each Western] is space, pure and absolute, materialized in the desert landscape" (70), a landscape "defined [in its purity] by absence" (71).

Emptiness or absence may very well come with connotations of moral clarity and purity, but once the landscape passes from the hands of the Western to those of science fiction, the connotations of these qualities change. While the Western celebrates empty spaces, science fiction invests them with a sense of agoraphobic uncertainty. Wide-angle shots of the desert landscape in films like *Tarantula* and *Them!* are often accompanied by ominous and eerie cues in the musical score. Neither one of these two films actually uses that campy staple of 1950s horror film scores, the theremin, on its soundtrack. But violin notes tend to rise and swell in an approximation of the theremin's ghostly wail whenever the camera contemplates the desert's emptiness; in *Them!*, the ants' idiosyncratic call is also heard during those scenes, a sound effect simulating echoes across vast open spaces that is oddly reminiscent of an air-raid siren. Despite this obvious gothicization of the landscape, there is also a strand of romanticism in 1950s science fiction films that harks back to the Western. Writing about the work of director Jack Arnold, for example, Blake Lucas notes that "the light over the expansive desertscape [in *It Came from Outer Space*] stands in contrast to the shadowy darkness of the horror films of Universal's past [. . .] In place of that kind of worn mise-en-scene the desert into which the spaceship crashes in the opening images has freshness and quiet beauty, and a new mystery" (Lucas 74). As the "mystery" of what inhabits the desert is gradually revealed, "freshness and quiet beauty" will yield to anxiety and paranoia—almost as if the film, in its depiction and use of landscape, moves from the optimism and moral clarity of one genre to the anxiety and paranoia of the other.

Emptiness, then, does not stand for moral purity. It stands for a version of the sublime in which horror and beauty are both present, with the former outweighing the latter. Describing *It Came from Outer Space*, Blake Lucas suggests that the "desert has *the appearance* of simplicity, yet hides things (the spaceship) and within the landscape, reality may mutate into illusion as relationships are redefined" (5, italics added). If the landscape's first impression recalls the Western, then the plot of a film like *It Came from Outer Space* is to undercut and subvert this first impression, and to rewrite it in the terms of a different genre. To the degree that the southwestern desert is an emblematic American landscape, the sublime mixture of horror and beauty also marks the convergence of the two genres. "America finds itself in that great southwest desert to which all of Southern California had once belonged," Hoberman reminds us. "Death Valley, the Mojave, the Great Basin, the Colorado Plateau, the Great Salt Lake, the Moab, White Sands. This territory is both distant past and onrushing future—the landscape where, as presaged by *Rocketship X-M*, the prehistoric merges with the postapocalyptic [. . .] this is the alien place that newsweeklies call the Most A-Bombed Area on Earth" (270). As time and space converge in the southwestern desert landscape, it is the transition from one genre to another that reveals how the nation's narrative has changed.

With enough historical hindsight, the inscription on the landscape would become increasingly legible. After his visits to atomic testing sites to take photographs that document these sites' strange inconspicuousness and evocative emptiness, Peter Goin confesses to sensations that appear to have been anticipated by science fiction films of the 1950s. "The landscape was charged, literally and figuratively," Goin muses, "and that irony was present in my mind. [. . .] This kind of landscape—profound in what it represents, politically controversial, *secluded from visual access*—provokes a similar response to the one I experience when I cross an international boundary. In such cases I become self-conscious, primarily aware of *the foreign quality and nature of the landscape*. At the test site, the physical threat, ubiquitous yet vague, informed my response" (Goin 82, italics added). In the absence of physical traces of nuclear test explosions, it is the invisible yet powerful mapping of the landscape that renders it uncanny, the drawing of symbolic boundaries that come with the essential secrecy of the nation's nuclear arsenal. Though seclusion from visual access would remain an essential feature of the military-industrial complex at work in the southwestern desert, social developments in the realm of transportation and leisure throughout the 1950s would begin to modify this insistence on secrecy in unexpected ways.

Until nuclear testing moved out of the American Southwest and to the Pacific, mushroom clouds rising over the desert horizon were a familiar sight to the locals. For a time, they even provided a tourist attraction, advertised by hotels that would offer rooms with particularly good views of the spectacle. Observable from a safe distance and starkly outlined against clear blue Western skies, these explosions would underwrite an odd thematic mixture. On the one hand, their full visibility suggested patriotic pride and the normalization of nuclear weapons within the framework of the military-industrial complex. On the other hand, they represented unknowability, predicated on physical distance and, more important, on military secrecy and the ideological control of information in the public sphere. The presence

Two nuclear tests in the Mohave Desert (1951): one visible from Las Vegas, the other observed only by the military. Source: National Nuclear Security Administration/Nevada Field Office.

of a tourist looking out a hotel window would validate this visual regiment just as much as an audience member at a cinema watching newsreels or a television viewer watching documentary footage. The aura of "being there," however, might have come with its own charismatic pull. Infrastructure necessary to increase the flow of tourists into the Southwest was certainly not a matter of nuclear testing. Odd as it sounds, though, nuclear spectatorship would end up profiting from the postwar economic boom. For one, there was the increasing availability and affordability of air travel, an industry fueled by reconverted military planes and the influx of scores of former military pilots. There was also the Federal Aid Highway act (1956), which would authorize "federal funding for constructing interstate highways and [create] an ongoing fund supported by a federal tax on fuel" (Rugh 17–18). While these investments encouraged and legitimized geographic mobility, they remained integrated into an overarching ideology of home and family; the family road trip became a staple of middle-class vacation during the 1950s. They also fed an ever-expanding realm of consumerism, fostering an ideology "that upheld the idea that consuming goods and experiences [e.g., that of travel] sustained national security" (Rugh 5). As David Halberstam put it, "the American Century was the same thing as the Oil Century—an era in which the economy was driven by oil instead of coal and in which, for the first time, the worker became a consumer as well" (*The Fifties* 117).

The expanding interstate transportation system, in collaboration with a booming American auto industry, would allow for widespread domestic travel, which, in turn, would gradually erode the geographic otherness of hitherto remote regions, like the southwestern desert.[9] Nuclear tourism was, admittedly, a small part of this migration. But even if it came to redefine the connotations of what had traditionally been a frontier landscape, these new connotations hardly deterred travelers and motorists who would come for more conventional forms of tourism. The theme in all of these geographic movements—from affordable travel by plane and automobile to the rising popularity of towns like Las Vegas and Lake Tahoe as tourist destinations—would be spatial mobility: a form of conspicuous consumption, and an expression of the American frontier spirit. Enabling this spatial mobility would be the opening up of this hitherto remote part of the domestic American space. Ideologically assured and technologically well-equipped, 1950s tourists venturing into the southwestern desert for the first time might still have embarked on their long road trips with some trepidation. But while the Western's assorted threats might have lost, as Tom Engelhardt suggested, their validity, the new and unfamiliar realities of the nuclear age, would still exercise a hold on the cultural imagination. Decades of travel and tourism would eventually erode the landscape's exotic otherness. But in the 1950s, it was still a place of unsettling empty spaces, of bizarre flora lining the sides of the interstate, and of the cinematic monsters bred by the sleep of technological reason, somewhere out there.

Military Homesteaders: The Origins of Occupation

While the 1950s may have been ringing in a new era of domestic tourism in the Southwest of the US, the historical origins of this process were established by the military not in the course of the Cold War but as part of the final phase of World War II. Atomic testing in New Mexico and Nevada began with the Manhattan Project. With it came an array of powers of territorial control the military would wield over the landscape: the ability to map, zone, and cordon off tracts of land, and to conceal activities within these regions behind a wall of security and secrecy. "If the race to win the war through superweapons created a threshold between worlds"—what historian David Beck calls "the pre- and post-bomb eras that bifurcate the twentieth century"—then "the nature of the installation at Los Alamos also established a precedent for the militarization of science and the military construction of secret zones of operation that would shape the permanent war economy in the West" (Beck 101). Not only did the Manhattan Project mark the beginning of the nuclear age, it also marked the beginning of the modern security state. The location for the secret government program was chosen for its distance from possible attack points along the US coastline, its sparse population density, and its inaccessibility to prying eyes. Garry Wills, in his discussion of the impact nuclear weapons have had on the American political system, also points out that its secrecy came as a direct result of the Manhattan Project being placed under direct control of the military, which would allow the concealment of its budget behind wartime security measures (Wills 11). Though production of the bomb was dispersed among various locations (Hanford in Washington State, Oak Ridge in Tennessee; and, eventually, the Tinian staging area in the run-up to the actual delivery of the bomb to Japan), Los Alamos (development) and Alamogordo (testing) in the New Mexico desert were going to provide the public with the iconography of the project as a whole. "The military-industrial complex," Wills concludes, "with a poisonous admixture of government and secrecy, had scored a triumph that would show the way to many other governmental activities" (23).

As much as the 1950s economic boom promised geographical mobility to a larger part of the US population by way of domestic tourism in areas like the southwest, the security mandates of the military-industrial complex in exactly this area worked in diametric opposition to this newly promised freedom. In the Southwest, more than anywhere else in the continental US, military prerogatives curtailed that geographic mobility in the interest of the emergent national security state. Oddly enough, the Manhattan Project, with its regional dispersal of development, testing, and production facilities, had generated a new kind of mobility in itself when it recruited workers in one location and deployed them in another. From the scientific to the security staff, and all the way down to secretarial and janitorial support, the personnel of the Manhattan Project was—for reasons of security—not from the area surrounding the Los Alamos laboratories. Like so many other parts of the military machinery of World War II, the Manhattan Project encouraged a geographic migration of labor that was to precede that of tourists in the Southwest by a good ten years. Within those ten years, the Southwest would provide the space in which enforced geographic mobility as a matter of military necessity would give way to voluntary geographic mobility as a form of leisure; a leisure which, nonetheless, would still be coded in terms of an ideology "that upheld the idea that consuming goods and experiences [e.g., that of travel] sustained national security" (Rugh 5).

Together with these mandatory and voluntary geographical migrations in the context of World War II, there are also the displacements of native populations in the Southwest to make room for the security perimeters surrounding installations like the one at Los Alamos. Later, this measure would also extend to the mining of uranium in the same areas throughout most of the Cold War. The same context would also include the internment of Japanese Americans, enforced in 1942 by Executive Order 9066. Many of the internees would end up in locations dispersed across the southwestern quadrant of the US. "If internment inadvertently produced new forms of Americanized identity due to the undermining of traditional Japanese cultural hierarchies," Beck concludes, "the conditions of life at Los Alamos also produced new social formations that prefigure in a number of ways Cold War society's internalized modes of self-surveillance and security-consciousness, and its celebration of managerial, corporate, and scientific elites as manifestations of a thorough-going patriarchal and paternalistic order" (102). From World War II on, then, the southwestern landscape functions as a regional example of a nexus of larger national phenomena. For good reason, Eisenhower's farewell address phrases its warning against the military-industrial complex in terms of its social, institutional, but also *geographic* distribution of agents and spaces. This was a national imaginary so vast that it might very well render invisible, unreadable, and thus incomprehensible the totality of operations routinely performed by the military-industrial complex, despite their plain visibility on the local and regional levels.

Science fiction films of the 1950s responded creatively to this reimagining of domestic spaces. In an overt homage to the Manhattan Project, the fictional Project Tic-Toc, the US government's top-secret time travel project, in the television series *The Time Tunnel* (Irvin Allen, 1966–67), is located in the southwestern desert. In the series' opening episode, a representative of the congressional oversight committee is brought to the location, a vast empty desert plain, by plane. Transferred to a limousine, he suddenly sees the ground opening beneath, as the car disappears down a ramp. In images reminiscent of the alien Krell machinery in *Forbidden Planet* (Fred M. Wilcox, 1956), the episode puts on display the seemingly endless vertical downward drops of transportation shafts, the complex mazes of tunnels and bridges. Most important, there is the series' eponymous device itself, a hypnagogic spiral vanishing toward infinity in black and white circles of ever decreasing circumference.[10] The personnel monitoring the device is dressed either in military uniforms or lab coats, illustrating the collaboration of technoscience and military might in the US projecting itself across temporal barriers. The fact that these facilities are nestled within the familiar space, that their discovery comes as an experience of, quite literally, the ground opening up beneath our feet, makes them perfect visual allegories of the military-industrial complex itself.

Like the eponymous Fort Apache in John Ford's Western, the vast installation of Project Tic-Toc in *Time Tunnel* is seen as a safe haven, a secure place in an insecure world. In several episodes of the series, its perimeters are compromised, usually by some force or agent that manages to reverse the direction of the time tunnel device and travel back from "somewhere out there" into the heart of the military-industrial complex. Every one of these intrusions confirms the space's positive connotations. Ensuring its security is as much a priority for the series' ideological agenda as legitimizing the two American time travelers as agents expanding the reach of US power (however much as their journey outward may be the product of accidents and their itinerary beyond the project's practical control). As invasions are staged and repelled, security is perpetually in peril. Without a doubt, *Time Tunnel* celebrates American technological ingenuity and superiority. But every reciprocal move by an enemy out there, every incursion into the supposedly safe space, adds a more sinister dimension to this technophilic celebration. In order to map this darker dimension, and thus to reconnect 1950s science fiction films with the horror film, we will return to the subcycle of giant creature films, to Gordon Douglas's *Them!*, and to that little girl wandering through the New Mexico desert.

The Blank Spot on the Map and the State of Occupation

As soon as the hunt is on in *Them!* for the giant mutated ants responsible for the death of the little girl's parents, the concerted efforts of law enforcement, science, and the military are geared toward one goal: to determine the location, somewhere out there in the southwestern desert, of the ants' nest. In military terms, this is their headquarters, their base of operations, the beachhead from which, following their biological imperative, they will launch their invasion of the rest of the world. What emerges from this horrific, apocalyptic prospect is the film's thematic focus and the source of its paranoid urgency—that, inside the familiar domestic space of the US, there is an alien enclave, a foreign body tucked away into the natural features of the landscape, cleverly concealed by those alien agents operating in it or from it by strategies of mimicry that pass it off as belonging there. In *Them!*, it is the nest, from which, eventually, the queen will spread her species throughout the world. In *The Monolith Monsters*, it is the first point of impact of the alien meteorite before its fragments begin to multiply and grow on their destructive march toward civilization. In *It Came from Outer Space*, it is the crash-landed alien spaceship, briefly glimpsed by our intrepid amateur astronomer, first when he arrives on the crash site, then when it is covered by a landslide down the walls of the crater dug by its impact.[11] In each film, finding the location of this alien enclosure is also a race against time—to find the ants' nest before the queen takes flight; to locate the direction in which the alien meteorites are marching before they can reach the next town in their path. And as the narrative clock is counting down, each film uses its allotted time to scan and survey the desert landscape.

Seen in the broader context of 1950s science fiction films, these alien enclaves do not necessarily have to be located in the southwestern desert. William Cameron Menzies's *The Whip Hand* (1951)—a spy thriller with a powerful dose of paranoia and melodramatic excess that operates on the border of the fantastic—takes place in a small lakeside resort in Minnesota. Winnoga is the base of operations for a cabal in which communists in cahoots with a former Nazi scientist are preparing for fifth-column germ warfare against the nation. Location is important to this and any other paranoid narrative; just as the backyard harboring the alien spaceship in *Invaders from Mars* is part of American suburbia, Winnoga, Minnesota, is nestled in what is called the "heartland" for good ideological reasons. And yet things are not what they seem. Having poisoned the lake, the town's traditional source of tourist income, in order to lower real estate prices, the communists have migrated into Winnoga en masse. They are aided by their collaboration with a powerful industrialist named Peterson (Lewis Martin), a traitor to his nation, whose fortified gothic mansion, ominously referred to as the Lodge, sits broodingly adjacent to the town, surrounded by a tight security perimeter. Beneath a thin veneer of Midwestern joviality and rosy-tinged Bradbury-esque nostalgia, the town is under constant surveillance;

every move, every phone call, and every social bond is closely monitored. Cultivating a paranoid atmosphere not unlike the one in his very own *Invaders from Mars* only two years later (1953), Menzies's film anticipates in its basic conceit the short film *Red Nightmare* (George Waggner, 1962). Financed and produced by a governmental agency named the "Department of Defense Directorate for Armed Forces Information and Education," *Red Nightmare* imagines what an ordinary American town would be like if it had been taken over by communists. Just as narrator Jack Webb continuously intrudes upon the film's eponymous red nightmare (and, finally, releases the audience from it), Menzies sends in courageous reporter Matt Corbin (Elliott Reid) to uncover the conspiracy and mobilize the FBI. In the film's climactic storming of Peterson's compound, the military-industrial complex goes up against the militant conspiracy, a conflict between institutional state power and its shadowy double.

Just like Waggner's nightmarish communist community, Menzies's imaginary alien enclave of Winnoga, Minnesota, in *The Whip Hand* figures as a powerful fantasy of a state of foreign occupation. Popular film and television during the 1950s has indulged this fantasy time and again in the context of the suburbs (e.g., in the *Twilight Zone* episode, "The Monsters are Due on Maple Street," or in Menzies's own *Invaders from Mars*). But films with a southwestern desert setting replicate the theme and transfer it to the imposing landscape of the southwestern desert with a slightly different historical point of reference.[12] In a key scene from Jack Arnold's *It Came from Outer Space* (1953), amateur astronomer John Putnam (Richard Carlson) and his fiancée Ellen Fields (Barbara Rush) are driving back through the desert after having visited what Putnam is certain to be an alien landing site. Along the side of the road, they spot two telephone linemen doing repair work on the wires that crisscross the desert. One of them, Frank (Joe Sawyer), invites Putnam to climb up and listen in with him on what he calls "the damndest noise ever" humming through the wires he has tapped. "Never heard anything like it on the wires before," he muses. As soon as Putnam climbs the ladder, Arnold cuts from high to low angle shots, and now there is no longer desert floor and country road cutting off the audience's view into the distance; instead, a vast empty sky opens up behind the character, who is framed in medium close-up. When Putnam asks what the sound might be, Frank replies, "It might be somebody up that way tapping the wires," his verbal cue coinciding with a point of view shot that tracks the wires as they recede toward the vast open spaces of the American Southwest desert and the distant horizon. As Putnam stares into the distance, both puzzled and

If You Listen to the Wires, The Wires Listen To You: Networked Surveillance in *It Came from Outer Space*

alarmed, Frank adds, as an afterthought, that the sound suggests someone listening, in turn, to them as they are doing their own listening. "Still hear it?" he asks Putnam, who replies, "No, it's gone . . ."

The scene, written by Ray Bradbury, resonates with the idea of the technological network inhabited or occupied by alien forces. Dominating the communication network that crisscrosses the desert and extends toward the larger continent and beyond, the alien presence raises suspicion that forces within the vast space act reciprocally. As Putnam and the telephone repairmen are tapping into the network, accessing its treasure trove of information and projecting themselves outward into the vast distances, the network is tapping into them. Suddenly, those vast distances are rushing toward them and come into alarming proximity. For better or worse, welcome or not, information is always and inevitably flowing in both directions at once. The aliens have turned the tables on the scientist tracking them; our network now works for them. As observers—or eavesdroppers, in this case—they are themselves being observed; someone is listening in on them. Surveillance, we discover, cuts both ways.

Though the significant plot twist in *It Came from Outer Space* is the revelation that the aliens have not come to Earth as invaders but as victims of a crash, and are thus eager to simply repair their craft and be on their way, they are invariably portrayed as an ominous, menacing presence. Their threatening nature stems exactly from their uncanny mobility through the networks mapping the desert landscape. The film emphasizes this point every time the camera travels alongside cars driving through the desert with telephone wires swinging rhythmically with the shot's forward movement at mid-level through the frame. The suggestion is that the aliens also somehow travel along the wires—whether they do so in some disembodied state or figuratively as they extend themselves through the network is something Bradbury's script and Douglas's direction never make clear. Nonetheless, as Douglas's camera keeps tracking the aliens' movements, it also measures and maps the desert in the search for the alien's base, their crashed ship hidden somewhere in the vast, empty landscape. Douglas works through this theme in the opening scene of that film as well; the same logic of surveillance, from the air and from the ground, is at work when law enforcement converges upon the little girl wandering around catatonically. Similar scenes also occur in *Tarantula* (Jack Arnold, 1955) and *The Monolith Monsters* every time characters scan the desert horizon in search of whatever mysterious forces are massing somewhere out there.

This scanning of the horizon is extremely significant as a trope in science fiction films of the 1950s. Read as a theatrical device, it is a form of teichoscopy—i.e., the gaze of a character into the visually inaccessible space off-stage, which is often accompanied by a verbal description of what is occurring in that space for the benefit of the audience. On a purely practical level, we have seen these shots occurring in films that work with military stock footage. Here, they tend to position a diegetic observer in the frame before cutting to the imported shots. More cinematically speaking, however, it is an image integrated into a sequence of multi-directional gazes by, in turn, audience, characters, and camera. These gazes integrate the audience's curiosity—the spectators' insistence to see the spectacular sight described or anticipated for themselves—into the progression of shots and edits that organize narrative coherence. Reverse-angle shots showing the desert empty are just as important to this "suturing" of the audience into the film as shots that, finally, reveal the presence of the monster. In the context of characters scanning the desert as a space of latent dangers, the suturing of the audience into these teichoscopic shots has clear ideological dimensions as well. It serves as a recruitment of the audience—or what critic Louis Althusser has called "interpellation"—into a mandatory and perpetual state of Cold War vigilance, reproducing the landscape as a field of surveillance and control.

In some cases, only one small location of the familiar landscape has been invaded and converted—as in *The Whip Hand* or *Invaders from Mars*. In other cases, the suspected presence of the alien enemy in the landscape renders that entire landscape strange and unfamiliar—as in the films that feature the southwestern desert, from *Them!* and *Tarantula* to *It Came from Outer Space* and *The Monolith Monsters*. All differences aside, though, the operative

The Southwest   147

Inside and Outside the Encampment: Territorial Occupation in *The Monolith Monsters* and *Fort Apache*

metaphor is always that of alien occupation. In the context of the Cold War, alien occupation is hardly an unusual topic; this will become obvious in the next chapter, which discusses US foreign policy. But it is one that usually attaches itself to spaces outside the US and thus comes with an entirely different set of thematic connotations. When, for example, the metaphor of occupation makes an appearance in the American Western—as it does in *Fort Apache* (John Ford, 1948), a film about a small and insignificant military outpost deep in "Indian country," shot in its director's favorite location, Monument Valley—its central spatial metaphor takes on meaning by way of its immediate historical context. As Hoberman points out, "Ford's cavalry Western opened in New York on June 25—one day after the Soviet blockade of Berlin created a beleaguered Western fort in the midst of hostile Red territory" (76). It does not take much imagination to read Berlin as the Cold War's premiere "frontier city" into Ford's cavalry encampment.[13]

British science fiction superficially resembles its American counterpart but uses the metaphor of alien occupation for its own ends. Expressing, for example, British postwar concerns about the presence of US bases in the country, Nigel Kneale's *Quatermass 2* (1955) tells the story of alien installations in the remote British countryside that are quietly preparing for an invasion on a massive scale. It is easy to read the film through the lens of reverse colonialism—i.e., the fantasy of Britain becoming the target of colonial conquest and occupation rather than being the colonizer herself. Kneale's story speaks as eloquently about anxieties about the loss of the British Empire in the wake of World War II as H. G. Wells's *War of the Worlds* did around the turn of the century. Despite being the "third nuclear power following the successful test of a British [nuclear] bomb in 1952," Tony Judt reminds us, Britain may have been part of Europe, but it also "had a very particular relationship with the United States. The British people tended to be ambivalent about America" (160). While US military presence in Britain during World War II had been largely welcome, its continuation as part of the US fortification of Western Europe as a bulwark against Soviet aggression was seen as a diminishment of British autonomy. This was especially true since the continued presence of military personnel in West Germany seemed to suggest an insulting equivalence between what had been a former ally and a former enemy of the US (all this "while Great Britain [during the 1950s] seemed somehow tighter, poorer, grayer and grimmer than any of the erstwhile defeated, occupied and ravished lands across the waters" [Judt 162]). With great topical acuity, Kneale's story attaches these anxieties about the loss of territorial self-determination specifically to the postwar handover of global power from Britain to the US. This was a context in which the alien installations came to resemble the US nuclear arsenal installed in Western Europe as a first line of defense against the Soviet Union. Finally, postwar British politicians would not be able to reverse the trend of decreasing international significance. In fact, a year after *Quatermass II*, Britain would suffer what might be considered the final blow sealing its demoted Cold War status with the Suez Crisis. Kneale's story, meanwhile, ends on a more reassuring note for its British audience. In it, Professor Bernard Quatermass infiltrates the alien enclosure and leads the successful revolt by the cowed villagers nearby who had been living under the shadow of the dangerous alien technology.

If American science fiction films take a different route in exploring the metaphor of alien occupation than their British counterparts, the point of departure seems to be not the general use of domestic landscapes but rather the specific use of American southwestern desert landscapes. The question that arises from this use is what exactly that state of occupation signifies whenever this mythical landscape is gothicized and rendered uncanny. One answer to this question leads back to the familiar interpretive patterns for films of the period—that, in other words, the aliens embody fears about communist invasion and subversion. But there is another side to this interpretation that is worth exploring if many of the films conceptualize alien occupation so strongly in terms of the military-industrial complex. It is true that conventional readings of these films discover the fear of communist subversion behind every butte, mesa, tumbleweed, creosote bush, and Joshua tree (and thus identify the alien pods in *Invasion of the Body Snatchers* or the alien impostors in *It Came from Outer Space* and *Invaders from Mars* as allegorical representations of communists). Yet more recent examples of critical discourse have accounted for an ambiguity in the representation that allows these alien others to be associated, with equal ease, either with communist infiltrators or with anti-communist crusaders. Critics like Tom Engelhardt and Peter Biskind have, in turn, read this ambiguity as a sign of the extreme polarization of 1950s political discourse; they detect in it a tendency to respond to the political fanaticism, real or imagined, of both political extremes with equal alarm and hysterical unease.[14] On the surface, this argument applies most directly to films that take as their setting tight urban or suburban communities. After all, the less densely populated a geographical space is, the less of a community there is to infiltrate. The more the open, empty spaces of the desert dominate a film, the less opportunity it has to allegorize the subversion of the nation. Though *It Came from Outer Space*, for example, features a small desert town which, in the throes of paranoia, sees its citizens turn into a violent lynch mob, the social decline takes place in the town, not in the open desert surrounding it. What critics like Robert Warshow and Jane Tompkins see as the Western's moral validation of the landscape applies just as well to science fiction films. Nonetheless, there is a way in which the critical argument about the political reversibility of Cold War paranoia revolving around the axis of "us versus them" can be carried over into the discussion of the southwestern desert setting in 1950s science fiction films.

On the surface, the mutated creatures and alien invaders that occupy the desert are representations of the political and ideological other—of communists, fifth columnists, subversives, and any other shade of villain produced by the bipolar ideological machinery of the Cold War. Upon closer inspection, however, this clear-cut divide begins to break down. Just as the eponymous giant tarantula is the result of technoscience gone awry, the giant mutated ants nesting somewhere in the desert in *Them!* are the result of nuclear testing, or, more specifically, of US nuclear testing. The film's imaginary threat, in other words, is arrived at by extrapolating from the activities of the military-industrial complex. *Them!* and many other films like it work very hard to suppress this aspect of their very own narrative logic. Instead, they ensure that the irony of the military having to defeat the threat that it had created itself never gets to occupy center stage. Still, the latent presence of this irony in the narrative lays the groundwork for readings of the film that go against the ideological grain of both "inclusionary" and "exclusionary" films of the 1950s. If we do not suppress or dismiss or disavow this narrative trace, we might arrive at a reading that takes the idea quite literally that the US is, in fact, occupied by a foreign nation. This "foreign nation," and the alien enclave into which it has withdrawn, however, would have to be part of its own political and economic system. Within this fantasy of alien occupation, part of the US' political and economic system has taken on a life of its own. Like science fiction's giant mutations—from ants and spiders to colossal men and fifty-foot women—it has grown to frighteningly inflated dimension disproportional to what its actual size should be. By way of its unnatural size, this particular mutation has acquired what Eisenhower's farewell address refers to as "unwarranted influence," and is now functioning, in effect, as a foreign agent of occupation.

On the microscopic narrative level, films like *Them!* treat the military enthusiastically or even deferentially; by and large, officers and enlisted men are sympathetic or even heroic figures; military hardware and efficiency are celebrated with technophilic, sometimes even fetishistic admiration, and scenes of military mobilization and action tend to be rousing and engaging. Reading all this macroscopically, however, might be a way to read 1950s science fiction films against the grain and to produce an understanding that reverses the militaristic allegory. Reading the giant tarantula or the giant ants haunting the desert landscape as a metaphor for the military-industrial complex would be one aspect of this redefined allegory. Another way to read the metaphor would be to expand it to encompass the interplay between these inflated monsters and the military that created them, their competition for control over domestic space, and the marginalization or exclusion of civilian presence in this systemic spatial occupation. Reading the films against their own patriotic, technophilic, and militaristic surface text is what might be needed in order to capture the full sense of unease or even horror they are expressing—an unease that stems from the recognition of how much friend and foe actually resemble each other. Isn't there a dystopian ring to the bureaucratic and technocratic institution—the Orwellian "Department of Defense Directorate for Armed Forces Information and Education"—which financed and produced George Waggner's anticommunist propaganda film *Red Nightmare*? Didn't the establishment of military bases and high-security perimeters, no-go zones, and blank spaces across the map of the Southwest inspire the Roswell alien landing mythology (as a local manifestation of the larger flying saucer panic throughout the 1950s) or the Area 51 mythology? Didn't the military occupation of domestic space undermine the most American of dreams, that of unlimited spatial mobility, just when the automobile industry and the Federal Highway Commission were about to make that dream come true for millions of American tourists? Doesn't the superimposition of this new geographic imaginary—driven by the military-industrial complex since the inception of the Manhattan Project—onto a landscape familiar to most Americans who had never set foot in the Southwest states but knew it intimately from decades of Westerns rewrite that landscape so that, from now on, it would no longer signify the open frontier but the closed surveillance system of the military-industrial complex?

Chapter Four

Decolonization

"Over There": Exporting the Military-Industrial Complex

At the heart of this chapter is a moment from George Pal's beloved adaptation of H. G. Wells's novel *The Time Machine* (1960). The story is quickly told. It's New Year's Eve 1899, the dawn of a new (American?) century. A British inventor, George Wells (Rod Taylor), invites a group of friends to his house in the London suburbs, ostensibly to demonstrate one of his new inventions. He arrives making a dramatic late appearance, disheveled and half-starved, and begins to tell the story of what happened to him, initiating a lengthy flashback that makes up most of the film. In this flashback, he recounts traveling into the future, observing a cataclysmic nuclear war, and arriving finally in the far future. In this future, all knowledge of history has been forgotten and humanity has been divided into the fair, docile Eloi, whose above-ground existence is sustained by the hideously deformed Morlocks below ground, who ensure the Elois' survival in exchange for culling their ranks periodically for slave labor and cannibalism. Falling in love with Weena (Yvette Mimieux), one of the Eloi, after saving her life, George descends to the Morlock tunnels below. Down there in the dungeons, George initiates the Morlocks' destruction. He even succeeds in rousing the Eloi from their complacency so that they eventually join in the fight. Before this task is completed, however, he is forced to return to the present. With some Morlocks still left undefeated, the film transitions back to the frame narrative of the beginning. Back in the present, George's task is now to tell the tale of his adventures in the future and recruit his friends to the ongoing revolutionary project. While nearly all of his friends remain incredulous, he returns to an uncertain yet hopeful future that awaits his guiding hand.

 The film's central image, the one that summarizes its central conflict and its resolution, is of the film's heroic protagonist, George (Rod Taylor), the time traveler. The insurrection he started among the hapless Eloi—humanity's kinder, gentler inheritors sometime in the far future—has

The Natives Escape and Organize: American Leadership in *The Time Machine* (George Pal, 1960)

been successful. Under George's leadership, the Eloi have freed themselves from exploitation by the sinister Morlocks. Now, hand in hand, the Eloi are marching off into a better tomorrow. At the center of the group are George and Weena, the girl who won his heart (and vice versa), unwitting ambassador of her people, the childlike companion to his lonely traveler, the Eve to his Adam. As much as this is the proverbial Hollywood ending, pat and predictable, it is also a moment of deep significance for Americans in the 1950s and how they would see themselves out there in the larger world. It is an ideal of benevolent intervention in the fates of an exotic people in an exotic place, started more or less by accident but followed through with moral conviction. The political naivete of this moment might ring false to those with the benefit of hindsight. However, if you were this American, the good American abroad, the disillusionment brought about by the Vietnam War would have been another ten odd years down the road.[1] If you were, figuratively speaking, an Eloi, the image might simply register as American hypocrisy; in a small but telling moment at the end of the film, George's friend Filby explains that George may have returned to the future "to help the Eloi build a new world," but also to "build a new world *for himself.*" An agent of gunboat diplomacy under the guise of benevolence, how

Measuring Global Space: The Gaze Toward the Horizon in *The Beast from 20,000 Fathoms*

could George not register with Morlocks and Eloi alike as an ambassador of a vastly superior foreign force meddling in their affairs? Complementary to what *Them!* and *It Came from Outer Space* could tell us about the military-industrial complex at home, *The Time Machine* provides a view of the military-industrial complex abroad.

The global perspective of 1950s science fiction films manifests itself in the choice of locations considered or constructed as "exotic." Science fiction films align this idea of the exotic with global spaces considered crucial to the national interest in the context of Cold War politics—from South America (*The Creature from the Black Lagoon* [1954], *The Black Scorpion* [1957], *Dr. Cyclops* [1957]) to Canada (*The Fiend Without a Face* [1958]), Europe (Italy in *20 Million Miles to Earth* [1957], Britain in *The Giant Behemoth* [1959], Switzerland in *The Trollenberg Terror* [1958]), and, time and again, the Arctic (*The Thing from Another World*, [1951], *The Giant Claw* [1957], *The Atomic Submarine* [1959]). Not surprisingly, these films teem with references to the imperatives of global surveillance. The opening montage of *The Giant Claw*, for example, details the construction of a radar shield in the extreme reaches of the northern hemisphere to guard against a Soviet sneak attack. *The Beast from 20,000 Fathoms* shows us American scientists carefully surveying the Arctic terrain selected for nuclear testing. The theme also appears in the underwater polar crossing in *The Atomic Submarine* where, like everywhere else, it indicates an extension of the military-industrial complex from the domestic to the global sphere. Studied and mapped, exotic locations outside the continental US are brought in line with the paranoid logic of surveillance superimposed upon the more remote domestic landscapes, like those of the southwestern desert discussed in the previous chapter. This "war beyond the war," as Dale Carter calls it, comes with a peculiar global logic. It

> develops, not as an imposition of front lines, rear areas, and safe havens, armed forces and non-combatants, tours of duty and furloughs blitzes and all-clears, but as a condition of immanent tensions and perpetual competition in which violation and sacrifice are endemic, neutrality is meaningless, and engagements prove obligatory but inconclusive; a state where what were once discrete combat zones dissolve into one continuous no man's land, boundless in its domain but besieged at all times, ostensibly unrestricted and demobbed but potentially hostile at all points. (69)

At home or abroad, the iconic image is the same: the military-industrial's watchful gaze across vast empty spaces toward the horizon.

A more distinct sub-cycle of 1950s science fiction films does not simply feature exotic locations but is explicitly predicated upon global travel. This cycle bears some of the marks that distinguish American postwar imperialism from its nineteenth-century European predecessors (and yet still signal to the audience that the US very much considers its own imperial project in the context of this historical tradition). As a sign of this indebtedness, European authors linked to a global perspective of Empire figure prominently among the sources from which filmmakers draw their attention. Most popular among these adaptations are Jules Verne's novels (ranging from the more realistic ones [*Around the World in Eighty Days*, Michael Anderson, 1956] to the more fantastic ones [*Journey to the Center of the Earth*, Henry Levin, 1959]), as well as those of H. G. Wells (from *The War of the Worlds* [Byron Haskin, 1953] to *The Time Machine* [George Pal, 1960] and *First Men in the Moon* [Nathan Juran, 1964]). By those choices alone, one might argue, American cinema reaffirms the nineteenth century's newly acquired global perspective as a matter of twentieth century global political expediency. All of these films revel in a playful historicism, an ironic sense of whimsy which seems to anticipate late-twentieth century steampunk. This attitude may signal an ironic detachment from the overtly political dimension of their material. But the films' substantial budgets—elevated in many cases to the proportions of the roadshow picture, (complete with extended running times and high-profile distribution and promotional practices)—testify to the seriousness with which they were treated by the studios that were producing them.

Decolonization   157

Jules Verne: Nineteenth-century Imperialism Alive and Well in the 1950s

Whereas many 1950s films set in remote and exotic locations reference America's presence in these spaces quite explicitly as matters of national security and military occupation (e.g., Joshua Logan's *South Pacific* [1958]), science fiction films depicting global travel tend to steer clear of global power politics enforced by military might as a motivation for the American travelers. Sometimes American travelers are driven by scientific curiosity and the heroic spirit of exploration, commonly portrayed as the epitome of humanitarian universalism, which is almost by definition apolitical. But even with those apolitical motivations, they often find themselves unwittingly transported to remote locations. The title of Irwin Allen's television series *Lost in Space* (1965–68) is almost programmatic in its retrospective description of Americans abroad in science fiction films. The time traveler in *The Time Machine* or the two time travelers in the television series *T Time Tunnel* (Irvin Allen, 1966–67) find themselves catapulted into sions of the past or the future, which had not been their original tion. Similarly, the group of travelers in *The Land Unknown* (Vi 1957) end up stranded in an unknown location as much as the astronaut in *Robinson Crusoe on Mars* (Byron Haskin, 1964).

unwitting travelers seem to reiterate the disavowal of any imperial agenda driving America's postwar presence in the larger world out there, films with global settings also tend to avoid the locations where early Cold War ambitions are writ large on the indigenous landscape and peoples (it is no coincidence that these itineraries often follow in the footsteps of World War II campaigns, especially in the Pacific theater). It is especially the latter factor—the presence of, and American encounter with, indigenous peoples—that tends to reveal the imperialist agenda operating from within its own ideological disavowal.

Looking back on 1950s nuclear culture from the lofty perspective of late Cold War Reaganite America, the documentary *The Atomic Café* (Jayne Loader, Kevin Rafferty, Pierce Rafferty, 1982) features snippets of an instructional film produced by the US military. This documentary shows the evacuation of the Bikini Atoll prior to the nuclear tests of Operation Crossroads (1946). Aided by a native translator, a navy officer explains to a group of native islanders, gathered around him, that they will leave their home and move to another island. The American officer is perched against a tree, the natives sitting on the ground. This arrangement is reminiscent of a classroom, just as the formal procedure of the islanders giving their collective consent to the evacuation evokes a town hall meeting. The scene is utterly unconvincing, stiff, and artificial, and obviously is the result of extensive rehearsals and repeated takes. As if to compensate for its shortcomings, the surrounding footage shows idyllic island life and happy villagers preparing for their impending diaspora. A voiceover informs the viewers that these natives are nomadic, and that, therefore, their relocation falls within the parameters of their traditional lifestyle. Great care is taken to ensure representations of the displaced that illustrate their consent and satisfaction. Nonetheless, the footage also invites melancholic, nostalgic reflection on the disappearance of a native culture under the influence of technological progress. If these people are victims, the film insists, they are not victims of US foreign policy but of a far more impersonal force from whose impact no one on the planet, including Americans themselves, are exempt—the nuclear age.

The satiric bitterness of *The Atomic Café* exposes the sentimental, nostalgic tone of the documentary footage as an ideological fiction. Still, the superimposition on the historical facts of a tragic story about the inevitable historical obsolescence of an indigenous people are familiar devices within a very American narrative harking back to the frontier myth and its coming to terms with the European genocide perpetrated on the native American population. The fact that the beauty, innocence, and nobility of a native population—whether on Great Plains or on a Pacific atoll—manifests itself in the very moment of their disappearance gives rise to an attitude of somber, abstract reflection. Historical and moral responsibility is transferred from the actual agent of the genocide to the more abstract and impersonal forces of history, which have deigned one the vehicle, the other the victim of progress. Lament over those vanquished by history further serves to ennoble the survivor. From James Fennimore Cooper's *The Last of the Mohicans*, an almost programmatic text about the frontier myth's processing of Native American genocide, the trope extends to all those 1950s science fiction films. *I Married a Monster from Outer Space* would be another example of such a story in which a dying alien race is dispatched with efficiency, ruthlessness, and a sentimental moment—albeit a rather short one—in which its imminent demise is remembered as if it has already occurred.

If the presence of a native population in one of those remote and exotic locations in 1950s science fiction films constitutes a problem, a challenge that needs to be narratively and thematically managed, then one way of management is simply to imagine that space as uninhabited. Again, this is a strategy that reaches back to foundational American mythology of "virgin lands," conveniently stripped of native inhabitants and thus ready for settling. Quite a number of films from the period chose this route. Notable among them are films that take place in either one of the polar regions; *The Thing from Another World* (Christian Nyby, 1951), for example, takes us to the Arctic, a space entirely free of native inhabitants. Nyby's change of locations from the Antarctic (in John W. Campbell's original novella, *Who Goes There?*) to the Arctic has inspired some discussion. Peter Biskind argues for the basic interchangeability of landscapes: "The vast, bleak Arctic wastes [of *The Thing*] play the same role here that the desert plays in *Them!*" (133), while Elizabeth Leane has a more differentiated take. In her reading of Campbell's novella, Leane speculates that the change of locations in the 1950s film is motivated by historical circumstances. "Critics [. . .] often read *The Thing from Another World* within a Cold War context as one of a series of anti-Soviet 1950s sf films; this makes sense of the relocation to the Arctic, a liminal space halfway between North America and the USSR" (229). Aside from this spatial reassignment registering as a Cold War update, however, the film's Antarctic also fits Leane's idea of a broader "trope of the male explorer conquering feminized land" (234).[2] Though this would apply to both Arctic and Antarctic, Leane's association of the Antarctic with abjection—a quality inherent in the mythology written onto the landscape

The Beast from 20,000 Fathoms: The Lure of the Polar Regions

and in the morphology of Campbell's "engulfing," "amorphous" monster (234)—implies a gendered configuration for Nyby's film. The story explores this configuration by having two aggressive male agents (the American team and the alien invader) struggle for control over the "virgin" Arctic, which is passively waiting for either conqueror to plant his flag.

In a critical discussion of Campbell's novella that takes off from Leane's alignment of geographic and mythical space with the fluid, abject morphology of the monster, Sherryl Vint has argued that "the story reveals through its anxiety about re-establishing a boundary between self and other the very precariousness of that boundary, a precariousness that is far more powerful than are the story's attempts to re-fix the meanings of self and other by destroying the monster/alien" (422). Although Vint is not primarily interested in the geographic space in which this negotiation of meaning takes place, her argument about boundary destabilization suggests an interesting line of critical inquiry. It would link the shapelessness of the Antarctic landscape with the imperialist objective of imposing structure upon it, imprinting and claiming it, against the attempts of an aggressive competitor who is all the more dangerous for evading military and technological means of surveillance and detection.

The whiteness of the landscape emphasizes its emptiness; it is a blank page waiting for someone to write on it. On this page, both Campbell's novella and Nyby's film go on to tell the story about the struggle for dominance between two conflicting forces. There is the alien invader, who has been in a deep freeze ever since he crash-landed here eons ago. Plotted against him is the American team, scientific in Campbell, military-scientific-civilian in

Mapping the Human Form onto the Blank Landscape: *The Thing from Another World*

Nyby. Having the alien immobilized during the millennia since his arrival serves as a way of discrediting his claim on the virgin territory. Ultimately, he too remains a recent arrival, a newcomer, an outsider, and thus a poor rival of the American research station, which, as a symbol of America's global ambition, controls the entire continent. Nyby's film features a famous sequence in which the team members map out with their bodies the shape of the crash-landed alien craft below the ice; their circular figures are mapped onto the comet-shaped outline of the alien craft's slide toward its final resting place. Meanwhile, the two figures are framed by the line of the distant horizon and the featureless whiteness of the snowed-in landscape on all sides.

Fred F. Sears's *The Giant Claw* (1957) provides a less abstract version of this symbolic planting of territorial flags in the eternal ice. The film begins with an introductory montage of stock footage that shows the construction "near the top of the world," as a voiceover informs the audience, of an early warning system of radar installations and air fields. They will be home to the fighter squadrons that will protect the US from enemy sneak attacks. The massive construction project is framed more as a struggle against the elements than a fight against the Soviet Union. As in Nyby's *The Thing from Another World*, it is the emptiness of the landscape that encourages the audience to regard the base as a legitimate claim to the territory. Eugene Lourie's *The Beast from 20,000 Fathoms* (1953) and Spencer Gordon Bennet's *The Atomic Submarine* (1959) also fit into this pattern. The blank landscape with the stark outline of the demonic other—a hostile shape-shifting alien, giant creatures awoken from their slumber, and, again, hostile aliens crash-landed in the Arctic ice—is clearly outlined as an allegory of a geographic otherness.

If the native population is conspicuously absent from this geographic fantasy—replaced by the fantasy of the land itself as the price of competition—what is always and inevitably present is the competitor himself. Between the American traveler and the land, or, respectively, the American traveler and the natives, there is an invisible agent, a third party operating against the US military. This "third man" is, of course, the Soviet Union. This is the Cold War enemy whose operations elsewhere in the world force the US to develop and possibly even deploy the nuclear weapons that are being tested in the native population's backyard. It is important to remember that the footage from the Operation Crossroads test in *The Atomic Cafe* omits all mention of the Soviet Union; in fact, it erases all national agency to the degree that it places responsibility for what is happening on Bikini squarely on the inhuman force of historical progress. This is a rewriting of a historical narrative in which nuclear testing in the Pacific plays an integral part. Obviously, the United States does not accept any blame for dispossessing and displacing an entire people. But, then, there is also no blame assigned to the Soviet Union for forcing the United States into an arms race which happens to come tearing through this remote part of the world and the lives of these indigenous people. The interaction depicted in *The Atomic Cafe* takes place exclusively between Americans and Bikini islanders, and so the historical narrative quickly begins to resemble the American myth of the frontier. Nuclear technology, a concrete manifestation of America's manifest destiny, drives a narrative of progress. Regrettably but inevitably, progress comes with casualties. In this story, the cultural extinction of a native people is infused with nostalgia. It displaces agency from the actual cause—i.e., US interests, political will, and the force necessary for implementing it—to an imaginary one that is assigned the status of an impersonal and irreversible historical destiny.

Whenever 1950s science fiction films do not imagine exotic spaces to be blank but instead imagine them as inhabited by native populations, Cold War conditions enforce a departure from classic frontier mythology by insisting that these native populations are not the direct enemy. In some films, a native population is present but is of little interest to the narrative. The Mexican characters in *The Black Scorpion*, for example, function largely as anonymous masses of fleeing civilians, unless they are providing local color. In *Creature from the Black Lagoon*, the native South Americans merely aid the American protagonists. In other films, native populations—the ones that are not historically obsolete and thus doomed to extinction—can appear quite vital and vibrant, even unsettling and alarming in their otherness. As soon as this otherness becomes positively menacing, however, they need to be actively exterminated if one's own survival is to be ensured.

As much as this may have played a role in traditional frontier mythology, not even the most alien or exotic native populations in 1950s science fiction films ever belong to this openly menacing kind. Instead, their agency tends to be subjugated to that of another party, a third agent which either competes for their attention and affection or directs their hostile actions—i.e., the Soviet Union. The triangular structure of these conflicts is thus less that of a classic antagonism between colonial subjects and objects, and more that of a classic romantic triangle. In this story, two suitors who may be aggressors to each other, but not to the object of their desire, compete for that object's attention, affection, and loyalty. Whether this competition for affection and loyalty is ultimately also a struggle for access to and control is a matter of political opinion. So is the question whether the object of affection really is the center of this struggle, or whether it is merely a pawn in the rivalry between the two suitors. In terms of George Pal's *The Time Machine* and its perfect Hollywood ending, described in the opening of this chapter, the question is whether this story is more about George finding Weena and falling in love with her, or George defeating the Morlocks and, incidentally, winning Weena as the prize of this struggle. In order to understand how *The Time Machine* operates among the available political opinions of its time, it is necessary to take a look at 1950s foreign policy—not so much toward the Soviet Union but toward the rest of the world.

American Foreign Policy: From Containment to Integration

The cultural narrative of US foreign intervention has roots that go deeper than the Cold War. One might think, for example, of Woodrow Wilson's 1917 congressional appeal to get involved in World War I so that "the world be made safe for democracy." As far as the Cold War is concerned, most historians date its explicit demand for intervention as a matter of US foreign policy after World War II to President Truman's address to Congress on March 12, 1947. In regard to the urgent cases of Turkey and Greece, Truman asserts that "it must be the policy of the United States to support free peoples who are resisting subjugation by armed minorities or outside pressures" (qtd. in Nadel 15). Originally geared toward rousing support for a

Greece in danger of veering away from American foreign policy interests, the Truman Doctrine not only aligns itself at that moment with postwar American initiatives like the Marshall Plan, but also echoes through the 1950s and beyond. Confirmed in its basic tenets in 1957 as the Eisenhower Doctrine, it would solidify US influence in the Middle East in the wake of the Suez War in 1957. This conflict had provided the US with an opportunity to demonstrate its global supremacy over what seemed like a last-ditch effort by Britain and France to reassert traditional imperial control over the region. Less overtly military interventions would follow a similar pattern. Historians like Odd Arne Westad have a clear picture of the extent and the motivation behind such policy matters: "The foreign aid that the United States provided to the Third World was primarily military—95 per cent of all aid in 1954 and more than 50 per cent in 1960—and the intention was both to prevent left-wing governments from coming to power and to help local elites resist Soviet pressure" (26). In practice and theory, postwar American foreign policy reflected the interests of the military-industrial complex, just as domestic policy did.

While there is little doubt that the mobilization for US participation in World War II required considerable efforts to overcome isolationist resistance, critics do disagree whether prewar American isolationism came with the trappings of militarism that were to characterize the American postwar posture. While Bacevich asserts that "the situation that had existed prior to World War II, when the American military profession was a marginal institution and senior military officers figures of marginal importance" (*New American Militarism* 52), Howard Zinn's account of US foreign policy challenges Bacevich's account (one that is also shared by C. Wright Mills). While Mills and Bacevich may be right about the cultural manifestations of militarism and their impact on politics, Zinn's list of foreign interventions at the hands of the US makes a compelling case for American realpolitik being very much that of a neocolonial power with global ambitions. Zinn lists wars with Mexico and Cuba, the occupation of Hawaii, Puerto Rico, Guam, and the Philippines, as well as the "opening" of Japan and China to aggressive market penetration, fostering revolution in Colombia, creating the state of Panama as a means of controlling the Panama Canal, and sending massive expeditionary forces to Nicaragua in 1926. His list concludes with similar interventions in Haiti, Cuba, Guatemala, and Honduras (Zinn, *People's History* 399).

Regardless of foreign policy positions on the part of the Soviet Union, which might have been equivalent in intention, design, and execution to those of the US, the two superpowers were not the only global player in this process of decolonization. Throughout the 1950s, various nations in the so-called Third World proceeded on their course toward national independence, individually and collectively, showing their formal colonial rulers that no cooperation or assent from them would be required. The scope and gravity of decolonization can best be understood by looking at the United Nations' Declaration on Granting Independence to Colonial Countries and Peoples, presented within the General Assembly on December 14, 1960—the year *The Time Machine* was released. Affirming the conviction "that all peoples have an inalienable right to complete freedom, the exercise of their sovereignty and the integrity of their national territory," the statement spells out in no uncertain terms "that the peoples of the world ardently desire the end of colonialism in all its manifestations." As these newly decolonized nations "freely determine their political status and freely pursue their economic, social and cultural development," they remove themselves from the crumbling or even obsolete structures of (largely European) colonial empires and become eligible for ideological, military, and economic recruitment into either one of the two global blocs.

The framework of the United Nations might have served US interests fairly well in justifying criticism of what appeared as Soviet imperialism among its Eastern European allies (or, as the parlance in the West had it, "satellite states"). Coming to the aid of a decolonizing nation, in turn, provided a persuasive pretext for American intervention as well. However, independent efforts of decolonizing nations promised a far more unpredictable or even inimical course of action. As Arne Westad points out, the US regarded with great skepticism events like the Asian-African conference in Bandung, Indonesia, in 1955, "the biggest and most influential gathering of Third World leaders held during the colonial era" (99). Ironically enough, the "sense of community among Third World countries was reinforced by attempts by the former colonial masters to get them to choose sides in the Cold War" (98). Both the Soviet Union and the US were equally alarmed about the destabilizing effects of such independent self-organization within a global framework. The balance of power among the two major players, as they themselves would define it, would automatically presuppose the recruitment and collaboration of what might otherwise have been independent agents. Even a Third World nation's theoretical ability to make its own choices constituted a degree of self-determination that caused intense anxiety within American foreign politics. Who could tell which way these new nations would turn? American interests on the global scale saw themselves threatened by countries falling under the spell of the Soviet Union, or choosing to do so voluntarily. But strong nationalist movements as the driving force behind decolonization increased this threat even further. It was exactly the freedom of political self-determination that "put decolonization in a new context," John Lewis Gaddis argues; the emergence of nationalism, from Washington's perspective, could cause as much trouble as the persistence of colonialism (123–24). The risk would emanate not only from recently decolonized nations that would *choose* to side with the Soviet Union, but also from nations that would settle on strategies of "non-alignment"—i.e., "to commit to neither side in the Cold War, but to leave open the possibility of such commitment," defending themselves against pressure from one superpower by "*threatening* to align with the other superpower" (124), thus becoming even more erratic and unpredictably self-interested agents. Despite the imposition of practical and ideological boundaries upon the willingness to tolerate non-alignment politics, the "very *compulsiveness* with which the Soviet Union and the United States sought to bring such states within their orbits wound up giving those states the means of escape" (128). These anxieties would be allayed by fantasies that decolonization would be followed by recolonization; or, even better, by recolonization *being demanded* by those who had recently cast off the shackles of empire (the demand for recolonization being the explicit "desire of the nation attacked," as the Eisenhower Doctrine put it).

Examples of the conundrum of non-alignment abound, most strikingly perhaps in cases in which the US eventually decided to take an assertive position as soon as it would become clear that non-alignment would pose a greater danger than a nation siding with the Cold War enemy. Cuba, in its early post-revolutionary days, is such an example. It is all the more striking because Cuba, by the early 1960s and culminating in the Cuban Missile Crisis in October of 1962, had initially been steering a course of non-alignment. In his pop-cultural history of the year 1959, Fred Kaplan describes Fidel Castro, during his two-week goodwill tour through the US in April 1959, as appealing successfully to a large American audience which accepted him as "an independent revolutionary [. . .] claiming to be neither communist nor capitalist" (94). Photographs of Castro during this goodwill tour show a politician winning the hearts and minds of many average Americans who, not long after, would turn against him. Though Vice President Nixon would meet with Castro (Eisenhower had excused himself), the governmental response to Castro was far less indulgent than the public one. "The very hope that Castro inspired" is identified by Kaplan thus: "that a country in the Caribbean might stay unaligned to either superpower—was itself a source of deep concern in Washington [. . .] The State Department's top regional specialist warned of Castro's tendency toward 'nationalistic neutralism, which the Communist will exploit to the fullest'" (97). Almost as if to steer clear of the far thornier problem of Cuban non-alignment, US foreign policy ratcheted up toward a more aggressive stance, which, in turn, edged Cuba toward alignment with the Soviet Union. Despite some steps toward the "normalization" of its relationship with Cuba during the second term of the Obama administration, US policy toward Cuba seems perpetually predicated on a vision that, even in the absence of the old Soviet Union, leaves little room for anything other than the Cold War model of recolonization.

The various American fantasies of recolonization, and the ways in which they engage with foreign cultures and their more or less reluctant acceptance of benevolent American intervention, are part of what Nadel has famously dubbed famously dubbed "containment culture": a national narrative unique to the Cold War

> in which insecurity was absorbed by internal security, internationalism by global strategy, apocalypse and utopia by a Christian theological mandate, and xenophobia—the fear of the Other—by courtship, the activity in which Otherness is the necessary supplement to seduction, whether that seduction is formal or illicit, voluntary or coerced, hetero- or homosexual, the product of romantic alliance, business transaction, or date rape. (14)

Not by coincidence is the language here evocative of that romantic couple at the heart of *The Time Machine*: George and Weena, brought together by a problematic courtship with elements of both seduction and coercion. Though Though Nadel's characterization characterization insists on the primary functions and effects of containment culture "to foreclose dissent, preempt dialogue, and preclude contradiction" (14), their use of the courtship metaphor, especially when read as a comment on US foreign politics, paves the way for a more profound revision in the historical understanding of the Cold War, and thus to a more nuanced understanding of Cold War science fiction films.

In her cultural history of the Cold War, Christina Klein sets out to modify the popular image of the predominance of what, in reference to Nadel, she calls the "global imaginary of containment" (22). Klein's reading is based on an understanding of containment which, in Nadel's terminology, places slightly greater emphasis on the coercive and illicit version of "seduction" than on the voluntary one. While most "cultural histories of the Cold War take the foreign policy and ideology of containment as their foundation" (23), Klein points out that it was, in fact, not the only one, but one of two co-existent approaches to foreign policy. Complementary to the global imaginary of containment, and interacting with it in complex ways, was an ideological stance articulated most clearly by Francis Wilcox, "a mid-level State Department official" (21). In a speech "to an audience of educators in Philadelphia" in 1957, Wilcox recasts "the problem of foreign resistance to US expansion into an issue of domestic pedagogy" (21). At its best, integration demanded that Americans were themselves to be transformed and refined so as to live up their own best national standards. Klein calls this complementary attitude "a global imaginary of integration" (22). She emphasizes that this view was not directed inward, smugly assuring Americans of their superiority and nervously pointing abroad to those hating America or resisting its advances. Instead, integration represented "the Cold War as an opportunity to forge intellectual and emotional bonds with the people of Asia and Africa" (22). Winning the hearts and minds of those nations, rather than conquering or militarily controlling them, would cleanse the US from the stigma of domestic racism. This was a sensitive issue in dealing with an antagonist whose internationalist agenda automatically promised to provide privileged access to this particular moral high ground. It would also exonerate the US from the critique of imperialism by distinguishing its global political ambitions categorically from those of the Soviet Union. In short, integration could provide a positive humanist and moral agenda—unlike that of mere "anti-communism," the concept upon which containment was predicated.

The "global imaginary of integration" makes an appearance in science fiction films whenever American travelers find themselves in geographic spaces in which encounters with the demonic other take place through mediation with or interpolation of a native population. In these films, the native population tends to wield more narrative power than in films from which it is either completely absent or for which it provides merely colorful background. As minor examples of the time-travel sub-cycle of the late 1950s, films like Ib Melchior's *The Time Travelers* (1964) and Edgar Ulmer's *Beyond the Time Barrier* (1960s) begin to explore "integration" as an ideological model rivaling "containment." Produced on minuscule budgets, the two films feature American military test pilots and scientists—i.e., representatives of the military-industrial complex, who discover that, at the end of their respective journey into the future, there is a native population under threat from an external enemy. Even though the geographically or temporally remote conflict has no direct impact on them, narrative logic demands that they get involved on the side of justice and in the fight against oppression and tyranny. While conflicts can have outcomes that range from the optimistic to the apocalyptic, it is invariably the involvement of the American protagonist which decides the conflict. The natives might function as a helpful sidekick, but the spark of revolution invariably burns red, white, and blue. As a central text within this sub-cycle, George Pal's *The Time Machine* (1960) stands out as a more carefully scripted, lavishly produced, and commercially successful exploration of "integration." Unlike Ulmer's and Melchior's films, *The Time Machine* also comes with the intertextual baggage of nineteenth century British colonialism, which gives the film's director a chance to explain why and how America in the twentieth century is unlike H. G. Wells's nineteenth-century Britain. Beloved as the film would become with general audiences, the critics were not as kind.

From Wells to Pal: *The Time Machine*

Any film adaptation of an immensely popular novel must take some liberties with its source material if it wants to use it for making a point about its own time and place. Small details do not seem to matter much to the critics. No one decries, for example, that Pal relocates the origins of subterranean Morlock existence from Wells's Victorian factories and slums to the air-raid shelters of the Cold War; conditioned by prolonged nuclear war, the Eloi willingly march underground whenever the Morlocks sound the sirens. Though a detail like this one is part of a larger allegorical structure, it is not the detail but the fact that Pal replaces Wells's central allegorical agenda with his own that gives critics the most trouble. John Huntington's comparative assessment of the film with "what Wells has achieved in *The Time Machine*" (54), for example, is based entirely on a petulant itemizing of Pal's crimes: that he "avoids facing the very conflicts that define Wells's work"; that he "ignores the biological issues so central to Wells" and instead "gives us a vague history of the first part of our century"; that his "myth lacks a logical base" (54), and that he has "robbed Wells's story of the essence of its conflict and replaced intellectual tension with melodramatic conventions that inspire unreflective affirmation" (55). Gary Westfahl chimes in, calling Pal a mediocre craftsman and accusing him of "seiz[ing] upon wonderful source material and shamefully butcher[ing] or trivialize[ing] it, as if unable to comprehend what made it special." Westfahl concedes that Pal was "once highly regarded in the science fiction community for his contributions to the genre," but ultimately accuses him of being "numb to the rhythms of film narrative and unable to attract or inspire capable actors."[3]

Answers do, of course, vary as to what exactly makes Wells's novel special or superior. But one recurring theme among those who dislike Pal's film is that it is either apolitical or that it replaces Wells's politics with Pal's. Many critics sound like Roger Berger when he complains that "Wells's novel at least recognizes the political problematics of the class situation of his times, utterly unlike the 1960 George Pal film version of *The Time Machine*" (qtd. in Berger 177). Fewer agree with Keith Booker, who at least concedes that *The Time Machine* is not alone in "shy[ing] away from such class issues," avoiding Wells's concern with social class "like most American cultural products of the 1950s" (171n14). Again, the omission of the theme of social class plays a particularly important role here, especially among scholars who otherwise recognize Pal as a filmmaker with an explicit political agenda. Donald Palumbo considers this omission a "thorough subversion of the novel's bleak themes [. . .] designed to make acceptable to a mass audience what was a cerebral story appealing originally only to a select following" (204).[4] Berger, while acknowledging that "the movie has usurped for the popular consciousness the message of the novel" (184), does not value the film's cultural centrality as evidence of the artistic or ideological power of Pal's adaptation. Instead, he concludes that the modified "image of the book attests to Pal's disservice to Wells" (184). Claiming that Pal's *Time Machine*'s "ideological mission" is "insidious" (177), he does not like the fact that Pal "essentially *domesticates* [sic] the novel and makes safe [its] threatening ideas for his late Fifties/early Sixties' audience" (184).

All in all, the erasure of social class in Pal's adaptation of Wells's novel provides the lynchpin of this virtually unanimous critical condemnation. Scholars who value the Cold War framework of Pal's adaptation are left with two options, both of which refocus attention to what Pal's thematic concerns actually are. Thomas Renzi identifies, in somewhat complimentary terms, "the imagined destruction of London by an atom bomb, the subsequent volcanic response from nature, and the hideous appearance of the Morlocks as possible mutant casualties" as "fear tactics to warn man to find alternatives to war before he annihilates himself" (4). Even after Renzi has identified the film's overall cautionary tone and its explicitly anti-nuclear agenda and has placed it in historical context, some critics are still not satisfied with Pal's handling of some of these narrative constituent elements. Donald Palumbo complains that, "[u]niformly blond, tanned, toned, and twenty-one, Pal's Eloi even—and quite inexplicably—speak English, albeit with some reticence and an economy of syntax" (207). Palumbo's insistence on realism when it comes to the linguistic prowess of the Eloi is all the more surprising in this instance because he recognizes that the structure of the narrative in both Wells and Pal is essentially allegorical, and yet he is the one who explains most clearly what this allegorical structure actually refers to. The audience of Pal's film, Palumbo states, "is invited to see [the Morlocks] as Russians and the Eloi as subjugated Eastern Europeans whom George [. . .] will ultimately, and magically, liberate" (207). In fact, Palumbo goes so far as to provide the proper historical context for this allegory as well when he claims that Pal's film "anticipates Kennedy's charge, given in his inaugural address, 'Ask not what your country can do for you, ask what you can do for your country.'" With an eye on the connection to the start of the Kennedy era, Berger takes Palumbo's idea one step further. According to him, Pal expresses "the dominant sensibility of the late 1950s" (182) by identifying "the Eloi [in the film], with their blond hair and vacuous manners" as representatives of the satiated, apolitical, hedonistic American youth populating "the seemingly infinite beach movies of the early 1960s" (181).

It is exactly this allegorical structure—in which "the Morlocks are, loosely, the Russians" (Huntington 54) and George, the time traveler, is, loosely, a postwar American entrepreneur in pursuit of global markets—that I would like to examine more closely. The following reading of the film will tie together many of the strands from the film's historical context I have outlined in the first half of this chapter. Against the backdrop of Cold War decolonization, the analysis will not focus on what Huntington dismisses as the "subtextual Cold War wish-fulfillment fantasy of revolt against totalitarian exploitation"; instead, it will examine the strategies outlined in the film by which a non-coercive, cooperative relationship is established between the US and the Third World. It is this theme—the allegory of Cold War decolonization against the backdrop of "integration"—that strikes me as relevant exactly because decolonization is an issue which, in the years preceding 1960, is far more urgently on the minds of Americans than the late 1950s moral unease about hedonistic youth (even though the Kennedy administration will eventually link the two concerns as a political matter). Secondly, by way of a critical re-examination of a changed discourse on the Cold War itself, I would also like to launch a defense of the allegory of decolonization—against Huntington's, Palumbo's, and Berger's claims that it is riddled with internal contradictions to the point of utter absurdity, and their complaint that it is too obvious, too plain, or too simple a retelling of what used to be a sophisticated allegory of social class in Wells. Against Palumbo's claim that Pal's film constitutes a crass dumbing down "to make acceptable to a mass audience what was a cerebral story appealing originally only to a select following" ("Politics of Entropy" 204), I would like to focus on this process of using cinema in order to "make acceptable to a mass audience" a political agenda that requires such support. Along the way, I will also return to the issue of audience interpellation and political recruitment already discussed at length in the first chapter of this book.

A Kinder, Gentler Nation: Learning from the Other

Even—or especially?—the critics who dislike Pal's *The Time Machine* have little doubt about the Cold War allegory in the film. We are invited, to quote Palumbo once again, "to see [the Morlocks] as Russians and the Eloi as subjugated Eastern Europeans whom George [. . .] will ultimately, and magically, liberate" (207). Perhaps a little less specifically than Palumbo would have it, the Eloi represent one of those nations anywhere in the world in dire need of aid from the United States in their struggle against the Morlocks. Pal's Morlocks are the enemy who represent, as Eisenhower put it in his farewell address, "a hostile ideology global in scope, atheistic in character, ruthless in purpose, and insidious in method." In returning to the future in order to help the Eloi build a new society after undermining or even toppling their domination by the Morlocks, George is a model to be emulated. Not only are his personal integrity and courage exemplary, but he also stands for responsible political action: the type of American the Cold War demanded—altruistic and self-sacrificing. It is important to note that there is nothing subtle about this allegory; audiences today would have as little trouble reading history writ large across the film as they did in the year of the film's release.

Nonetheless, critics who associate Pal's Eloi with 1950s American teenagers also have a point. When Berger asserts that "they all—zombie-like—march toward the sphinx when the Morlock controlled air raid siren sounds" (181), there is in that assertion a hint of disdain for what Frankfurt School critics like Theodor Adorno and Max Horkheimer would call "the culture industry."[5] Following the call of that air-raid siren throughout the 1950s, teenagers were increasingly interpellated as consumers.[6] As a result of their rising economic enfranchisement, their concerns would increasingly surface in American popular culture. Hollywood and other corporate media were trying to tap into the teenage market, and these attempts would be part of a larger demographic and economic shift. The 1960s counterculture would be a high point of that shift, albeit with a range of available political positions that would exceed those offered in 1950s popular culture. Berger's criticism falls short of the fact that, alongside the Annette Funicellos and Gidgets populating "the seemingly infinite beach movies of the early 1960s" (181), there is also a substantial set of fictional teenagers in 1950s American cinema who are not just brave little consumers. They are either juvenile delinquents, such as the ones in *The Wild One* (Laslo Benedek, 1953), *Rebel Without a Cause* (Nicholas Ray, 1955), or *Blackboard Jungle* (Richard Brooks, 1955), or they represent the anxiety over the juvenile delinquent in a broader context of incipient threats to the social order, such as the demonic children in science fiction films like *The Bad Seed* (Mervyn LeRoy, 1956), *Village of the Damned* (Wolf Rilla, 1960), and *These Are the Damned* (Joseph Losey, 1963). Though Pal's Eloi lack the penchant for violence the culture was so worried about in its teenage population, they eventually prove that, with the proper coaching, they have the capacity to become violent. When the first Eloi, late in the film, finally decides to come to George's aid in his fight against the Morlocks, the film applauds this behavioral change.

Oddly enough, though, there is a lack of distinction between children and teenagers in the film's portrait of the Eloi. Berger reads this as a comment on the cultural extension of childhood into the teenage years during 1950s America. The actors and actresses chosen for the film are clearly in their late teens and early twenties—hence, Berger's association with 1950s beach movies. Child actors might have communicated the Eloi's vulnerability via the Morlocks more efficiently. But then they would have also caused problems for showing the romantic attraction George feels for Weena. As if to give wide berth to this potential problem, George and Weena's relationship is chaste, with Weena as the one awaiting sexual initiation. While Weena is all potential, George is clearly a mature adult, and his advantage over the Eloi is one of life experience and attitude. He may be an idealist, but his idealism remains tempered by practical self-interest. Standing next to Yvette Mimieux (playing Weena) or the extras cast as Eloi, actor Rod Taylor looks—as I am sure was Pal's intention—a few sizes larger: like a parent standing next to a child. To the critics who read the Eloi as spoiled American teenagers, the difference might register as being generational. Given his age, George represents the older American generation, hardened and disciplined by the experience of World War II, which still retains a memory of the Great Depression anchored somewhere even deeper in its background. The

Softened by a Life of Luxury: The Eloi as Postwar Teenagers in *The Time Machine*

Eloi, in contrast, are a generation whose lives have been free from violence and deprivation. They are incipient baby boomers, untried, untested, inexperienced, soft, naïve, and self-indulgent. Seen through the eyes of their parents' generation, they must have appeared dangerously ill-equipped for the harsh realities of the Cold War.

While Pal's critics may be right in reading 1950s generational conflicts into the film's portrait of the Eloi, this reading does not necessarily contradict the idea that the film might ultimately offer a different allegory. The generational metaphor and the larger allegory of decolonization are not mutually exclusive. Within this allegory, native populations are the children and teenagers standing next to the American adult. Like children, they are helpless, docile, unable to act in their own best interest, and incapable of defending themselves. The metaphor, with all its racist implications, is borrowed from conventional nineteenth-century colonial discourse. Yet its Cold War variant comes with a slight internal shift, one that does not condemn native populations to an unvarying, ahistorical state of perpetual childhood where they require perpetual supervision and guidance by their colonial masters. Fey and effeminate as the Eloi might be, they are also healthy and nature-bound. Their bodies are not only intact and toned; they are beautiful. Their androgyny is that of adolescence at its moment of transitioning toward the next stage of maturity. It is a state of potential, of something coming into its own, taking its intended shape. The Elois' passivity turns them into sleepwalkers awaiting some event that will rouse them. Berger uses the term "zombie," which is misleading because it implies a developmental dead end. Pal, however, wants to keep open the possibility that the Eloi could actively appeal to George, or anyone else, for help, for outside interference must be effective before the Eloi can explicitly embrace and welcome their delivery into independence. Ultimately, the film suggests, their inability to help themselves and to ask for help from others is a tragic feature of their condition. It demands our empathy rather than our pity or condemnation. It is a tragic feature they are about to overcome, given the right conditions.

While the Eloi are presented as a nation under foreign domination, the Morlocks are the oppressor—technologically advanced beyond the Eloi, barbaric, inhuman, and animalistic. While George may be a few steps ahead of them technologically, George has the bad luck of having to operate alone and without the support of his native culture. Pal makes sure that we, together with George, recognize our shared humanity with the Eloi, all the while cutting off all such paths toward similar identification with the Morlocks. They, as Huntington puts it, "represent nothing but horror" (54). There is no interest on the part of the narrative to explore Morlock culture or politics beyond the simple fact of its penchant for aggression and domination. We never find out what exactly those vast, thumping Morlock machines down there in the dungeons actually *do*. But mid-twentieth-century American engineering they are not. Similarly, the film evades the fact that the Eloi are, properly speaking, a postindustrial culture. Visually it tries to amalgamate post- and preindustrial imagery within one broad prelapsarian metaphor. But the metaphor never comes together as a coherent picture of what Eloi culture actually is, just as it shows little interest in working out the details of Morlock society. Politics is irrelevant. The film does not have to show the Morlocks as communists in order to have them register as representatives of the Soviet Union. Showing them as oppressors is sufficient to identify them and assign them their position within the larger political allegory.

Unlike the Eloi as H. G. Wells imagines them in the novel, Pal's Eloi are not really that different from someone like George. In both the novel and the film, they are the final product of a long process of evolution. But, unlike Wells, for whom the product of this process amounts to something like a new species, Pal conceives of the evolutionary process primarily as cultural and social. Biology may be irreversible, but social evolution is not. It is the Elois' adaptability, their capacity for change, that the film keeps emphasizing tirelessly. It is written into their teenage bodies, unfinished yet already intimating their perfect, beautiful final shapes, as it is written into their social evolutionary matrix. And, in the logic of the film, it provides the moral imperative to George to return to the future and complete the process of their emancipation which he has set in motion. Whether this is a reasonable course of action is never in question. To the degree that success is possible, any attempt to redeem the Eloi is reasonable. But whether it is also a prudent course of action—that is the question which, Pal feels, deserves explicit deliberation, both in the narrative and the outcome of the plot.

Looking at the Eloi as a native population in need of rescuing from the Soviet Union's pernicious grasp, viewers will quickly realize that Pal frames the Eloi in what appear to be contradictory terms. On the one hand, they are clearly not like George; they are a people in need of change and aid and reform, and yet subtly different from us. On the other hand, they are "just like us," with their otherness skin-deep, their potential for transformation palpable even to a recent visitor like George. Though this construction may initially appear internally inconsistent, both of its constituent elements are necessary to the Cold War allegory because the narrative arc the film pursues will gradually close the gap between them. For this narrative to gain momentum, the Eloi need to be *different from us*; for it to conclude, they need to be *just like us*. In order to enable this process, Pal sets out to emphasize at all available opportunities the morphological, linguistic, and racial similarities between the Eloi and George.

In racial terms, this means that the Eloi clearly represent members of nations in the process of decolonization, yet their bodies do not mark them as racially different from that of the American who is coming to their rescue. The 2002 adaptation of *The Time Machine*, directed by Simon Wells, clarifies this point by casting the black actress Samantha Mumba in the role of Weena (called Mara in this version) and "Africanizing" Eloi culture by way of digitized sets and overall production design. To be clear, casting non-white actors would have been an option for a late 1950s film. Many Westerns of the same period tend to use non-white actors to play Native American characters as representations of the racial other in their enactment of both containment and integration fantasies (though they generally do not use actual Native Americans). Similarly, science fiction films like Byron Haskins's *Robinson Crusoe on Mars* (1964) fall back on racial differentiation in their choice of actors; Haskins's Martian character of Friday (played by actor Victor Lundin), for example, is emphatically dark-skinned, with dark hair, and an accent reminiscent of Native American characters in the Western. Despite these available alternatives, Pal's representation of both the Eloi and the Morlocks remains committed to whiteness. Applied to a Third World nation, this whiteness stands in contrast to the "claim of racial superiority that was built into the imperialist project" and to which, according to Westad, the colonized themselves "were subject to relentless propaganda" (74).[7]

The Power of Romance: The American Adam with his Eve

Pal may have had several reasons for departing from this easily available visual motif. For one, the whiteness of the Eloi allows them to function as stand-ins for European nations—like Hungary, Czechoslovakia, or Yugoslavia—which would have been subject to Soviet imperialist control. Outrage over Soviet imperialism would be bolstered by a conception of the Soviet Union's victims as visually compatible with white Americans (the flipside of this racial fantasy is the frequent rendering of Russians in Cold War discourse as exotic, "oriental," or racially other). Meanwhile, the larger allegorical framework, which has the Eloi frolic in an Edenic natural environment associated with the more "natural" landscapes of Africa and Asia, ensures a broader resonance that renders them representative of "nations everywhere," i.e., "the Third World." Pal's conspicuous avoidance of making the Elois racially exotic in his casting of *The Time Machine*, which allows Roger Berger to identify them as American teenagers so readily, speaks to Pal's priorities. It indicates that the suggestion of proximity between George and the Eloi is a thematic concern overriding that of a more explicit reference to decolonizing nations in Africa or Asia. In the final instance, what matters to Pal is that, as exotic and different as the Eloi might be, the gap between them and us can be bridged, their otherness neutralized.

Incidentally, the same rationale based upon the constant emphasis on the redeemability of the Eloi also accounts for the detail that so bothers Huntington and Palumbo: the fact that the Eloi speak English. While it may appear strange to demand that a film about time travel conform to strict laws of realism when it comes to the language spoken in an imaginary future, the absence of communication problems between the time traveler and the natives is significant beyond simple convenience. Unlike the Morlocks, who, despite their technological superiority, seem barely capable of grunting, the Eloi have language, and an immediately intelligible one to boot. The metaphor is almost too obvious: George and the Eloi literally speak the same language. As with their racial features, their language places them in closer proximity to the film's central perspective and illustrates their potential to be redeemed from their current state.

Along the same lines, it is also important to remember how explicitly the film recognizes and validates the Elois' former historical glory. George discovers, scattered throughout their Edenic environment, traces of the culture from which they emerged. The spectacular architecture, libraries, and sophisticated technologies for recording and preserving memory he comes across speak of the glory of these forgotten ancestors. None of these artifacts, however, do the Eloi of this generation deserve, understand, or know how to apply. Either they do not care, or they are clueless as to how certain artifacts work. Nonetheless, the reference to the substantial accomplishments of the earlier culture from which the Eloi eventually developed tells the audience that they are not savages undeserving of George's affection and support. The film's production design makes sure that we recognize in their ruins those of the Acropolis, Angkor Wat, or Machu Picchu. The film reminds its American viewers that indigenous cultures they encounter may have reached maturity and flourished long before their own. The Eloi, therefore, are merely in a temporary, and thus reversible, state of cultural decline.[8]

Taken on their own merit, these thematic elements in *The Time Machine* might suggest the traditional patterns of containment culture, within which American global interests see themselves anticipated, reflected, and welcomed wherever they project themselves. Yet this is an attitude Pal decries as narcissistic, voyeuristic, and unproductive.[9] Compared to how little interest the film shows in the Morlocks, it is deeply invested in the transformation of George Wells, its representative American. If Pal's film departs from containment ideology, it does so by way of harnessing its agenda to one of the central conventions of Hollywood filmmaking—the positing of a romantic love interest for the male main character in order to complete his oedipal trajectory.[10] Significantly enough, Pal provides George with Weena as an object of desire, whose ideological significance he needs to establish against the paternalistic consensus among the elderly male captains of industry that make up his circle of friends. And, as an exotic (though not too exotic) woman, Weena is also the embodiment of otherness whose presence is necessary for George to undergo a sentimental, moral, and ideological education. Even though the age difference between the two initially produces an uneasy incestuous subtext, the film goes on to elaborate on their relationship as a narrative arc that takes George from cultural narcissism to a recognition of the cultural other.

Upon his arrival in the idyllic landscape of the future, for example, George interrupts his reflections on the place's natural abundance and perfection by telling himself, "But it would be no paradise if it belonged to me alone." This remark confirms the biblical theme by anticipating the arrival of Weena on the scene—she is the Eve to his Adam. It also speaks of the recognition that, without the presence of the other, George's interaction with this space would remain essentially narcissistic. As much as it might allow for a recasting of the American frontier mythology as "virgin territory," the emptiness of this landscape troubles George. The space is not incomplete, waiting for the human/American inscription, in the same sense that those vast and empty Arctic and Antarctic landscapes in *The Thing from Another World* and *The Giant Claw* are. It is not hostile but lush and fertile, and yet George's presence alone is not enough to ensure his claim to ownership and control. The film then reiterates this idea in the next scene, transposing it from the natural to the cultural world, when George discovers one of the Elois' decrepit gathering places. Inside this dome, George accidentally discovers that a dropped plate produces as much of a perfect echo as the sound of his own voice. The empty replication of the sound does little to animate the space, or, for that matter, to produce meaningful narrative. Instead, it produces an uncanny moment in which George recognizes how alone he really is. This recognition leads directly to him, increasingly panicked by the absence of other human beings, running through the depopulated landscape. Suddenly, this landscape, which struck him as a veritable Garden of Eden not too long ago, is robbed of all its previous natural charms.

What Pal is doing here is indicting the idea of the natural and cultural space eliciting colonization by way of its emptiness as a form of pathological narcissism. As the empty landscape incites panic rather than triumphalism, it sets the stage for George to supersede this transitional phase through his incipient relationship with Weena. Not by coincidence does the panic attack lead him to the group of Eloi and to Weena. Their first encounter casts George in the role of the voyeur, spying on the group, which is unaware that they are being watched. The moment of contemplation is not just one of unabashed visual pleasure, enjoyed by the film and its protagonist alike. It also produces a certain amount of knowledge about these strangely alluring creatures. Unassailable in his concealment behind the low-hanging branches of a tree, George studies the Eloi like an anthropologist. There is enjoyment mixed in with his curiosity, but his attention is not erotically focused on any specific member of the group. It is the group and its internal interactions as a whole that interest him. His contemplative

Eye Contact: The Third World Under Western Eyes

pleasure, however, is quickly disrupted, as much as his illusion of knowledge is quickly dispelled, when he discovers that no one is coming to Weena's aid when she slips and threatens to drown in the river.

The quick dramatic progression from voyeuristic dissociation to active involvement marks the overcoming of yet another stage in George's development. The chain of events is moving him quickly from narcissism and voyeurism to an active engagement with the other. That Weena really *is* the other, however, does require one more obstacle, lest the entire process feels too much like a contrivance or a foregone conclusion. Rescued from drowning by George, Weena fails to show gratitude or appreciation for his actions. Her eyes failing to make contact with his, she simply gets up and wanders off. Only when George finally succeeds in overcoming her inability to acknowledge his presence does genuine interaction between George and the Eloi begin. This is a crucial moment: he has made himself the object of *her gaze*, and thus become the other from her point of view. From conversations in which the Eloi educate George about the political and economic organization of their world, to his active intercession on their behalf against the Morlocks, Pal turns the conventional oedipal trajectory into a condensed sentimental education. The goal of this process is, first, the recognition of otherness, and, second, its disavowal in a gesture of mutual identification. In other words, what happens in George and Weena's courtship is that each one of them, in turn, acknowledges the presence of the other and sees him or her for the stranger he or she is. As they learn about each other, recognize that their similarities outnumber their differences, and thus gradually fall in love, their differences are resolved and their otherness is eliminated. From the personal to the political, this is the story of integration in a nutshell.

As an internationalist, inclusionary ideology that could compete with the more aggressive stance of containment, integration might have been forged by political elites. Still, as Christina Klein reminds us, it depended for its efficiency on "a broad base of public support" (28). George, the representative of his own culture cast out into the world, has to undergo an informal educational process which gradually remakes him in the image of integration. This educational process would have been too important to be left to chance; hence, it needed to be established, institutionalized, and encouraged at home. Sending Americans abroad in the hope that they would eventually find their way toward the desired mode of interaction would be impractical.[11] The broad base of support Klein mentions would have to be integrated into an educational effort, formally or informally. American attitudes toward foreign cultures would have to be reshaped on the basis of real or perceived similarities with these very cultures. This recognition was then to produce new Americans, who would be accepted and embraced as formal or informal ambassadors of their nation whenever they were to leave the US and travel abroad. Though not universally accepted or enthusiastically embraced, this ideology of integration became a point of reference for American popular culture from the late 1950s on.

In hindsight, overtly didactic Cold War texts, like governmental educational films of the *Duck and Cover* variety, or television events documenting the use of nuclear devices like *Operation Ivy*, may have usurped collective memories of Cold War culture when it comes to pedagogy (or, one might say, demagogy). Nonetheless, much of American popular culture during the Cold War was not content with simply representing (allegorizing, narrativizing, visualizing, documenting) the issues of the time. Beyond the documentary impulse, it would resort to a variety of means and devices with a direct appeal to its audience.[12] Berger, for example, is quite clear about *The Time Machine* "attempt[ing] to conscript its intended audience into a larger ideological force" (178); he sees the film actively aligning its rhetorical structure with Kennedy's appeal to ask "what you can do for your country." Keith Booker goes one step further by pointing out that much Cold War science fiction falls into the category of the cautionary tale which "seem[s] genuinely designed as attempted *interventions* in contemporary debates concerning the Cold War arms race" (65, italics added). Peter Biskind's discussion provides both the goal for such active interventions and the emotional and affective leverage exercised in the pursuit of their goals. Science fiction films, he writes, "often presented America in the grip of an emergency, and once again, these emergencies dramatized the necessity of consensus, of pulling together" (*Seeing is Believing* 102).

Against this general backdrop, audience interpellation in *The Time Machine* would be specifically a matter of which foreign policy stance to endorse and which to reject. In trying to enlist its viewers to the cause of integration, the film would, first, have to acknowledge the more popular stance of containment, and then, second, assert itself against opposition from the camp of containment supporters. Pal shows all the signs of having been fully aware of the fact that the ideology he was to put forward in *The Time Machine* was a contested one; that it was placed alongside other, perhaps more compelling visions of how the US should interact with nations in the process of decolonization. This becomes noticeable when the film shows George trying to interpellate his circle of friends into the interventionist fable presented to them in his lengthy flashback. This circle consists of a representative cross-section of the social, financial, and technocratic elite, a microcosmic version of the military-industrial complex. None of these characters are explicitly identified as politicians. But all of them are upper-middle-class pillars of society, well-off, established, and perhaps a little too self-assured and ideologically complacent. Focused on sustaining personal comfort, and thus easily inconvenienced, they show themselves to be disinterested in a distant future to be won or lost. In political terms, this would make them isolationists. Conversely, they are only interested in military applications of the new technology; the moment when one of the men praises the use of chronometers for the navy, he reveals himself to be a supporter of containment. The men fail to see that, even now that the Morlocks have essentially been defeated, the Eloi cannot be left to their own devices. They might be likable, but they are far from being able to decide their own path into the future independently. George must enlist his friends' support to return and guide Weena and her community in making the right choices. Without the imminent threat of the Morlocks, this guidance can be gentle and flexible. But while the political course in Weena's world is open to some degree of experimentation, the enlistment of George's friends comes with overtones of military stridency. Describing the act of ideological interpellation performed by containment culture, the critics cited previously resort to military metaphors like "conscription" (Berger) and "intervention" (Booker). These are measures that occur under conditions of crisis and emergency. But despite its great urgency, this discourse fails. Unconvinced of the case out before them, George's friends walk

George's Interventionist Fable: Overcoming American Complacency

off into the cold night. With one exception, the circle is unable to achieve ideological consensus and agree on a reasonable course of action.

However, where conscription and intervention fail, romantic courtship succeeds. As George returns to Weena, at great personal risk—George might have won a decisive battle against the Morlocks but not (yet) the war—there is a sense that the progress of their relationship provides a far more successful model of interaction. It is integration in action, a practical step removed from the verbiage, the after-dinner talk among men. In those terms, George has neither been "conscripted" nor performed an "intervention." Though, at first glance, their romance seems to meet Nadel's definition of Cold War "containment" ideology—i.e., that "courtship [is] the activity in which Otherness is the necessary supplement to seduction" (14)—he has also been neither the seducer nor the seduced. Weena is far too guileless to be a seductress, just as George is too much of a gentleman to take advantage of so guileless a girl. But George has been transformed by falling in love. For American film audiences, this is a state as mysterious (and as maddeningly imprecise and ideologically overdetermined) as it is plainly comprehensible and obvious. She has made him a better person, and for that, he gets to change the course of her life. As a matter of national policy, this is, of course, woefully insufficient. As a utopian ideal, however, it might be inspiring. As a political metaphor, it marks Pal's point of departure from containment culture. It is his move toward a kinder, gentler America winning over decolonizing nations within the framework of the Cold War by America being more lovable than its competitors.

Conclusion
The Long Shadow of the Fifties

By the early 1960s, the science fiction film that had dominated the previous decade was on the decline. As cinematic cycles go, its subject matter was starting to show signs of creative exhaustion. The audience was growing tired of seeing the same monsters being defeated by the same military heroics time and again. What used to be that added generic ingredient to 1950s science fiction—supernatural and psychological horror—was beginning to gain currency. As things turned out, films like Jacques Tourneur's *Night of the Demon* (1957), Jack Clayton's *The Innocents* (1961), or Sydney Hayer's *Night of the Eagle* (1962) were closer in spirit to what was to come in the following decade than the alien invasion and bug-eyed monster films made alongside them. In 1960, Alfred Hitchcock's *Psycho* and Michael Powell's *Peeping Tom* initiated a cycle of films in which the subjective and horrific depth of human psychology were to replace nuclear weapons as the source of monstrous transformations. At the same time, the horror film would undergo a shift back to the prewar gothic traditions that had run their course when Universal Studios stopped making "classic" monster movies and started, as Universal-International, making Cold War science fiction. The move away from technological and back to gothic horror would culminate with the rise of the British Hammer studio. After contributing some important science fiction films to the 1950s cycle (*The Quatermass Xperiment* [1955], *Quatermass 2* [1957], *Quatermass and the Pit* [1967], *X the Unknown* [Joseph Losey, 1956]), Hammer would go on throughout the 1960s to make a name for itself by reworking classic 1930s Universal horror tropes. In the US, Roger Corman's Poe adaptations (*The Pit and the Pendulum* [1961], *The Premature Burial* [1962], *The Tomb of Ligeia* [1964]) would follow the same trend. On the science fiction side of things, Rachel Carson's book *Silent Spring* (1962) would inject new life into the monster movie, reorienting the 1950s cycle away from Cold War concerns toward the environmental horrors of nature gone haywire. As late as the 1970s, horror and science fiction stalwarts like Bert I. Gordon and American International Pictures were still cranking out films like *Food of the Gods* (1972) or *Empire of the*

Ants (1977). Superficially, these films replicated themes and methods of the 1950s cycle—from the giant mutated creatures to the evocation of H. G. Wells's cultural prestige. But science fiction had taken a turn with Stanley Kubrick's *2001: A Space Odyssey* (1968), which was to leave even these last remnants of the 1950s cycle looking cheap, outdated, and irrelevant. To make a genuine comeback, the 1950s cycle would need a new historical context in which its familiar tropes and anxieties would take on new life. In order to discover what this new context was going to be, let me switch briefly to the historical side of my argument, and see what happened to the military-industrial complex after the 1950s.[1]

In the final chapter of his book on the military-industrial complex, James Ledbetter tracks the historical use of the term since it was coined by Eisenhower in his presidential farewell address. For the time being, this history ends with the term's sudden resurgence in the popular debate during the eight years of the George W. Bush presidency. "By early 2010," Ledbetter points out, "video versions of [Eisenhower's] address had been viewed more than half a million times on YouTube" (189–90). Refined and updated versions of the term were also making the rounds, some facetious neologisms, others seriously thought-out extensions of the original. So far we have seen the "prison-industrial complex" and the "real estate-industrial complex," the "climate-industrial complex" and the "organic-industrial complex," and, as a highlight of the term's triumphant return to public consciousness, a "2008 book by Nick Turse [carrying] the tongue-in-cheek title *The Complex: Mapping America's Military-Industrial-Technological-Entertainment-Academic-Media-Corporate Matrix*" (190).[2] Ledbetter traces the origins of this renewed interest in Eisenhower's term back to "the 2005 feature-length documentary *Why We Fight*, which marks something of a renaissance for Eisenhower's farewell" (188). The concept had already played a crucial role in Michael Moore's documentaries *Bowling for Columbine* (2002) and *Fahrenheit 9/11* (2004), but only with Jarecki's film did it become "the most popular expression of the notion that that a military-industrial complex was largely responsible for the Iraq war that began in 2003" (189). Or, as Stephen Prince put it, *Why We Fight* "suggests that, when the language about preserving freedom or establishing democracy is stripped away from modern conflicts, one of their primary engines is seen to be profit-taking by the industries that have forged deep bonds with the officials who define foreign policy and who take the nation to war" (187).

In the context of this book, it is important to note that director Eugene Jarecki chose as a title for his documentary not a catchphrase from the Cold

Eugene Jarecki's *Why We Fight*: Updating Frank Capra

War but from World War II (i.e., the title of government-commissioned World War II propaganda films overseen and partially directed by Frank Capra). Given the reversal of politics in Jarecki's and Capra's respective films, Stephen Prince concludes that Jarecki's choice of title "introduces some irony" (185), an irony which, however, leaves Capra's films untouched. There was a good reason for "why we fought" in Capra; there's no such good reason in Jarecki. It is also worth noting that a single documentary may itself be part of a larger cultural trend, but does not single-handedly kick it off. Ledbetter's larger point, however, is well taken. In order for the term to return to prominence, it took a very specific set of external circumstances to come together: a US administration with a particularly belligerent posture in matters of foreign policy, and, consequently, two extensive foreign wars in the course of which the US, against strong diplomatic and popular opposition within the international community, invaded and occupied sovereign nations halfway around the globe without an official declaration of war. These two wars would then produce one of the highest numbers of injured veterans, with the highest number of post-combat suicide rates, in US history. In the case of the administration in charge of all this, "the connections between military infrastructure provider Halliburton and Vice

President Dick Cheney" (Ledbetter 189) provided a textbook example of the dreaded revolving door between military, political, and corporate power. Among the exacerbating circumstances were also the government's close ties with private contractors like Blackwater, the series of annually expanding defense budgets, and the often non-competitive assignment of vastly profitable contracts to corporations (not just Halliburton but also Bechtel and others). However, while the Bush administration may be a particularly egregious example of mishandling public relations for the military-industrial complex, its handling of the nexus between the military, corporate power, and politics was, according to Ledbetter, not a categorical exception from the way America does business. If Ledbetter is correct, then post-9/11 America under Bush might have seen a return of Eisenhower's (in)famous term. America may have stopped talking about the military-industrial complex for a while, but that did not mean that the military-industrial complex had, quietly, gone away. The return of the term marked a new awareness of political and economic conditions for which it had always been the most apt description.

Tracking the continuities of political and economic practices, Ledbetter points out that the last time in American history when the term "military-industrial complex" had enjoyed similar currency was during the Vietnam War. Vietnam was yet another war conducted under the menacing shadow of Cold War nuclear escalation yet fought entirely with conventional weapons. Back then, organized resistance to the war would apply Eisenhower's term to companies like Dow Chemicals, which, "along with United Technology in Connecticut, had received an Air Force contract to manufacture 75,000 tons of Napalm-B" (165) to help the US conduct its most highly visible war since Korea. Domestic policies intended to raise support for, or suppress opposition to, this war included the "FBI's domestic spying and dirty tricks under COINTELPRO, whereby disinformation was circulated to discredit American radical groups" (184). Law enforcement's increasing interconnections helped to establish the military-industrial complex's transition to the national security state. As Ledbetter is tracking the rise and fall in popularity of the term "military-industrial complex" in the public debate, it becomes apparent that a time of war, especially an unpopular war meeting with increasingly vocal popular opposition, provides fertile ground for the term to return to public consciousness. As the US moves from World War II, through the Korean War, toward the Vietnam War, and, finally, on to the two wars initiated by the Bush administration—the one in Afghanistan and the one in Iraq—the consistency with which the military-industrial complex returns to the spotlight at certain times suggests that it is an indispensable part of American life in the twentieth and into the twenty-first century. The popularity of the term might wax and wane, depending on a political discourse shaped by a variety of complex forces; the phenomenon it refers to, however, remains constant.

After September 11, 2001, the conditions determining the visibility of the term as part of American culture would improve considerably. Critics of contemporary US policy have diagnosed the increased levels of militarization as a cultural turn toward what Andrew Bacevich has called the "new American militarism." According to Bacevich, this is a phenomenon "manifesting itself in a romanticized view of soldiers, a tendency to see military power as the truest measure of national greatness, and outsized expectations regarding the efficacy of force" (*New American Militarism* 2). Bacevich's critique covers both actual foreign policy and general attitudes toward these policies, variously distributed among decision-makers and the larger population. After the 1950s had been overseen by a president whose major credentials for political office had been his high rank in the military during World War II, only his direct successor in the White House was still measured by that very standard; Kennedy's tour of duty in the navy helped to shape him as an electable public persona, offsetting both his relatively young age and his religious background. Johnson, Nixon, Ford, Carter, Reagan, and Clinton won their respective bids for the presidency without ostentatious displays of military credentials in their biographies. The post-9/11 political careers of presidential hopefuls like John Kerry and John McCain, however, are unimaginable without the candidates trying to capitalize on their military experiences. However, as the cases of Kerry and McCain also demonstrate, military credentials are not in themselves a guarantor of political capital. Following his dismissal after the initial phase of the Korean War, Douglas MacArthur had not been successful in parlaying his enormous popularity (outweighing that of the president who had dismissed him) into a political career. Conversely, George W. Bush gained the presidency despite dubious military credentials. Cynical observers would go on to speculate that Bush's displays of military aggression might very well have been an overcompensation for his unimpressive record; many will remember the political pageantry of Bush dressing up in the flight suit of a fighter pilot to deliver the erroneous declaration on board the USS *Abraham Lincoln* on May 1, 2003, that the US' mission in Iraq had been accomplished. Meanwhile, John Kerry's case demonstrates that having or not having actual military credentials is more a matter of massaging public perception than historical record. Regardless of all these biographical and contextual historical permutations, what supports Bacevich's assertion that pervasive militarism rules contemporary American politics, especially after 9/11, is the fact that a candidate's military record is *again*—after decades or relative irrelevance—a matter of considerable political weight.[3]

Bacevich's second assertion—the one about the "outsized expectations regarding the efficacy of force" (*New American Militarism* 2), and thus about the use of military force as a default setting of US foreign policy—is supported by the historical record of both the Cold War and its aftermath. Here is a thumbnail sketch of US foreign policy after World War II and before 9/11:

> After the Korean War (1950–53), the U.S. engaged in the Vietnam War (1961–73), the Iran hostage rescue attempt (1980), deployment in Beirut (1982–84), the invasion of Grenada (1983), the raid on Tripoli (1986), the invasion of Panama (1989), the Persian Gulf War (1991–92), the invasion of Somalia (1992–93), the invasion of Haiti (1994), the air raids on Bosnia (1995), and Operation "Allied Force" in the Kosovo (1999). ("Chronology of U.S. Military Interventions")

Aside from the wars in Afghanistan (2001–) and Iraq (2003–), which provide the flashpoint for Jarecki's *Why We Fight* and Moore's *Fahrenheit 9/11*, the US has also engaged in military action in Libya (2011) and drone strikes in Middle Eastern countries like Yemen and Pakistan. If this overview appears either incomplete or hyperbolic, it is because formal declarations of war, as issued at the onset of World War I and World War II, are largely a thing of the past. They have been replaced in the discourse of US foreign relations by a more euphemistic vocabulary in which war figures, for example, as a constructive contribution to the process of "nation building" (war in Iraq, 2003–) or a "kinetic military operation" (US military action in Libya, 2011) (Hantke, "Military Culture" 329–30). Bacevich himself counts nine major operations until 2006, which makes America going to war "just about an annual event" ("Andrew J. Bacevich with Lewis Lapham").

Given the public attention to the role of the military-industrial complex in the first two major American wars of the new millennium, post-9/11 America seemed like an uncanny repetition of 1950s Cold War America. In reference to atomic testing by the Manhattan Project, the post-attack site of the World Trade Center quickly became "Ground Zero." Henry Luce's famous editorial about the dawn of the "American Century" in *Life* magazine (February 17, 1941) would replay itself in the naming of the "Project for the New American Century," a neoconservative think tank co-founded by William Kristol, boasting political celebrities like Dick Cheney, Donald Rumsfeld, and Paul Wolfowitz among its contributors and advocating "a set of muscular policies America must pursue in order to remain the world's military dominant power" (Prince 185). Anxieties over Soviet nuclear sneak attacks and McCarthyite communist hysteria would replay themselves in the widespread public paranoia about terrorist attacks from outside the US, like the ones directed at the World Trade Center and the Pentagon, and about embedded terrorist "sleeper cells" awaiting instructions to launch fifth column campaigns of domestic sabotage. Even the postwar founding of the CIA by way of the 1947 National Security Act resonated with the consolidation of the national security state, via the passing of the Homeland Security Act in 2002 and the structural streamlining of the state security apparatus under the ideological umbrella of the strangely antiquated, yet mythically resonant label of "Homeland Security." Anticipating the key argument in Shane Harris's *@War: The Rise of the Military-Internet Complex* (2014), Ken Hollings's insights into historical continuity regarding the national security state are particularly relevant here. "I would argue," Hollings muses,

> that we have entered a kind of negative dialectic with the culture of the 1950s, where robotics, AI and data storage have taken over from LSD, UFOs and atomic radiation as our new collective fantasies of science [. . .] If, for example, you wanted to find the basis for a comparison between Cold War paranoia and the prevailing War on Terror, I would suggest that it can be found in the development of the network over the past 50 or 60 years: from SAGE and similar long-range detection systems organized around the digital processing of data in graphic terms to the US military's use of networked simulators and the NSA's vast surveillance systems, it becomes clear that the network has always been defined by the enemy within it—in other words the presence of the enemy defines that network and helps focus its operations [. . .] I would still see the expanded network as a key expression of how our urge to inhabit both inner and outer space developed out of Cold War strategies of the 1950s and 1960s. (Ken Hollings, personal email, February 28, 2014)

Writing about post-9/11 America, Wheeler Winston Dixon has summarized this uncanny return of a past decade by asking: "What do the 1950s mean to us now, and why are so many of the decade's most intriguing films resolutely marginalized?" Dixon speculates that, "in their authenticity and direct appeal, [1950s films] bring us into contact with the 1950s in a manner that strips away our preconceptions and nostalgia of the era in a way that makes us uncomfortable with our cultural origins" (*Lost in the Fifties* 184). Idiosyncratic as Dixon's cinematic taste might be, it is doubtful whether he would include *I Married a Monster from Outer Space* or *Tarantula* in his list of "the decade's most intriguing films." Thus, in his conclusion, he returns to the uncanny similarities between the Cold War and the so-called war on terror. "In many respects," he argues,

> we are living in the 1950s right now: repressed, obsessed with "terror alerts," eagerly seeking phantom security in ever-increasing hypersurveillance, reverting to the patriarchal order for a measure of safety and reassurance, retreating to our digital home entertainment centers to experience the world as filtered through a variety of "news" filters rather than experiencing the joys and sorrows of the human community firsthand.

Dixon is neither the first nor the last to notice that more than any other decade, the years following 9/11 seem like a replay of the 1950s. But even if we agree with him, things are not as simple as that because the 1950s were not as simple as that. The question we need to ask ourselves is: which 1950s are we talking about?

After the 1950s had passed, and were receding fast in the historical rearview mirror, there would always be two competing assessments of the decade—one by those who loved it, one by those who hated it. The one endorsed by its defenders would be infused with a conservative nostalgia that casts Eisenhower's America in the rosy glow of happy nuclear families, idyllic suburban homes, a booming consumer culture, and an uncomplicated patriotism stemming from World War II triumphalism. As conservatives would claim the decade for themselves, it became the moment when the Greatest Generation would reap its well-earned rewards. The 1950s would be the calm before the storm; the 1960s would unleash social, racial, and political violence on the nation. It would be the period when Ronald Reagan would remake himself from a mediocre actor into the politician that was to become the greatest Republican president of the twentieth century. Those looking back on the 1950s with a less charitable eye would paint a less idyllic picture. For them, the 1950s would be the decade of cultural conformity and boredom, of grievously insufficient rights for women and minorities, of waves of social panics about flying saucers, juvenile delinquents, comic books, communist subversion, and nuclear war. A nervous, twitchy decade with a psychotic smile plastered perpetually across its face. While a

Conclusion 193

Psychotic Cheerfulness in the Face of
Annihilation: The Pleasures and Horrors
of the 1950s

nostalgic endorsement of the 1950s would retrospectively sanitize science fiction films from the period as charmingly bungling, hilariously hyperbolic, campy entertainment, the more critical perspective would construe them as a cinematic record of the darker side of the decade for generations to come. From this perspective, the films provide a historical counter-narrative that would render the 1950s useful for narratives not enthralled by conservative nostalgia. Even to critics of the 1950s, the conservative narrative is still visible in this cinematic record. But it is a narrative with a twist. For every happy family in the conservative version, there would be an oppressive patriarchal regime in the counter-narrative. In every idyllic suburban home there would be an alienated, brooding, and potentially abusive war veteran. Every shiny new automobile would come with its uses as a possible vehicle to escape from the smoldering ruins of a once great American metropolis. And every facet of American patriotism would be enforced and co-opted by the military-industrial complex.[4]

Celebratory films about the military-industrial complex would remain a staple of Hollywood production after the 1950s, with the war film as action-adventure spectacle first in line. Most notably (or notoriously), screenings of *Top Gun* (Tony Scott, 1986), a film made with enthusiastic logistical support by the air force, were accompanied by air force recruitment stands pitched directly in front of American multiplexes. Reaching back to the militaristic themes of *Pearl Harbor* (2001), Michael Bay's *Transformers* franchise (with four films, starting in 2007) would receive considerable aid in personnel and material by the military. The wars of the Bush administration seemed conducted to the drumbeat of a war narrative in another genre, the *Lord of the Rings* trilogy (Peter Jackson, 2001, 2002, 2003), its literary source material inspired by the British experience of World War II tailored to the specific interpellative demands of the "war on terror." Similarly, the relative success of adaptations of C. S. Lewis's *Chronicles of Narnia* (*The Lion, the Witch and the Wardrobe* [2005], *Prince Caspian* [2008], *The Voyage of the Dawn Treader* [2010])—especially in contrast to the failure of what was to be the first installment of the Philip Pullman *His Dark Materials* trilogy (*The Golden Compass* [2007])—suggests that source material derived from World War II seems to resonate more closely with the ideological demands of the "war on terror" than, for example, Pullman's contemporary critical take on established hierarchical authority. While Jackson's massive undertaking with *The Lord of the Rings* was shifting the genre emphasis away from science fiction and toward heroic fantasy, the genre blend of horror and science fiction elements popularized during the 1950s remained a staple at the box office.

Conclusion 195

Enriched with military spectacle and packaged as summer blockbusters, it would launch films like *Battle Los Angeles* (Jonathan Liebesman, 2011) and *Battleship* (Peter Berg, 2012). Together with an increasingly militarized array of superhero films and franchises, which in an endless replay loop seem to celebrate military hardware and spectacle, television series like *Battlestar Galactica* (2004–2009) would join the fray. While digital effects have made Hollywood largely independent of Pentagon support, the internal logic of the Hollywood blockbuster, more militarized than ever, now extends to the heirs of 1950s science fiction films. With or without direct support or explicit approval from the military-industrial complex, the landscape of the contemporary Hollywood blockbuster is loud, fast, and heavily armed, a battlefield mapped out by the 1950s science fiction film cycle.

For a film like *Battle Los Angeles* (2011) to register as a latter-day version of Byron Haskin's *War of the Worlds* (1953)—for the more literal-minded, Steven Spielberg's actual remake of *War of the Worlds* (2005) will work just as well—contemporary audiences would have to bring a finely-tuned historical awareness to the film. Bridging a period of roughly fifty years, this historical awareness would have to be constructed by way of a larger, coherent historical imaginary called "the fifties." This historical imaginary can include anything and everything—from academic historiography to high school textbooks, from *Mystery Science Theater 3000* to those beehive hairdos worn by Kate Pierson and Cindy Wilson of the B-52s. In order to develop a specific and self-conscious genealogy in which post-9/11 horror and science fiction films explicitly hark back to the 1950s cycle as their origin, it would be necessary for "the fifties" itself to come into focus as a distinct historical and cultural phenomenon. Like all historiography based on decades, "the fifties" are the product of hindsight. But even the Cold War itself was, after all, not an entirely homogeneous period. How thoroughly even the latter half of the Cold War was to break away from the 1950s can be read in a film like *The Atomic Café*, a documentary about the 1950s produced and released in the early 1980s. Witty and insightful, the film plays on the double themes of nuclear anxieties and communist paranoia. It does so by assembling original footage from civil defense films, military instructional and promotional footage, newsreels, and television programs into startling and often ironic juxtapositions. In one memorable sequence late in the film, we see Vice President Nixon ring the Liberty Bell as part of the opening ceremonies of National Mental Health Week. The scene is followed by a prolonged sequence that recapitulates the progression of an imaginary nuclear attack on the United States. It opens with the ominous shadows of planes overhead, moves on to scenes of urban panic and evacuation, and closes with school classes ducking and covering right before the nuclear explosion itself. The extended sequence emphasizes the insanity, the self-delusion, and the schizophrenia at work behind much of the strategic and cultural efforts to contain Cold War anxieties. With Nixon at the helm, the scene articulates in a nutshell the film's general stance—that of psychologizing 1950s America. In effect, the film places the nation on the psychiatrist's couch, a neurotic, obsessive-compulsive mental patient, dissociated from reality, rocking reassuringly back and forth while barely holding it together. On the chair next to the couch sits the 1980s psychologist, well-informed, realistic, and stripped of all comforting illusions. The figure's authority comes with historical hindsight; he is calm and resigned in the face of a reality even worse than the one upsetting the patient. He is a bit amused by the patient's hysteria, patronizing perhaps, but if so, his condescension is tempered by empathy. Post-9/11 America would have that patient return to the couch yet again, hyper-vigilant and ready to lash out, with a case of collective PTSD.

Considering how historically specific the image of the 1950s in *The Atomic Café* is, there are surprisingly few horror and science fiction films produced and released after the 1950s which reference the decade explicitly as a historical origin. Horror auteurs who happened to be baby boomers would foray into the 1950s periodically. After establishing his interest in the 1950s by directing a remake of William Cameron Menzies's *Invaders from Mars* (1986), Tobe Hooper would go on to *Spontaneous Combustion* (1990), a film that traces its present day telekinetic horrors back to the naïve governmental atomic experiments of the 1950s. Another baby boomer transforming 1950s childhood horrors into cinema is Joe Dante. With *Matinee* (1993), Dante made not a horror film but a film *about* 1950s horror films (the same goes for *Psycho Beach Party* [Robert Lee King, 2000] or *Alien Trespass* [R. W. Goodwin, 2009]). Less personal approaches to 1950s horror and science fiction, however, would prove problematic; though parts of Roland Emmerich's *Godzilla* (1998) attempted to embed the film's cutting-edge CGI extravagance in a nostalgic framework of 1950s references, the film failed to hit a nerve with the audience. Suffice it to say that lacking the topical urgency of the Cold War and its nuclear hysteria and communist paranoia, the film did not connect with the audience. An alien invasion film like *Mars Attacks* (Tim Burton, 1996) might have been trying to reboot Byron Haskin's *War of the Worlds*, but it was mostly Burton's auteurist credentials that brought audiences to the theater. An alien impostor film like Stuart

Conclusion 197

June Cleaver Reimagined by Rod Serling: *Pleasantville* (Gary Ross, 1998)

Orme's *The Puppet Masters* (1994) might have been trying to revive 1950s classics like *Invaders from Mars*, but went down as a lackluster exercise in genre nostalgia. The same goes for the 1990s attempt at remaking *I Married a Monster from Outer Space*, Rand Ravich's *The Astronaut's Wife* (1999), a forgettable film that was to remain a minor entry on the resumes of the major stars (Johnny Depp, Charlize Theron) recruited to enhance its box office. Emmerich's *Godzilla* (1998) was certainly trying to do its part for the giant creature film, but it would take the Fukushima Daiichi nuclear disaster in 2011 to generate topical relevance for Gareth Edward's take on *Godzilla* in 2014. Emmerich's film, meanwhile, seemed to be about nothing else than computer-generated effects and relentless product placement and merchandizing. Looking back on the 1990s, it seems fair to say that American audiences did not really care about "the fifties," especially not in the incarnation of its dark, dystopian counter-narrative. Whatever progress special effects had been making throughout the 1990s, their impact on 1950s remakes turned out to be rather counterproductive. "Action movies in the nineties," Kim Newman complains, "use walls of flame as pretty backdrops, and one of the most pernicious clichés of the age—easily on a par with the suggestion in fifties films that ducking behind a rock a hundred yards from Ground Zero is protection enough from an A-bomb blast" (261–62). On a smaller scale, one might see films like *Pleasantville* (Gary Ross, 1998) as more successful in instrumentalizing the 1950s for political reasons. In the case of *Pleasantville*, the 1950s backdrop is explicitly construed as a television series come-to-life, a mass-mediated utopia that, upon closer inspection, turns out to be rather dystopian. Except for the film's commentary on mass media, it is not concerned with the military-industrial complex. Rather, its gist is a cautionary tale about the resurgence of the political right after the 1994 Congressional elections, which Ross portrays as Republicans trying to take the nation back to a dull, lifelessly cheerful black-and-white 1950s that keeps a tight lid on sexual liberties and racial equality.

In contrast to these playful meta-historical evocations of the 1950s, the decade was to leave its mark on science fiction in other ways. For one, it spawned a host of films that, without any self-conscious historical attribution, operate in the space of "technohorror" where science fiction and horror operate alongside each other. Though mad scientists and dangerous science had already been running through horror films of the 1930s and '40s, it was the formation of technoscience during World War II and the consolidation of the military-industrial complex in the 1950s that would bring these mythical characters and emblematic spaces into focus. The 1950s legacy are films with a take on technoscience that is distinctly pessimistic, technophobic, or dystopian. Steering directly toward abjection in their exploration of the interactions between bodies and technologies, Ridley Scott's *Alien* (1979) was to prove as influential for science fiction cinema as Kubrick's *2001* had been roughly a decade before. Though the *Alien* franchise had roots reaching back as far as pulp SF (A. E. Van Vogt's fix-up novel *Voyage of the Space Beagle* [1950]), it would come into its own in the cinema during the 1950s with *It! The Terror from Beyond Space* (Edward L. Cahn, 1959) and, subsequently, with *Planet of the Vampires* (org. *Terrore Nello Spazia*, Mario Bava, 1965). Springing from these roots, the *Alien* franchise was to become a vehicle for the permanent entrenchment of 1950s-style technohorror in American popular culture.[5] The explicit reference to the military-industrial complex is even more pronounced in the *Resident Evil* franchise (with five films so far, starting in 2002, and one scheduled for 2015), which also provides an example of how the gaming industry has expanded the range of science fiction cinema even further. In all these multi-platform franchises, the interplay of powerful corporations with military or para-military organizations, configured around science and technology, with a good dose of abject spectacle, makes these films direct descendants of the 1950s cycle (without demanding from its audience the recognition that the material derives specifically from the 1950s).

The turn toward historical self-awareness was to come with 9/11. Suddenly science fiction films seemed to foreground the 1950s as exactly that historical reference point by which they would orient themselves. If films were referencing the 1950s, it now mattered whether you caught the reference or not. Even the seriousness of 1950s science fiction films—their lack of self-irony, which had still been a target of mockery during the 1990s—suddenly seemed to hit a nerve.

> Virtually all of these films turn away from the irony that pervades giant creature films from the 1990s [. . .] Like Francis Lawrence's 2007 *I Am Legend* (the third and so-far only post-Cold War adaptation of Richard Matheson's 1954 novel by the same title), Oliver Hirschbiegel's *The Invasion* (2007, the third update of Don Siegel's 1956 *Invasion of the Body Snatchers*), or Scott Derrickson's *The Day the Earth Stood Still* (2009, the first ever remake of Robert Wise's 1951 Cold War classic), contemporary adaptations or recreations of 1950s films treat their various preposterous central premises not with the tongue-in-cheek humor of [a campy low-budget mockbuster like] *Mega Shark* [*versus Giant Octopus*] but with grimly serious efficiency. (Hantke, "Cloverfield" 238)

Superficially, this shift in tone, away from campy humor and toward a new seriousness, seemed to validate the slogan about "the end of irony" that circulated through media and public debate for a time after the 9/11 attacks. More important, though, this new seriousness drew attention to the rapid increase in paranoia and militaristic hysteria post-9/11 under the Bush Administration, and then linked this tense, twitchy mood to that of the Cold War during the long 1950s under Eisenhower. Post-9/11, there would be little space for campy takes on 1950s horror and science fiction; *The Lost Skeleton of Cadavra* (Larry Blamire, 2001) would end up a casualty of its ill-timed release date, while *Alien Trespass* (R. W. Goodwin, 2009), released eight years later, would garner little public resonance. The lighthearted animation film *Monsters versus Aliens* (Rob Letterman/Conrad Vernon, 2009) did better at the box office, but, being a movie for children, did not even register as a political film. What *Monsters versus Aliens* did accomplish beautifully, however, was to capitalize on the long reception history of 1950s horror and science fiction iconography, which it inventories with considerable wit and affection. Even if the film fell short of figuring in any substantial relationship to 9/11, it did enshrine the canonical status of films like *Attack of the 50 Foot Woman*, *Creature from the Black Lagoon*, and *The Fly*, introducing a whole new generation of viewers to some of the classic tropes of 1950s science fiction.

Among the post-9/11 films that succeed in investing the analogy between Bush's and Eisenhower's America with considerable political gravity is the

Retro-Fifties, Post-9/11: The Modern Security State Then and Now in *Fido* (Andrew Currie, 2006)

horror comedy *Fido* (Andrew Currie, 2006). Though the film resorts to the zombie apocalypse as its central idea—an idea that comes into cultural circulation after the end of the 1950s cycle and with the start of neo-horror at the end of the 1960s—Currie superimposes this metaphor upon a retro version of 1950s suburban America. The film's major location, an idyllic small town with little pink houses and white picket fences, is under permanent occupation of the military-industrial complex in exchange for protection from roaming hordes of zombies. The film's exploration of paternalistic, militaristic, and corporate control over a population of women and children—all conceptualized visually and tonally in ways reminiscent of *I Married a Monster from Outer Space*, *Invaders from Mars*, and an endless array of *Twilight Zone* episodes—wields the historical analogy with sharp satirical precision. The price of security, Currie reminds his audience, is a return to standards of traditional authority that make post-9/11 America look like an advertisement for TV dinners from the pages of *Life* magazine.

Another film that successfully reworks 1950s horror and science fiction trope—this one in the category of giant creature films with a genealogy that reaches back to films like *The Black Scorpion* or *20,000 Miles to Earth*—is Gareth Edwards's *Monsters* (2010). The film is a creature feature shot on a very moderate budget, which distinguishes it from similar films that either aim for blockbuster status (e.g., *Cloverfield* [Matt Reeves, 2008]) or announce their blockbuster status proudly (Edwards's own 2014 *Godzilla*). Taking its cinematic clue from Neill Blomkamp's *District 9* (2009), and bending the source material away from science fiction and more toward horror, *Monsters* imagines a South American landscape traversed by North

American tourists, confined by no-go zones under command by the military-industrial complex. With its conceit of found digital footage, *Monsters* is clearly not driven by the spectacular display of digital effects. Instead, the film reconnects 1950s concerns about the military-industrial's control over domestic geographic spaces to neoliberalism's rezoning of the global sphere. This rezoning would have been felt with particular acuity in the wake of the economic crisis starting in 2008 and brought to wider attention with academic crossover bestsellers like David Harvey's *A Brief History of Neoliberalism* (2005) and Naomi Klein's *The Shock Doctrine* (2007). *Monsters* expresses this new political sensibility by developing the occupation metaphor that runs through 1950s films like *Them!* and *It Came from Outer Space*.

As in the 1950s, post-9/11 science fiction films would also position themselves across a spectrum of political opinions. They still fall roughly into the two categories proposed by Tom Engelhardt for 1950s popular culture ("The exclusionary films were apocalyptic and hysterical about them; the inclusionary ones about us" [106]). Between the polar extremes lies a vast middle ground of popular entertainment that negotiates—sometimes deftly, sometimes dully—the risky territory of public discourse. Some films might aim to intervene constructively in the public debate while others are just looking for a broad consensus that promises high ratings and solid box office.[6] On the conservative end of the spectrum are films like *I am Legend* (Francis Lawrence, 2007), which ultimately embrace the newly militarized, digitally fortified, xenophobic America under the guidance of Homeland Security. On the progressive end, we find films like *The Mist* (Frank Darabont, 2007), which grimly gesture toward the social and psychological casualties of this new perpetual war on terror itself. As if trying to literalize one of the key ideas about nuclear war in the 1950s, Darabont constructs an ending for his small band of Americans in which the survivors truly envy the dead. Among the two extremes, it would be the more conciliatory "inclusionary" films and television series that find themselves muted. These are the texts that would advocate "integration" rather than "containment"; the texts that concede that aggression against America might have been blowback from some (covert) US intervention elsewhere, and not the actions of irrational, demonic "evildoers" from somewhere along the "axis of evil." The more "exclusionary" ones, meanwhile, would ramp up their aggressive, xenophobic pitch. Politically speaking, the ending of *The Mist* is about as "inclusionary" as it gets, indicting an unholy alliance of military and technoscience in a fatal feedback loop with rampant irrational paranoia. Compared to the cautiously hopeful ending of Stephen King's original

1980s novella on which the film is based (itself harking back to 1950s creature features), Darabont comes up with an ending which speaks of a despair and pessimism so profound that audiences might wish for a taste of corny 1950s optimism. To many viewers, *The Mist* may stand as an example of what was to be the major difference between 1950s and post-9/11 culture. While the Cold War looked like a prolonged wait for the ultimate catastrophe, post-9/11 culture would begin with the ultimate catastrophe and go on from there. As this book has been arguing all along, the trauma driving 1950s American culture was not the perpetually deferred nuclear apocalypse, but instead the very real and painfully remembered disruption of World War II and the imposition of a new militarized regime as the new postwar American normality. As postwar America eventually settled in to these new routines, so post-9/11 America seems to settle in to something eerily familiar: a perpetual state of crisis and a routine of normalized militarization reminiscent of the long 1950s.

Notes

Introduction

1. The definition of science fiction draws from Eric Rabkin's discussion of the fantastic, especially in *The Fantastic in Literature* (Princeton, NJ: Princeton University Press, 1976).

2. Though definitions of this term abound, Donna Haraway has provided this brief definition: "Technoscience extravagantly exceeds the distinction between science and technology as well as those between nature and society, subjects and objects, and the natural and the artificial that structured the imaginary time called modernity" (Haraway, *Modest Witness* 3). As an ideology, a mode of operation, a modality (to use Haraway's word), technoscience strikes me as particularly well aligned with the integrative and expansionist concept of the military-industrial complex, being both its foundation and one of its structural components.

3. For a full discussion of the problem of genre, see Sobchak, "Transylvania on Mars: Science fiction," in *Screening Space*, 26–63.

4. "Adapted to the screen, [the Jules Verne novel *20,000 Leagues Under the Sea*] would provide action, exotic location scenery, and even some spectacular violence [. . .] These elements clearly aligned the film with the wave of science fiction films marked by what Susan Sontag famously termed 'the imagination of disaster' and 'an aesthetics of destruction'" (Telotte 67).

5. "In 1955 only 7 were distributed, 1.3 per cent of the total, and broadly the same figure as throughout the early fifties. In 1956 that figure doubled to 15 (2.8 per cent), and a year later doubled again to 33 (6.9 per cent). Over the five year period there are 139 horror-movies; there were only 30 in the previous half-decade" (Tudor 25).

6. For a detailed overview of box-office stars during the 1950s, see Peter Lev, 306.

7. Cynthia Hendershot reminds her readers how dissociated popular perceptions about Americans' priorities in the 1950s could be from actual historical reality. "As Haynes points out, only three per cent of the public in 1949 cited Communism as 'the most serious issue facing the nation'" (65), citing instead such issues as "'preventing war, inflation, government spending, taxes, relations with the Soviet Union, nuclear war, housing, and union-management turmoil'" (Haynes qtd. in Hendershot 56).

8. Tony Shaw has made the argument that specifically dissenting opinions require this protective measure of metaphor and allegory. "At the beginning, in the late 1940s and early 1950s, dissent largely came in allegorical or semi-allegorical form. As the 1950s progressed, and with the broad outlines of the Cold War consensus now firmly

established, a number of filmmakers grew more openly critical of Cold War orthodoxy" (136).

9. In his extensive filmography of the war film, John Shelton Lawrence has documented the war film's postwar slump, listing just two films—William Wyler's *The Best Years of Our Lives* (1946) and Theron Warth's and Richard Fleischer's *Design for Death* (1947)—in the period between the end of the war and the resurgence of the genre with the 1949 release of Henry King's *Twelve O'Clock High* (Lawrence 529–65). Heralding the end of the slump for the war film, the Korean War was, as Biskind calls it, the "answer to a prayer" (*Seeing is Believing* 59). Schatz's overview of wartime production trends, meanwhile, limits discussion of the horror film during World War II to two paragraphs, noting the exhaustion of the Universal franchises and the creative, nourish low-budget productions by Val Lewton at RKO (Schatz 232–33). Science fiction does not merit a single mention.

10. Peter Biskind reads this as an even more complex expression of "not one but several warring ideologies, so that it is possible to speak of radical (left- and right-wing) as well as mainstream films" (*Seeing is Believing* 4), while Kim Newman sees a political divide opening up between films produced by major studios and those independently produced ("The major studios present simple soldier heroes who act by the book and never question orders, but the independents are actively anti-military" [*Apocalypse Movies* 85]).

11. To cite just one example of such critical variety, Tony Williams, in an essay engaging with critic Robin Wood, reads *The Thing from Another World* as a continuation of Howard Hawks's "exploration of a professional group that fascinated him so much throughout his career. It is an ideal group existing beyond society and his conception of military professionals in both *Air Force* and *The Thing* would be unthinkable today, if not impossible in practice" (Williams, *CineAction* 58). While Wood, according to Williams, would have read this community as an "ideal democracy"—a view in line with auteurist continuity in Hawks's work but rather out of sync with military reality, which is anything but democratic—Williams himself goes one step further, calling the Hawksian military community "more relevant to an ideal conception of Marxism which is what Hawks unconsciously offers as a utopian community" (Williams, *CineAction* 58).

12. Particularly striking among these stories is one that explains with an eerie matter-of-factness the invention and use of napalm, entitled "Jellied Gasoline" (*Life*, July 9, 1945). The story points out the use of the material in the Pacific theater: "Flamethrowers have scorched and suffocated *suicidal* Japanese soldiers in their caves and underground forts" (47, italics added). Except for the odd detail about the scorched and suffocated victims of Napalm having been "suicidal" to begin with, the tone of the reporting is stripped of any awareness of the weapon's inhuman cruelty. That association would come with the Vietnam War, especially with Associated Press photographer Nick Ut's Pulitzer Prize-winning images of burned children running from the village of Trang Bang after it had been set ablaze by US troops on June 8, 1972. The use of napalm in torching the giant ants in *Them!* (1954) and the giant spider in *Tarantula* (1955) is still tonally and politically

consistent with *Life*'s reporting on the Pacific campaign in World War II. On protests against Dow Chemicals, the manufacturer of napalm, as part of resistance against the military-industrial complex, see also Ledbetter, 165–66.

13. Another possible point of reference would be the social acceptance and popularity of war toys among children. Analyzing his own childhood in the late 1950s and early 1060s, Tom Engelhardt links war toys directly to American political culture, pointing out that there "had been a burst of professional and parental concern about when 'play goes warlike' during World War II" but that this concern had dissipated by the time Engelhardt himself found his own childhood toy chest taken over by the military imagination (82)

14. "By the end of the Korean War it was abundantly clear to General Eisenhower that there were limits to the sacrifices most Americans were willing to make in order to extend Americanism abroad. His policies of using covert interventions combined with alliances with local elites—rather than US military forces—proved successful in toppling moderate left-wing governments in Iran and Guatemala" (Westad 26). While Edward Said, for example, is struggling in *Orientalism* with the fact that US imperialism differs in its methods, especially in regard to direct military, from its European predecessors, his analysis in *Culture and Imperialism* (published in 1993, in the wake of the first Gulf War) is clearly based upon the recognition, indebted to historian Richard Barnet, that "a United States military intervention in the Third World had occurred every year between 1945 and 1967" (Said, *Culture and Imperialism* 285).

15. Further off to the margin of the spectrum of critical positions might be Michel Foucault's analysis of power, which would have the military as one of the institutions—together with the school, the prison, and the hospital—through which power flows and which power aligns according to a series of core principles of agency and interaction. Structurally aligned with Hardt and Negri's conception of Empire as a form of global politics in which the US has lost its privileged position, Foucault's concept would explain the spread of military structures but would not assign the military a central position per se.

16. The version of history Chomsky is taking issue with is not so much the one put forth by Westad, whose analysis is more nuanced, but by Paul Nitze in NSC 68, especially in regard to the moral framework surrounding US foreign policy. "Within this framework, the United States was identified as the guarantor of Western security, the regenerator of its economy, and the instigator of a period of freedom and prosperity. Precluded from this framing were alternative narratives that explained the hostilities [i.e., resistance against US interference within European politics] as a function of US economic, political, ideological and cultural expansion across the Atlantic [. . .] rather than recalling the immediate past of cooperation with the Soviets and economic engagement with the Nazis or other awkward colonial relationships, the initial and most powerful Cold War narratives called on the sacred documents of US diplomacy, providing continuity, benevolence, comprehension and closure to the unfolding story" (Ryan, *Mapping Containment* 61).

17. In regard to US foreign policy in the Third World, historians have often made reference to the possible disparity between actual political goals and ideological framing

whenever US interventions failed to produce their desired results because of the misreading of colonial or post-colonial wars as local symptoms of the Cold War. David Halberstam, for example, makes the case for the US misreading the conflict on the Korean peninsula as a manifestation of the Cold War, while it was, in reality, "a pure colonial war" (94), precipitated by the nation's postwar division and by driven by national rather than international political motives (*The Coldest Winter* 91–94). While this particular misreading might have been understandable in the context of the "loss of China" in 1949, adherence to this position might have exacerbated US involvement in Vietnam and other wars since. Because, by the late 1940s, "America cared nothing about Korea" without the threat of global communism, reading just that threat into a civil war was what was needed "so that Americans were willing to fight and die for it" (63).

18. Ian Buruma has pointed out that the concept of the "zero hour," applied mostly to Germany being reconstituted as a democratic state by the Allieds after 1945, is a convenient political fiction. "The year 1945 would be a blank slate," Buruma writes; "history would be happily discarded; anything was possible [. . .] Of course, anything was not possible. There is no such thing as a blank slate in human affairs. History cannot be wished away" (242–43). To the same extent that Germany's zero hour failed to meet the standards of a historical break, the argument can be made about the US and the impact of nuclear weapons on the transition between World War II and the incipient Cold War.

19. "The facts about the destructive power of the atomic bombs dropped on Hiroshima and Nagasaki in August 1945 had slowly percolated down through American society. First reports of the bombs' effects had been heavily censored. After the war ended, reporters were barred from the bombed Japanese cities. Some sneaked in ahead of occupation troops and filed stories, but these were embargoed by General MacArthur's censors in Tokyo. Pictures showing the flattened cities appeared in newspapers, but there were few eyewitness reports describing the human toll or the effects of radioactivity. And after all, the only eyewitnesses were Japanese survivors, and their reports in the press were dismissed as propaganda. Japanese newsreels showing the human toll were confiscated; US Army films of the ruined cities were classified secret. The radiation issue did not emerge until the atomic bomb tests at Bikini Atoll in the summer of 1946" (Lingeman 270–71).

20. As detailed as John Hersey's reporting on Hiroshima for *Life* magazine in 1946 is—especially its graphic detail about the human devastation—it lacks the impact of the visual image. Hersey also points out that "General MacArthur's headquarters systematically censored all mention of the bomb in Japanese scientific publications, but soon the fruit of the scientists' calculations became common knowledge among Japanese physicists, doctors, chemists, journalists, professors, and, no doubt, those statesmen and military men who were still in circulation. Long before the American public had been told, most of the scientists and lots of non-scientists in Japan knew [about the technical details of the drop, the weapon, and the potential for further generations of the same weapon]" (Hersey, *Hiroshima* 108).

21. Though the first detonation of a hydrogen bomb on November 1, 1952, occurred under military secrecy and without a television audience, news reporting on the

event was extensive, using maps of American heartland locations to demonstrate blast and fallout range of the device within easily recognizable spatial and geographic dimensions (this device was to be used in later broadcasts as well, and became a standard representational trope of nuclear war). At the end of a show devoted to this event, the host, Edward R. Murrow, "apologizes not for the message but for the medium. Regrettably, 'so far there is no film available and there is not likely to be any available of the first hydrogen bomb'" (Doherty 11).

22. While one might argue about the cultural impact of this underdog narrative in, for example, the *Star Wars* franchise, its political value is undisputed; e.g., the military consequences of the so-called "missile gap" theory—positing the US erroneously as outgunned by the Soviet Union's arsenal—which was handed over from the Eisenhower to the Kennedy administration, ultimately served as a legitimization for a massive increase of the defense budget.

23. Cinematic genres like the Western, barred by their nineteenth-century setting from having to come to terms with the idiosyncrasies of nuclear weapons, would have fewer problems imagining war during the 1950s. John Ford's *Fort Apache*, for example, would merge "the nineteenth-century war against the Indians with the World War II combat film" (Hoberman 77), a move that would do justice to US foreign interventions in Korea but suppress the larger Cold War context in which conventional regional conflicts could blossom into global nuclear ones.

24. Other media at the time were facing similar representational challenges. Paul Boyer recounts the case of a radio program, broadcast on June 30, 1946, "presenting a chillingly realistic depiction of the outbreak of a future atomic war" (Boyer, *Bomb's Early Light* 65). After an "'unearthly roar,'" signaling the atomic blast, the following voiceover was heard: "'Silence—complete and total silence. The infinite silence of death.'" Though Boyer characterizes this depiction as "frightening fare," the most memorable signifier in the program's crucial moment is not the roar but the silence; i.e., the gap, the void, the rupture in the text, which, in the larger context of visual representation, corresponds to cinematic devices establishing distance, muting or altogether erasing the textual presence of the bomb.

25. "After the bomb was dropped on Hiroshima, the first pictures that appeared on front pages of newspapers and magazines across the country were tightly controlled, official government releases of the mushroom cloud, not of the destruction on the ground in Japan or of the bomb itself" (Titus 105). Beyond the issue of information control, the mushroom cloud's aesthetic has a similar effect. "Spectacular imagery, poetic references, and colourful hyperbole focused the public's collective eye on the aesthetics of the mushroom cloud and glossed over the dangers that resulted from radioactive fallout" (107).

26. Christian G. Appy, in a discussion of what he calls "sentimental militarism," notes that films like *Mister Roberts* (John Ford, 19), *The Caine Mutiny* (Edward Dmytryk, 1954), and *White Christmas* (Michael Curtiz, 1954) address the issue, familiar to millions of US soldiers without direct combat experience; that, quoting a line of dialogue from *Mister*

Roberts, "'the unseen enemy of this war is boredom'" (Appy, "Sentimental Militarism" 91). Appy links this observation not only to a film's potential appeal to a larger audience—i.e., to a selective and thus highly ideological referencing of World War II "as a site of fantasy and nostalgia as much as stress" (95)—but also to "postwar critiques of corporate tedium and alienation" (90). While cinema prefers dramatic action, "the challenges of the Cold War were more likely to involve patient, undramatic, everyday service without a clear or decisive end in sight" (90)—a dramatic problem a film like *Bombers B-52* recognizes and yet fails to resolve. In reference to *Strategic Air Command*, Appy also suggests that the audience's understanding of "dramatic action" may be gendered, citing his wife's verdict ("excruciatingly boring") about the film's fetishistic celebration of military hardware—akin to that in *Bombers B-52*—in contrast to James Stewart being "utterly seduced and challenged by the latest military hardware" (93).

27. The emphasis on daytime precision bombing is curiously reminiscent of the emphasis so many histories of the Korean War place on that war's first year only (see, for example, David Halberstam, *The Coldest Winter*). In both cases, the dramatic emphasis on one aspect of the respective military campaign helps to distract from the more significant later period, in which "strategic" bombing—i.e., saturation bombing of areas regardless of the presence of essential military or industrial installations—emerged as the dominant strategic component.

28. *Strategic Air Command* is discussed in detail by Biskind (*Seeing is Believing* 64–69).

29. For a full discussion of father-daughter relationships in Cold War films of the period, see Christine Cornea, *Science Fiction Cinema: Between Fantasy and Reality* (2007), 53–57.

30. The melodramatic narrative of families under generational duress is cast explicitly against the background of the military-industrial complex. Throughout the entire film, there is only one set of characters who are not members of the military, the Slater family in San Francisco, whom the Brennans visit during their vacation. Having left the military, Slater is the one proposing a corporate job to Brennan, showing off his lavish house as evidence that leaving the military and transitioning into private enterprise is a sure path to upward social mobility. It is, however, the introduction of the new bomber which retains Brennan's loyalty to the air force.

31. Later examples of the same dilemma are visible in films like *Top Gun* (Tony Scott, 1986) and *Heartbreak Ridge* (Clint Eastwood), shot in periods that either had to imagine a microscopic "warlike" conflict for Tom Cruise's character to prove himself in, or resort to the less-than-impressive "war" against Grenada to provide the recruits trained by Clint Eastwood's character with an actual field of battle. Douglas, aware that "real conflict" might be a complex and potentially divisive issue, opens the film with documentary footage of aerial combat during the Korean War, showing a dogfight that ends with one plane dramatically spiraling toward the ground and crashing. The sequence prefigures the two near-crashes of B-52s during test flights the film is about to dramatize—a dramatization that will use documentary footage shot by Gordon with permission of the air force but lacking in comparable visual impact.

32. For a full discussion of "trauma," see Stephen Prince, *Firestorm*, 10–16.

33. In *Specters of War: Hollywood's Engagement with Military Conflict* (2012), Elisabeth Bronfen has mapped out a model for the reflection of traumatic war experiences in cinema. As her key example, Bronfen chooses text John Huston's long-suppressed documentary on traumatized World War II veterans, *Let There Be Light* (1946). She argues that it is the "irrepresentability of any actual experience of war" (109)—i.e., the audience's affective "detachment from the heightened anxiety of battle" (108)—which allows "the war film to pass as movie entertainment [. . .] regardless of how realistic it strives to be" (108–109). Cinema can restage or re-enact the original trauma in a "scenic reconstruction" of what must inevitably be "fragmented internal images" (110). These images can be "unequivocally perceived as being different from the original experience" (110), and thus reintegrated into a coherent narrative. Narrative externalization and reintegration allow for a representation of trauma—not trauma itself—to be communicated from the affected subject to a cinematic audience, a process that is always and inevitably ideological in nature.

Chapter One

1. At the time of this writing, the most recent and detailed account of this cooperation between the federal government and Hollywood has been Mark Harris's book-length study of five directors, *Five Came Back* (2014). While Worland characterizes the process of the film industry's "recruitment into the government's far-reaching war-information campaign" as "uneasy" (48), Harris goes to great lengths to work out the idiosyncratic factors combining in each of his five director's cases that make up for an overall picture of cooperation driven by patriotism, career considerations, and biographical coincidences, all encompassed within an industrial framework of studios maneuvering to ensure profits under rapidly changing conditions.

2. Worland's essay focuses largely on low-budget productions by poverty-row producers (e.g., *Black Dragons* by Monogram Pictures [1942]) or productions by the low-budget divisions of major studios (e.g., Columbia Pictures' Bela Lugosi vehicle *Return of the Vampire* [1944]).

3. This is not to say that science fiction films were not produced en masse at shoestring budgets, but that science fiction generated a market niche for more lavishly budgeted prestige projects (starting with William Cameron Menzies's *Things to Come* [1936], finding its form with Irving Pichel's *Destination Moon* [1950], and extending itself via Stanley Kubrick's *2001* [1968] toward contemporary blockbusters like Christopher Nolan's *Interstellar* [2014]). Though there have been expensive and prestigious horror films, they are, by and large, neither typical nor canonical for their genre.

4. For a brilliant overview of World Wars II on the development of the horror film, see David Skal, *The Horror Show*, Chapter Seven, "'I Used to Know Your Daddy': The Horrors of War, Part Two," 210–27.

5. Ideological concerns are not the only framework in which 1950s cinema operates. For one, there is the fact that Hollywood, since the 1930 and certainly throughout the

1950s, has been making films under the auspices of the Motion Picture Production Code. There is also the shake-up of the industrial landscape that came with the Paramount Decision in 1948, the antitrust legislation that forced Hollywood studios to divest themselves from their theatrical distribution networks, reshuffling the power structure in a way that would give rise to the independent producer.

6. Commenting on the opening credit sequence of the television series *The Outer Limits*, Rick Worland has pointed out that the "disembodied Control Voice [addressing the viewer directly] becomes a threatening presence from the outside world that forcible seizes our television set right in our homes where we though [sic] we were safe, and commands us in authoritarian fashion to 'sit quietly and we will control all that you see and hear'" (Worland, "Sign-Posts up Ahead" 111). While this device played directly to the interpellative power of television itself—quite in opposition to warmth with which it was welcomed by a steadily increasing audience—it linked these media-specific anxieties to the "Emergency Broadcast System tests and announcements with which Americans had become uneasily familiar" after the system had been established "by President Truman at the behest of the Defense Department in October 1951, amidst fear that combat in Korea might escalate into a disastrous U.S./Soviet clash" (Worland 111).

7. For further information, see also Joel Frazier and Harry Hawthorne, "20,000 Leagues Under the Sea: The Filming of Jules Verne's Classic Science Fiction Novel," *Cinefantastique* 14 (May 1984): 32–53.

8. In an interview with Tom Weaver, Robert Wise recounts Pentagon disapproval of *The Day the Earth Stood Still*, forcing the production to use National Guard equipment (Weaver 55).

9. Cooperation between the military and the media would be carried over to television as well. "Military experts were loaned out to shows with military themes, weaponry and soldiers were on call for battle reenactments, and special help was offered to network news programs" (Engelhardt 76).

10. Blair Davis draws attention to the fact that the seamless integration of stock footage also depended on which budgetary level of filmmaking is using the practice. "High-end Bs are normally able to disguise the use of stock footage more easily than lower-tier Bs," Davis argues. "Larger budgets allow for the creation of more seamless transitions between the stock shots and regular footage [. . .] The use of stock shots in middle- and low-end Bs is often quite jarring because of their failure to convincingly suture the stock footage into the film" (177).

11. Michael J. Shapiro raises the question of what exactly constitutes "military" stock footage; whereas, for example, the case of combat footage is fairly unambiguous, Shapiro wonders whether footage of Robert McNamara holding a press conference in Errol Morris's *The Fog of War* would qualify as military stock footage as well (*Cinematic Geopolitics* 75–83).

12. It is worth noting that much of the stock footage in *Atomic Submarine* was originally shot for a World War II film, Delmer Daves's 1943 *Destination Tokyo*, and was acquired for subsequent reuse by Alex Gordon, the producer of *The Atomic Submarine* (Alex Gordon, Commentary Track).

13. It is also important to note that the angle is not directly 90 degrees but remains slightly tilted, presumably because the footage was shot from airplane windows and doors, suggesting civilian planes, rather than through a literal bombing sight, which would allow a straight downward look at the ground below.

14. Mark Harris credits specifically John Ford's propaganda film *The Battle of Midway* (1942) with creating this aesthetic. "The juddering, jolting, damaged images captured at Midway had, it turned out, created a new standard for realism in which, for the first time, lack of polish was taken as a benchmark of veracity" (173). It would not even take until the end of the war, Harris points out, for filmmakers to turn these features into stylistic tools that could be used in exactly those cases from which actual historical veracity would be missing.

15. See, for example, C. L. Moore's *Doomsday Morning*, with its "Five Days' War" (qtd. in Newell and Lamont, "Rugged Domesticity" 434).

16. Extrapolating these attitudes half a decade into the future, it is hardly a stretch to hear John F. Kennedy's inaugural address in January 1961 in which he would admonish his audience, "Ask not what your country can do for you—ask what you can do for your country!"

17. Kim Newman has pointed out that, just as "World War II remains the central metaphor of most mass invasions" (123), films about alien occupation following the successful invasion "borrow heavily from the resistance-and-collaboration clichés developed during the war" (124).

18. In the immediate postwar years, war films "had become box-office poison, and from 1945 to 1949 Hollywood virtually stopped making them" (Biskind, *Seeing is Believing* 59). This initial disinterest transformed itself into a slightly more sublimated form of disavowal and displacement. "Then came Korea, the answer to a prayer. The fresh crop of fifties war films started hopefully, even nostalgically [with many war films, however, still] set in World War II (a more compelling war than Korea)" (*Seeing is Believing* 59).

19. In his account of postwar labor strife, Thomas Childers itemizes the industries affected: "in November 1945, [. . .] 320,000 automobile workers walked out on General Motors" (207). In May of that year, "coal miners went out, followed by electrical workers and meatpackers. Later than month, the country experienced a national railroad strike; 250,000 workers walked off the job, shutting down rail traffic all across the country" (208). In line with my own larger argument about the militarization of American life, Truman "reacted by seizing control of the railroads, threatening to use the Army as strikebreakers and to draft the strikers into the military" (208).

Chapter Two

1. Cashing in on the previous year's *I Was a Teenage Werewolf*, also directed by Gene Fowler, and *I Was a Teenage Frankenstein* (Herbert L. Strock), the title also alludes to anti-communist films like *I Was a Communist for the FBI* (Gordon Douglas, 1951), highlighting the film's political allegory of space aliens as Soviet fifth columnists.

2. The three remakes of Don Siegel's original film are far more explicit about the original human body being turned into refuse. While Philip Kaufman's version (1978)

features garbage trucks quietly hauling away the human remains, Siegel's film remains somewhat cagey about showing or explaining what happens to the original bodies. Stephen King has also pointed out that Kaufman goes a long way in emphasizing the abject nature of the alien impostors, citing a "repulsively horrible" moment when an impostor's "face breaks in with sickening ease, like a rotted piece of fruit" (King, *Danse Macabre* 5).

3. David A. Smith reads widespread and hyperbolic, or even hysterical, American conceptions of "Soviet leaders [having established] mind control over their subjects" (219) as a form of psychological transfer. In the course of this transfer, anxieties about postwar America in the throes of "rapid technological change, standardization, bureaucratization, and gigantism" (Smith 225) are embodied in an assembly of negative images that make up the portrait of the ideological enemy. The parts of this composite that Smith assembles from bestsellers, advertising, and nonfiction of the period have all the trademarks of the alien impostor, from the dull, glassy stare to the robotic movement, lack of emotion, and absence of conventional morality.

4. J. Hoberman traces this compensatory fantasy back to another narrative rooted deep in American mythology. "In popular culture, brainwashing was the post-Korean War Korean War scenario. The notion of the brainwashed American prisoner tapped into the most deep-rooted of national myths, expressed in the late seventeenth- and early eighteenth-century New England 'captivity narratives,' wherein white settlers—usually women—were abducted by Indians and even went native" (307–308).

5. For further discussion, especially in regard to hypnotism as a theme aligned with cinematic audience interpellation in science fiction films throughout the 1950s, see Kevin Heffernan, "The Hypnosis Horror Films of the 1950s: Genre Texts and Industrial Contexts" (2000).

6. Wilson's sentimentalization of this wartime romance and its resulting illegitimate child back in Italy—a child for whose support the novel's main character eventually gains his own wife's willing cooperation—bring to the forefront a narrative that replays on a personal scale the political narrative of the Marshall Plan. As this wartime romance and its resolution are taking center stage, edging out another part of the novel's war memories that foregrounds physical and mental trauma, they also help to suppress more radical issues like wartime atrocities suffered by, but also committed by, US troops during the liberation of Italy. While Sloan Wilson's Tom Rath must fight the occasional irrational impulse to burst into violence ("He had a sudden, immediately controlled impulse to Kill Ogden. He knew just how he could do it" [Wilson 113]), he also tells himself that the war "was incomprehensible and had to be forgotten" (96).

7. Other scenes that show the replacement of humans with alien impostors take place in the film's city setting, in transitional non-spaces like back alleys and abandoned nighttime streets that provide the urban equivalent of the opening scene's country road.

8. "Critical attitudes toward military service, in fact, helped explain why enlistment lagged in the late 1940s and why the armed forces were forced to offer better benefits and take steps to moderate the deep division between officers and enlisted men that

characterized the war years" (Bodnar 72–73). As an example of the conflicting forces surrounding the veteran, Bodnar discusses the rivalry between the more left-leaning American Veteran's Committee (AVC) and the more conservative, hawkish American Legion and the Veterans of Foreign Wars, which were to advocate not only strong Cold War anti-communist stances but also fell behind on broader issues of social equality and justice (e.g., the active recruitment of African American veterans). See Bodnar, 69–71.

9. Incidentally, another issue of *Life* (July 23, 1945, 55–59) published not much earlier had featured an article entitled "Divorce Mill: Los Angeles Frees Many more Mismatched Couples Than Reno," that reflected, in surprisingly sympathetic terms, the rising divorce rate attributed to "mismatched" wartime marriages, a term broad enough to include marriages troubled by the psychological problems of the husband returned from the war.

10. In his characterization of the issue, Mark Harris goes one step further: "In the press [in 1945] much of the coverage of veterans tended toward lurid examples of what the historian Joseph Goulden called 'The War-Crazed Veteran theory . . . the following [headlines] were not atypical: 'Veteran Beheads Wife with Jungle Machete,' 'Ex-Marine Held in Rape Murder,' 'Sailor Son Shoots Father'" (Harris, *Five Came Back* 397).

11. In the closing remarks of her monograph on the film, Sarah Kozloff emphasizes what she sees the lack of closure in *The Best Years of Our Lives*: one wife's inability to prevent her husband's descent into alcoholism, another's failure to alleviate her husband's economic woes, and another's helplessness when faced with her husband's physical injuries (Kozloff 97). Though these objections capture the film's complexity, Kozloff closes her own remarks by adding, "All [these wives] can truly offer is love and acceptance" (97)—a conclusion which acknowledges the sentimental melodramatic move by which the film ultimately contains its pessimism.

12. *Quatermass II* (BBC, 1955; remade by Hammer as *Quatermass 2* [1957]) provides another such blueprint, with its extended paranoid fantasy of the alien beachhead hiding in the British countryside; this trope of alien occupation, discussed in detail in Chapter 3, would go on to be an influence on alien invasion and impostor films like *Invaders from Mars* and *Invasion of the Body Snatchers*.

13. Howard Zinn, writing about the use of napalm by US forces during the Korean War, quotes a BBC journalist's description of its effects on the human body: "In front of us a curious figure was standing [. . .] He had no eyes, and the whole of his body, nearly all of which was visible through tatters of burnt rags, was covered with a hard black crust speckled with yellow pus . . . He had to stand because he was no longer covered with a skin, but with a crust-like crackling which broke easily" (Zinn, *People's History* 419). This description could very well be the direct inspiration to the make-up effects in a film like *First Man into Space*.

14. "It is an interesting perception of perceived pressures for closure in narratives of this period that the film's [i.e., *Invasion of the Body Snatchers*] original ending—the 'pods' taking over everywhere and our hero unable to convince anyone that the threat is real—was changed before distribution. In the distributed version the authorities accept his

story and begin to act against the invasion, a resolution in line with all other examples of this type, where victory over the invader is invariably assured" (Tudor 44).

15. Some episodes take on the issue of war trauma more directly. "The Purple Testament" (February 12, 1960) deals with a soldier during World War II who develops the ability to foretell which one among his comrades will die next in battle, while "The Encounter" (May 1, 1964) describes a random meeting of a World War II veteran with his Japanese gardener, in the course of which both characters slide back into violent behavior patterns established during the war.

Chapter Three

1. A case in point here might be the disproportionate attention paid by histories of the Korean War to the first year of the conflict (with its dramatic reversals in territorial gain and loss). This tight analytical focus comes at the expense of the prolonged bombing campaign against North Korea, which would dominate the latter period of the war but tends to drop out of the picture. David Halberstam's *The Coldest Winter* would be one example of this recurring pattern.

2. Clifford Simak's fix-up novel *City* (1952) opens with an eponymous short story that ponders the abandonment of cities as a form of organized social life as a result of new transportation and agricultural technologies. In *The Martian Chronicles* (1950), another fix-up novel, Ray Bradbury returns time and again to the trope of the abandoned city, as mass migrations from town to country and from one planet to another render cities obsolete. Jack Finney's work is, on the whole, shot through with the same nostalgia that runs through Simak and Bradbury, a nostalgia that turns to the celebration of the mythical American small town at the expense of urban life in short stories like "Of Missing Persons" (1955) and "I Love Galesburg in the Springtime" (1960).

3. Boucher explains the ranch style's antisocial stance (the houses turning "their back to the street," not having "traditional welcoming porches"), with the search for privacy by the occupants, many of whom "had grown up in overcrowded urban housing where family and neighbors were constantly present" (20).

4. Though none of these films are made by what one might call a cinematic auteur, it is important to note the role that Gordon Douglas, director of *Them!*, played in some of the other films as well. "A movie like *Them!*" Blake Lucas points out, "followed *It Came* in using [the] desert (for its first half and with a somewhat more literal effectiveness in the hands of non-specialist Gordon Douglas). Significantly, it is the setting also for the two later movies of the U-I cycle on which Arnold gets co-story credit, *Tarantula* and *The Monolith Monsters*, only the first of which he wound up directing himself" (75).

5. For a discussion of the thematic overlap between the classic Indian Captivity Narrative and modern stories about alien abduction, see Michael Sturma, "Aliens and Indians," *Journal of Popular Culture* (November 2002).

6. "Still others have deciphered the genre beneath the disguise of the road movie [. . .] These arguments depend on the trick of promoting a key component of the genre—its

operation as morality play, its journey structure—to the status of a defining feature of the form" (Kitses 3).

7. The intersection of both genres could be quite jarring, as Hoberman notes: Andre De Toth's "*Springfield Rifle* was mainly shot on location in the Sierra Nevada, where production had to be halted one day when a mushroom cloud appeared on the horizon. (Across the state line, the army was testing tactical nuclear weapons)" (Hoberman 212).

8. Reemes lists as a "particularly clever example" of Arnold's "confident and inventive *mise en scene*" the recreation of the desert on set. "Built on Stage 12," Reemes recounts, "the largest on the lot, the set used forced perspective to create the illusion of a distant horizon" (29). Although Reemes does not go into detail about the use or significance of the desert setting, she describes a specific scene in which the desert setting allows for a horizon shot of a character with "eerie and frightening implication[s]" (29). Here and elsewhere in Reemes's account of Arnold's use of setting, atmosphere is the predominant factor, just as eeriness is the prevailing mood (79). She quotes Arnold, defending his use of setting as a way of involving the audience in an atmosphere that overrides their difficulties in suspending disbelief in regard to a preposterous (science-) fictional premise: "That's why I like to shoot in the desert or ocean beaches, locations that will help me create an atmosphere. Most of *It Came from Outer Space* was shot in the desert. I looked for places in the desert that engulfed me in an atmosphere and that is where I would shoot" (Arnold qtd. in Reemes 203).

9. For a full discussion of the link between increasing incentives for automotive travel, geographic mapping, and Cold War paranoia in popular culture, see Hantke, "The Road Movie on Television, and the Cold War Mapping of America: *Route 66, The Fugitive, The Invaders,*" *Journal of Popular Film & Television* (2014).

10. The series' iconography would reverberate through later decades' worth of horror and science fiction films. Similar images of inconspicuous buildings that serve as entrances to vast governmental facilities also appear in *The Satan Bug* (John Sturges, 1965) and *The Andromeda Strain* (Robert Wise, 1971), just as the underground missile bases in films like *Twilight's Last Gleaming* (Robert Aldrich, 1977) or *The Day After* (Nicholas Meyer, 1983) follow the same iconography.

11. Biskind argues that the film is eager to abandon its southwestern settings: "*Them!* goes on to build this whisper of regional rivalry [between "the desert of the Southwest" and the "federal authority from the East"] into a structural contrast by cutting between shots of desert locales, with the ants wreaking havoc [. . .], and shots of Washington, D.C. When the dry, dusty landscape of the Southwest fades away and the U.S. Capitol Building [. . .] fades in, we breathe a sigh of relief" (123–24).

12. In a discussion *of Invaders from Mars*, Rob Latham has pointed out that 1950s suburbanization, with its segregation along lines of class and race, contributed to the defusing of conflicts at odds with the interest of the military-industrial complex. The "need for a vigilant military-industrial complex—one which itself strongly undergirds suburban life in its provision of jobs for middle-class professionals" (Latham 200)—is displaced onto the presence of the alien ship concealed underground yet increasingly

dominating social and institutional interactions within the community. In emphasizing the similarities between the Martians and the military-industrial complex, Latham lays the groundwork for a reading of suburban space in the light of surveillance and occupation that aligns itself with the one outlined in this chapter specifically in regard to the southwestern desert.

13. Hoberman reads the Indian territory surrounding the film's eponymous military base as a complex imaginary space on which a variety of thematic forces converge. On the one hand, it is staging area for "a vision of total mobilization with an appropriate emphasis on order and eternal vigilance: militarized suburbia" (79). On the other hand, he also sees in the film "a new fascination with the post-atomic southwestern landscape [being] set in a mobilized world and dominated by the personalities of rival military leaders" (77), a Cold War battleground in which the lack of clear borders and boundaries is projected onto the emptiness of the southwestern landscape.

14. Engelhardt refers to these extremes as "inclusionary" and "exclusionary" modes of the same discourse. On the one hand, "exclusionary villains came from the other side of borders previously unimagined and unerringly headed for (or burst to life in) the United States with mayhem in mind [. . .] On the other hand, in the inclusionary mode, similar beasts or robots or space aliens turned out to be, if not lovable, then far wiser than Americans [. . .] The exclusionary films were apocalyptic and hysterical about them; the inclusionary ones about us" (Engelhardt 102).

Chapter Four

1. Ironically enough, the complementary term—the "ugly American"—would have already entered the public debate thanks to Eugene Burdick and William Lederer's 1958 novel by the same title.

2. J. P. Telotte makes the same argument about the cinematic adaptation of the Jules Verne novel *20,000 Leagues Under the Sea*: "While the film shifts the action's location from the world's various oceans and seas solely to the South Pacific, in part to capitalize on a general postwar fascination with the region, but also to evoke recent atomic testing there, which had lately drawn national headlines" (68). Needless to say, the South Pacific was already familiar to a mid-1950s audience that had followed the US campaign "island hopping" its way toward the Japanese islands in the course of World War II.

3. In contrast, Susan Sontag calls Pal "technically the most convincing and visually the most exciting" of all directors working in science fiction at the time, capable of raising the genre "to another level" (102)—no small praise from a critic of Sontag's caliber.

4. Nonetheless, Palumbo has devoted another article to tracing some of the mythical implications of Pal's film; see Palumbo, "The Monomyth in Time Travel Films," 211–18.

5. While *The Time Machine* has moved away from concerns about social class, other films from the period do return to this category, sometimes in ways that are reminiscent of Wells's Eloi and Morlocks. In *This Island Earth* (Joseph M. Newman, 1955), for example, the alien society of Metaluna is divided into an ethereal, highly intellectual upper class

and a monstrous working class. Like Wells and Pal, Newman eventually reveals that what at first appeared like a sublimely confident upper class exercises very little control over its own fate, living in fear of the working class it has created. In its attention to social class, Newman's film operates far more in the spirit of Wells than Pal's does.

6. For a detailed discussion of the teenage demographic in 1950s cinema audiences, see Blair Davis, "Hollywood in Transition: The Business of 1950s Filmmaking," in *The Battle for the Bs*, 19–42.

7. While other genres, like the Western, are commenting on race relations and the civil rights movement during the 1950s, science fiction films are oddly quiet on the issue. Race matters might be legible in the allegorical subtext of some films from the cycle, but they most certainly are not an explicit part of the cycle's overall political agenda. Though the Hollywood star system did produce notable African American actors at the time—such as Sidney Poitier, Paul Robeson, and Harry Belafonte—Belafonte is the only one who was to appear in a science fiction film: *The World, the Flesh, and the Devil* (Ranald MacDougall, 1959). Not surprisingly, the film deploys its post-nuclear survival scenario primarily as a means of examining race in America, and thus may have taken its cue from an earlier post-apocalyptic survival film, Arch Oboler's low-budget production *Five* (1951, distributed by Columbia Pictures), which features among its eponymous band of survivors one African American character. The conspicuous whiteness of the Eloi in *The Time Machine*, whatever its other allegorical functions may be, thus serves to suppress the racial dimension of the material, a dimension in which the treatment of native populations abroad by the US serves to comment directly on the treatment of the US' African American population at home. US administrations from Eisenhower to Kennedy were acutely aware of how domestic race conflicts were detracting from the US' claims to democratic equality in its bid for global markets. If critics of the film decrying its erasure of H. G. Wells's class politics have little to say about the film's racial politics—or, for that matter, about the racial politics of the entire cinematic cycle the film is part of—it is not a matter of reiterating the film's erasure of the issue. Rather, it is a reflection of the entire cycle's disinterest in the issue. As the 1960s progressed, a later generation of science fiction film would begin to tackle the racial theme directly, which had been too sensitive for the 1950s. It would take almost a decade for Richard Matheson's 1954 novel *I am Legend* to morph from the very white *The Last Man on Earth* (Ubaldo Ragona, 1964) into the racially conscious *The Omega Man* (Boris Sagal, 1971). For a broader discussion of race in Cold War cinema, see Tony Shaw, "Turning a Negative into a Positive," *Hollywood's Cold War* (2007), 167–98; for breaking new ground in reading race in 1950s science fiction films, see Patrick Gonder, "Like a Monstrous Jigsaw Puzzle: Genetics and Race in Horror Films of the 1950s" (2003): 33–44.

8. Several critics have commented on the cyclical model of historiography in Wells, adopted by Pal and Duncan for the film. See, for example, Renzi, 9–12, or Palumbo, "Politics of Entropy," 204–11.

9. One illustration of this attitude would be an "official survey, taken in the spring of 1958 [which] revealed that fewer than half of the State Department's foreign service

officers had the ability to speak a foreign language" (Kaplan 125). Incidentally, Eugene Burdick and William Lederer's novel *The Ugly American* was published in 1958.

10. For a brief working definition of the critical terminology, as well as bibliographic references to more detailed discussions of classic Hollywood narrative, see Susan Hayward, "Oedipal trajectory," *Cinema Studies: The Key Concepts*, 261–63.

11. Kennedy's Peace Corps initiative would try to take the necessary steps to ensure that volunteers would go out into the world carefully prepped. Still, as a matter of historical accuracy, it is important to note that the Kennedy administration supplemented this initiative with a political refocusing of the US Army's School of the Americas in Fort Benning, Georgia, toward the goals of training for anti-communist counterinsurgency in aid of Third World regimes. Many of these regimes would, subsequently, come under intense scrutiny for human rights abuses. David Ryan also identifies the US exporting its cultural products to the Third World as a strategy somewhere between integration and containment. To the degree that the "construction of cultural narratives was fundamental to facilitate [the] extension of US power" (53), it also allowed those profiting from such construction to cast their own motives and objectives in a more favorable light. Consequently, US "concepts of leadership, responsibility and manifest destiny echoed the paternalistic language of nineteenth-century imperialism, but avoided its explicit characterisation" (53). Whether, ultimately, the relationship between the more aggressive "containment" policies and the more conciliatory "integration" policies were supplementary or contradictory remains for historians to argue.

12. See, for example, Spencer Weart, *Nuclear Fears: A History of Images* (Cambridge: Harvard University Press, 1988) or Patrick Mannix, *The Rhetoric of Antinuclear Fiction: Persuasive Strategies in Novels and Films* (Lewisburg, PA: Bucknell University Press, 1992).

Conclusion

1. For a more detailed discussion of the end of the 1950s cycle, see Hantke, "Science Fiction and Horror in the 1950s," in *A Companion to the Horror Film*, ed. Harry Benshoff, 255–76.

2. At the time of this writing, the most recent extension of the term comes from journalist Shane Harris with his book on national cybersecurity, entitled *@War: The Rise of the Military-Internet Complex* (New York: Houghton Mifflin, 2014).

3. As unimaginable as this state of affairs would be in European politics, it is also revealing to consider singular exceptions. The military service of the male members of the British royal family, for example, points to a more symbolic or ornamental function of the military within the (democratic) political imaginary of European nations.

4. Dixon's own take on the 1950s clearly follows the lead of the decade's science fiction films: "The 1950s were a complex decade but a decade that was ultimately dominated, especially between 1950 and 1955, by an almost unquestioning acceptance of the status

quo and reified by a culture of fear and air-raid drills, similar to the 'terror alerts' of the early twenty-first century" (*Lost in the Fifties* 185).

5. In a public talk about the work of Philip K. Dick, Jonathan Lethem has argued that Scott's *Alien* established one of the two default settings of Hollywood science fiction ever since: the science fiction film as horror film (he traces the other setting back to James Cameron's *Terminator* films: the science fiction film as action spectacle). As original as *Alien* might be in many ways, I think the case can be made that it gets its central conceit— the one appreciated by Lethem—from its 1950s predecessors. For the full discussion, see Lethem, "The Literary Imagination."

6. For an example of such political maneuvering without a clear political resolution, see Hantke, "Bush's America and the Return of Cold War Science Fiction: Alien Invasion in *Invasion*, *Threshold*, and *Surface*" (Fall 2010): 143–51.

Works Cited

Althusser, Louis. "Ideology and Ideological State Apparatuses (Notes Toward an Investigation)." 1970. Accessed December 3, 2014. <http://www.marxists.org/reference/archive/althusser/1970/ideology.htm>.
Appel, John. "Incidents of Neuropsychiatric Disorders in the United States Army in World War II." *American Journal of Psychiatry* 102.4 (1946): 433–36.
Appy, Christian G. "'We'll Follow the Old Man': The Strains of Sentimental Militarism in Popular Films of the Fifties." In *Rethinking Cold War Culture*, eds. Peter J. Kuznick and James Gilbert. Washington: Smithsonian Books, 2001. 74–105.
Bacevich, Andrew J. *The New American Militarism: How Americans Are Seduced by War*. New York: Oxford University Press, 2005.
———. and Lewis Lapham. 28 June, 2006. Audio recording. Lannan Podcasts. <http://podcast.lannan.org/2006/07/06/andrew-j-bacevich-with-lewislapham/>.
Bapis, Elaine M. *Camera and Action: American Film as Agent of Social Change, 1965–1975*. Jefferson, NC: McFarland, 2008.
Beck, David. *Dirty Wars: Landscape, Power, and Waste in Western American Literature*. Lincoln: University of Nebraska Press, 2009.
Benshoff, Harry, and Sean Griffin. *America on Film: Representing Race, Class, Gender, and Sexuality at the Movies*. Second edition. Malden, MA: Wiley-Blackwell, 2009.
———. *Monsters in the Closet: Homosexuality and the Horror Film*. Manchester: Manchester University Press, 1997.
Berger, Roger A. "'Ask What You Can Do for Your Country': The Film Version of H. G. Wells's *Time Machine* and the Cold War." *Literature/Film Quarterly* 17.3 (1989): 177–87.
Biskind, Peter. *Seeing is Believing: How Hollywood Taught Us to Stop Worrying and Love the Fifties*. New York: Pantheon, 1983.
Bodnar, John. *The 'Good War' in American Memory*. Baltimore: Johns Hopkins University Press, 2010.
Booker, Keith M. *Monsters, Mushroom Clouds, and the Cold War: American Science Fiction and the Roots of Postmodernism*. Westport, CT: Greenwood Press, 2001.
Boucher, Diane. *The 1950s American Home*. Oxford: Shire Publications, 2013.
Boyer, Paul S. *By the Bomb's Early Light: American Thought and Culture at the Dawn of the Atomic Age*. Raleigh: University of North Carolina Press, 1994.
Bradbury, Ray. *The Martian Chronicles*. New York: Doubleday, 1950.
Bronfen, Elizabeth. *Specters of War: Hollywood's Engagement with Military Conflict*. New Brunswick: Rutgers University Press, 2012.
Burdick, Eugene, and William J. Lederer. *The Ugly American*. New York: McGraw-Hill, 1958.

———. and Harvey Wheeler. *Fail Safe*. New York: McGraw-Hill, 1962.

Buruma, Ian. *Year Zero: A History of 1945*. New York: Penguin, 2013.

Carter, Dale. *The Final Frontier: The Rise and Fall of the American Rocket State*. London/New York: Verso, 1988.

Childers, Thomas. *Soldier from the War Returning: The Greatest Generation's Troubled Homecoming from World War II*. Boston/New York: Houghton Mifflin, 2009.

Chomsky, Noam. "Cold War: Fact and Fancy." In *Deterring Democracy*. New York: Hill & Wang, 1991. 9–68.

"Chronology of U.S. Military Interventions." *Give War a Chance*. PBS, *Frontline*. Accessed December 8, 2011. <www.pbs.org/wgbh/pages/frontline/shows/ military/>.

Cornea, Christine. *Science Fiction Cinema: Between Fantasy and Reality*. Edinburgh: Edinburgh University Press, 2007.

Davis, Blair. *The Battle for the Bs: 1950s Hollywood and the Rebirth of Low-Budget Cinema*. New Brunswick: Rutgers University Press, 2012.

"Declaration on Granting Independence to Colonial Countries and Peoples, 1960." Modern History Sourcebook: United Nations. Accessed May 28, 2008. <http://www.fordham.edu/halsall/mod/1960-un-colonialism.html>.

"Divorce Mill: Los Angeles Frees Many More Mismatched Couples Than Reno." *Life* (July 23, 1945): 55–59.

Dixon, Wheeler Winston. *Lost in the Fifties: Recovering Phantom Hollywood*. Carbondale: Southern Illinois University Press, 2005.

Doherty, Thomas. *Cold War, Cool Medium: Television, McCarthyism, and American Culture*. New York: Columbia University Press, 2003.

"Eisenhower Doctrine." Modern History Sourcebook: President Eisenhower: The Eisenhower Doctrine on the Middle East, A Message to Congress, January 5, 1957. Accessed May 26, 2008. <http://www.fordham.edu/halsall/mod/1957eisenhowerdoctrine.html>.

Engelhardt, Tom. *The End of Victory Culture: Cold War America and the Disillusioning of a Generation*. New York: HarperCollins, 1995. Revised edition. Amherst: University of Massachusetts Press, 2007.

Evans, Joyce A. *Celluloid Mushroom Clouds: Hollywood and the Atomic Bomb*. Westview Press: Boulder, 1998.

Finney, Jack. "I Love Galesburg in the Springtime." 1960. In *About Time: Twelve Stories by Jack Finney*. New York: Simon & Schuster, 1986. 17–36.

———. "Of Missing Persons." 1955. In *About Time: Twelve Stories by Jack Finney*. New York: Simon & Schuster, 1986. 75–93.

Frazier, Joel, and Harry Hawthorne. "*20,000 Leagues Under the Sea*: The Filming of Jules Verne's Classic Science Fiction Novel." *Cinefantastique* 14 (May 1984): 32–53.

Gaddis, John Lewis. *The Cold War*. New York: Penguin, 2005.

Gannon, Charles A. "Silo Psychosis: Diagnosing America's Nuclear Anxieties Through Narrative Imagery." In *Imagining Apocalypse: Studies in Cultural Crisis*, ed. David Seed. New York: St. Martin's Press, 2000. 103–118.

Genter, Robert. "'Hypnotizzy' in the Cold War: The American Fascination with Hypnotism in the 1950s." *Journal of American* Culture 29.2 (June 2006): 154–69.
Goin, Peter. "The Nuclear Past in the Landscape Present." In *Atomic Culture: How We Learned to Stop Worrying and Love the Bomb*, eds. Scott C. Zeman and Michael A. Amundson. Boulder: University Press of Colorado, 2004. 81–101.
Gonder, Patrick. "Like a Monstrous Jigsaw Puzzle: Genetics and Race in Horror Films of the 1950s." *Velvet Light Trap* 52 (Fall 2003): 33–44.
Gordon, Alex. Commentary Track. *The Atomic Submarine*. 1959. Criterion Collection, 2007.
Halberstam, David. *The Coldest Winter*. London: Pan MacMillan, 2007.
———. *The Fifties*. New York: Random House, 1993.
Hantke, Steffen. "Bush's America and the Return of Cold War Science Fiction: Alien Invasion in *Invasion, Threshold,* and *Surface*." *Journal of Popular Film & Television* 38.3 (Fall 2010): 143–51.
———. "Military Culture." In *The Oxford Handbook of Science Fiction*. London/New York: Oxford University Press, 2014. 329–39.
———. "The Return of the Giant Creature: *Cloverfield* and the Political Opposition to the War on Terror." *Extrapolation* 51.2 (Fall 2010): 235–57.
———. "The Road Movie on Television, and the Cold War Mapping of America: *Route 66, The Fugitive, The Invaders*." *Journal of Popular Film & Television* (2014).
———. "Science Fiction and Horror in the 1950s." In *A Companion to the Horror Film*, ed. Harry Benshoff. New York/London: Wiley-Blackwell, 2014. 255–76.
Haraway, Donna. *Modest_Witness@Second_Millennium.FemaleMan_Meets_OncoMouse*. New York/London: Routledge, 1997.
Harris, Mark. *Five Came Back: A Story of Hollywood and the Second World War*. New York: Penguin, 2014.
Hayward, Susan. "Oedipal trajectory." In *Cinema Studies: The Key Concepts*. Second edition. 2001. London/New York: Routledge, 2000. 261–63.
Heffernan, Kevin. "The Hypnosis Horror Films of the 1950s: Genre Texts and Industrial Contexts." *Journal of Film and Video* 54.2/3 (Summer/Fall 2002): 56–70.
Hendershot, Cynthia. *Anti-Communism and Popular Culture in Mid-Century America*. Jefferson, NC: McFarland, 2003.
Hersey, John. *Hiroshima*. First published in the *New Yorker* in August 1946. New York: Alfred A. Knopf, 1985.
Hoberman, J. *An Army of Phantoms: American Movies and the Making of the Cold War*. London/New York: The New Press, 2011.
Hollings, Ken. Personal email. February 28, 2014.
———. *Welcome to Mars*. <https://archive.org/details/Welcome_to_Mars>.
Huntington, John. *The Logic of Fantasy: H. G. Wells and Science Fiction*. New York: Columbia University Press, 1982.
Jancovich, Mark. *Rational Fears: American Horror in the 1950s*. Manchester/New York: Manchester University Press, 1996.
"Jellied Gasoline." *Life* 19.2 (July 9, 1945): 47–48, 50.

Johnson, Chalmers. *Blowback: The Costs and Consequences of American Empire*. New York: Henry Holt, 2000.

———. *The Sorrows of Empire: Militarism, Secrecy, and the End of the Republic*. New York: Metropolitan, 2004.

Judt, Tony. *Postwar: A History of Europe since 1945*. 2005. London: Vintage, 2010.

Kaes, Anton. *Shell Shock Cinema: Weimar Culture and the Wounds of War*. Princeton, NJ: Princeton University Press, 2009.

Kaplan, Fred. *1959: The Year Everything Changed*. Hoboken, NJ: John Wiley & Sons, 2009.

King, Stephen. *Danse Macabre*. New York: Berkley Books, 1981.

Kitses, Jim. *Horizons West: Directing the Western from John Ford to Clint Eastwood*. London: BFI Publishing, 2004.

Klein, Christina. *Cold War Orientalism: Asia in the Middlebrow Imagination, 1945–1961*. Berkeley: University of California Press, 2003.

Kozloff, Sarah. *The Best Years of Our Lives*. BFI Film Classics. London: Palgrave Macmillan, 2011.

Latham, Rob. "Subterranean Suburbia: Underneath the Smalltown Myth in the Two Versions of *Invaders from Mars*." *Science Fiction Studies* 66.2/2 (July 1995): 198–208.

Lawrence, John Shelton. "Filmography." In *Why We Fought: America's Wars in Film and History*, eds. Peter C. Rollins and John E. O'Connor. Lexington: University Press of Kentucky, 2008. 529–65.

Leane, Elizabeth. "Locating the Thing: The Antarctic as Alien Space in John W. Campbell's 'Who Goes There?'" *Science Fiction Studies* 32.2 (July 2005): 225–39.

Ledbetter, James. *Unwarranted Influence: Dwight D. Eisenhower and the Military-Industrial Complex*. New Haven/London: Yale University Press, 2011.

Lenihan, John H. *Showdown: Confronting Modern America in the Western Film*. Urbana/Chicago: University of Illinois Press, 1980.

Lethem, Jonathan. "The Literary Imagination: Jonathan Lethem and Kim Stanley Robinson on Philip K. Dick." Youtube.com. Posted June 27, 2013. <http:// www.youtube.com/ watch?v=EcaQmNyxGPs>.

Lev, Peter. *The Fifties: Transforming the Screen, 1950–1959*, ed. Peter Lev. Berkeley: University of California Press, 2003.

Lewis, Tom. *Divided Highways: Building the Interstate Highways, Transforming American Lives*. New York: Viking, 1997.

Lingeman, Richard. *The Noir Forties: The American People from Victory to Cold War*. New York: Nation Books, 2012.

Lucas, Blake. "U-I Sci-Fi: Studio Aesthetics and 1950s Metaphysics." In *The Science Fiction Film Reader*, ed. Gregg Rickman. New York: Limelight, 2004. 68–98.

Luciano, Warren. *Them Or Us: Archetypal Interpretations of Fifties Alien Invasion Films*. Bloomington: Indiana University Press, 1987.

Mannix, Patrick. *The Rhetoric of Antinuclear Fiction: Persuasive Strategies in Novels and Films*. Lewisburg, PA: Bucknell University Press, 1992.

Masco, Joseph. *The Nuclear Borderlands: The Manhattan Project in Post-Cold War New Mexico*. Princeton, NJ: Princeton University Press, 2006.

May, Elaine Tyler. *Homeward Bound: American Families in the Cold War Era*. New York: Basic Books, 1988.
Mills, C. Wright. *The Power Elite*. 1956. Oxford: Oxford University Press, 2000.
Nadel, Alan. *Containment Culture: American Narratives, Postmodernism, and the Atomic Age*. Durham/London: Duke University Press, 1995.
Newell, Dianne, and Victoria Lamont. "Rugged Domesticity: Frontier Mythology in Post Armageddon Science Fiction by Women." *Science Fiction Studies* 32.3 (November 2005): 423–41.
Newman, Kim. *Apocalypse Movies: End of the World Cinema*. New York: St. Martin's, 2000.
O'Donnell, Victoria. "Science Fiction Films and Cold War Anxiety." In *The Fifties: Transforming the Screen, 1950–1959*, ed. Peter Lev. Berkeley: University of California Press, 2003. 169–97.
Old Gold. Advertisement. *Life* 19.6 (August 6, 1945): 77.
Palumbo, Donald E. "The Monomyth in Time Travel Films." In *The Celebration of the Fantastic: Selected Papers from the Tenth Anniversary International Conference on the Fantastic in the Arts*, eds. Donald Morse, Marshall B. Tymn, and Bertha Csilla. Westport, CT: Greenwood, 1992. 211–18.
———. "The Politics of Entropy: Revolution vs. Evolution in George Pal's 1960 Film Version of H. G. Wells's *The Time Machine*." In *Modes of the Fantastic: Selected Essays from the Twelfth International Conference on the Fantastic in the Arts*, eds. Robert Latham and Robert Collins. Westport, CT: Greenwood, 1995. 204–11.
"Post-Traumatic Stress Disorder (PTSD)." National Institute of Mental Health. January 3, 2013. <http://www.nimh.nih.gov/health/publications/post-traumatic-stress-disorder-ptsd/index.shtml>.
Prince, Stephen. *Firestorm: American Film in the Age of Terrorism*. New York: Columbia University Press, 2009.
Rabkin, Eric. *The Fantastic in Literature*. Princeton, NJ: Princeton University Press, 1976.
Reemes, Dana M. *Directed by Jack Arnold*. Jefferson, NC: McFarland, 1988.
Renzi, Thomas C. *H. G. Wells: Six Scientific Romances Adapted for Film*. Second edition. Lanham, MD: Scarecrow Press, 2004.
Rolinson, Dave, and Nick Cooper. "'Bring Something Back': The Strange Career of Professor Bernard Quatermass." *Journal of Popular Film and Television* 30.3 (2002): 158–65.
Rosenberg, Aaron. "Specters of Totality: The Afterlife of the Nuclear Age." In *The Silence of Fallout: Nuclear Criticism in a Post-Cold War World*, eds. Michael Blouin, Morgan Shipley, and Jack Taylor. Newcastle: Cambridge Scholars Publishing, 2013. 45–58.
Rugh, Susan Sessions. *Are We There Yet?: The Golden Age of American Family Vacations*. Lawrence: University Press of Kansas, 2008.
Ryan, David. "Mapping Containment: The Cultural Construction of the Cold War." In *American Cold War Culture*, ed. Douglas Field. Edinburgh: Edinburgh University Press, 2005. 50–69.
Said, Edward W. *Culture and Imperialism*. New York: Vintage, 1993.
Schatz, Thomas. *Boom and Bust: American Cinema in the 1940s*. History of the American Cinema. Volume 6: 1940–1949. Berkeley/Los Angeles: University of California Press, 1997.

Schlosser, Eric. *Command and Control: Nuclear Weapons, the Damascus Accident, and the Illusion of Safety*. New York: Random House, 2013.

Sebald, W. G. *Luftkrieg und Literatur/On the Natural History of Destruction*. 1999. Frankfurt: Fischer, 2001.

Seed, David. *American Science Fiction and the Cold War*. Chicago/London: Fitzroy Dearborn, 1999.

Shapiro, Jerome F. *Atomic Bomb Cinema: The Apocalyptic Imagination on Film*. New York/London: Routledge, 2004.

Shapiro, Michael J. *Cinematic Geopolitics*. London/New York: Routledge, 2009.

Shaw, Tony. *Hollywood's Cold War*. Edinburgh: Edinburgh University Press, 2007.

———. and Denis J. Youngblood. *Cinematic Cold War: The American and Soviet Struggle for Hearts and Minds*. Lawrence: University Press of Kansas, 2010.

Simak, Clifford. *City*. New York: Gnome Press, 1952.

Skal, David. *The Horror Show: A Cultural History of Horror*. New York: Penguin, 1993.

Smith, David A. "American Nightmare: Images of Brainwashing, Thought Control, and Terror in Soviet Russia." *Journal of Popular Culture* 33.3 (2010): 217–29.

Sobchak, Vivian. *Screening Space: The American Science Fiction Film*. New Brunswick: Rutgers University Press, 1987.

Sontag, Susan. "The Imagination of Disaster." 1965. In *The Science Fiction Film Reader*, ed. Gregg Rickman. New York: Limelight, 2004. 98–114.

Sturma, Michael. "Aliens and Indians: A Comparison of Abduction and Captivity Narratives." *Journal of Popular Culture* 36.2 (November 2002): 318–34.

Telotte. "Science Fiction as 'True Life Adventure': Disney and the Case of 20,000 Miles Under the Sea." *Film & History: An Interdisciplinary Journal of Film and Television Studies* 40.2 (Fall 2010): 77–79.

Titus, Costandina A. "The Mushroom Cloud as Kitsch." In *Atomic Culture: How We Learned to Stop Worrying and Love the Bomb*, eds. Scott C. Zeman and Michael A. Amundson. Boulder: University Press of Colorado, 2004. 101–23.

Tompkins, Jane. *West of Everything: The Inner Life of Westerns*. Oxford/New York: Oxford University Press, 1992.

Tudor, Andrew. *Monsters and Mad Scientists: A Cultural History of the Horror Movie*. Oxford: Blackwell, 1989.

Valantine, Jean-Michel. *Hollywood, the Pentagon and Washington: The Movies and National Security from World War II to the Present Day*. London: Anthem Press, 2005.

Vint, Sherryl. "Who Goes There? 'Real' Men Only." *Extrapolation* 46.4 (2005): 421–38.

Warshow, Robert. "Movie Chronicle: The Westerner." In *The Immediate Experience: Movies, Comics, Theatre and Other Aspects of Popular Culture*. Cambridge/London: Harvard University Press, 2001. 105–125.

Weart, Spencer. *Nuclear Fears: A History of Images*. Cambridge: Harvard University Press, 1988.

Weaver, Tom. "*The Day the Earth Stood Still*: Interview with Robert Wise." 1988. In *The Science Fiction Film Reader*, ed. Gregg Rickman. New York: Limelight, 2004. 50–60.

Westad, Odd Arne. *The Global Cold War: Third World Interventions and the Making of Our Times*. Cambridge: Cambridge University Press, 2007.

Westfahl, Gary. "Pal, George." *Gary Westfahl's Biographical Encyclopedia of Science Fiction Film*. Accessed May 28, 2008. <http://www.sfsite.com/gary/palgo1.htm>.

Williams, Tony. "Encountering *The Thing from Another World*." *CineAction* 84 (2011): 56–61.

Wills, Garry. *Bomb Power: The Modern Presidency and the National Security State*. New York: Penguin, 2010.

Wilson, Sloan. *The Man in the Grey Flannel Suit*. 1955. New York: Thunder Mouth Press, 2002.

Worland, Rick, "OWI Meets the Monsters: Hollywood Horror Films and War Propaganda, 1942 to 1945." *Cinema Journal* 37.1 (Fall 1997): 47–65.

———. "Sign-Posts up Ahead: *The Twilight Zone*, *The Outer Limits*, and TV Political Fantasy 1959–1965." *Science Fiction Studies* 23.1 (March 1996): 103–22.

Wylie, Philip. *Tomorrow*. New York/Toronto: Rhinehart & Company, 1954.

Zinn, Howard. *A People's History of the United States: 1942–Present*. 1980. Revised and updated edition. New York: Harper Collins, 1995.

Index

abjection, 6, 8, 10, 159, 198
Adorno, Theodor, and Max Horkheimer, 172
"agit-prop," 68
Alcoholics Anonymous, 91
Alfred Hitchcock Presents, 9
Alien, 198, 219n5
Allen, Irvin: *Land of the Giants*, 57; *Lost in Space*, 157; *Time Tunnel*, 14, 57, 141–42, 157; *Voyage to the Bottom of the Sea*, 10, 57
Alligator People, The, 13
Althusser, Louis. *See* interpellation
American Century, 11, 12, 24, 50, 139, 153, 190
Andromeda Strain, The, 215n10
Appel, John, 97
Appy, Christian, 40, 207n26
Area 51, 151
Arnold, Jack: *Creature from the Black Lagoon*, 5, 162; *It Came from Outer Space*, 45, 51–52, 87, 129, 135–36, 143, 144–46, 215n8; *The Man from Bitter Ride*, 135; *Red Sundown*, 135; *Tarantula*, 8, 128, 214n4
Around the World in Eighty Days, 156
Atomic Attack, 33–34, 66
Atomic Café, The, 158, 195–96
Atomic Submarine, The, 7, 13, 155, 210n12

B-52s, 195
Bacevich, Andrew, 164, 189–90
Bad Seed, The, 10, 173
Bapis, Elaine, 133
Barker, Clive, 6
Barker, William. *See* Bridey Murphy

Battle Los Angeles, 195
Battle of Midway, 72, 211n14
Beast from 20,000 Fathoms, The, 155, 160
Beck, David, 140, 141
Bedford Incident, The, 9, 34
Beginning of the End, The, 128
Bennet, Spencer Gordon. *See Atomic Submarine, The*
Benshoff, Harry, 91, 92–93, 96
Berger, Roger, 170–72, 177
Beyond the Time Barrier, 168
Biskind, Peter, 59, 149, 159, 181–82, 204n9, 204n10, 208n28, 211n18, 215n11
Black Scorpion, The, 128, 162
Blake, Linnie, 43
Bloch, Robert, 9
Bodnar, John, 19, 93–94, 98, 212–13
Bonus March, 98
Booker, Keith M., 29, 170, 181
Boucher, Diane, 214n3
Boyer, Paul, 78, 207n24
Bradbury, Ray, 9, 125, 145, 214n2
Bridey Murphy, 91
British Film Institute, 3
Bronfen, Elisabeth, 43, 209n33
Bureau of Motion Pictures, 48
Buruma, Ian, 206n18
Bush, George W., 186, 189

Cabinet of Dr. Caligari, The, 51, 80, 110
Campbell, John W., 8, 159–60
CARE packages, 22
Carson, Rachel, 185
Carter, Dale, 25, 156
Castle, William, 51–52
Castle of Otranto, The, 4

Castro, Fidel, 13, 166
Catch 22, 124
Childers, Thomas, 211n19
children, 56–57, 173–74
Chomsky, Noam, 26–27, 42, 205n16
cinematic cycle, 3–4, 58, 185–86
Cold War, 17–28, 83, 90, 129, 158–60
Condon, Richard. See *Manchurian Candidate, The*
"containment," 25, 78–79, 167, 183
Corman, Roger, 185
Cornea, Christine, 208n29
Cronenberg, David, 6
Crowley, Aleister, 11
Cuban Missile Crisis, 25, 35, 166
Cult of the Cobra, 10, 13, 101–2
Curtis, Adam, 12

Dante, Joe, 196
Davis, Blair, 210n10, 217n6
Day After, The, 32, 215n10
Day the Earth Caught Fire, The, 10
Day the Earth Stood Still, The, 13, 16, 60, 210n8
Derrida, Jacques, 30, 34
Destination Moon, 9, 209n3
Destination Tokyo, 210n12
Dixon, Wheeler Winston, 191–92, 218n4
Doherty, Thomas, 31–32, 206n21
"Don't Fence Me In," 127
"Doom Town," 32
Douglas, Gordon: *Bombers B 52*, 9, 36, 38–39, 124, 207n26, 208n31; *I Was a Communist for the FBI*, 211n1; *Them!*, 10, 13, 45, 51–52, 53, 127–28, 142–43, 214n4, 215n11
Dow Chemicals, 188, 204n12
Dr. Strangelove, 9, 36
Duck and Cover, 181

Earth vs. the Flying Saucers, 64–65, 70
Edwards, Gareth, 200–201

Eisenhower, Dwight D., 17–20, 23, 26–27, 76, 125, 141, 172, 186, 192, 205n14; doctrine, 50, 164, 166
Emmerich, Roland, 196–97
Engelhardt, Tom, 15, 134, 139, 149, 201, 205n13, 210n9, 216n14
exclusionary/inclusionary films, 15–16, 150, 201
Evans, Joyce, 36–37, 216n14

Fail Safe (Sidney Lumet), 9, 34, 35
Fail Safe (Eugene Burdick and Henry Wheeler), 13
Federal Aid Highway Act, 125–26, 138
Fido, 200
"fifteen minute war," 74
Finney, Jack, 125, 214n2
First Man in the Moon, 156–57
First Man into Space, 13, 64, 104–5, 213n13
Five, 34, 217n7
Five Against the House, 118
"Five Days' War," 211n15
flying saucers, 11, 62–65
Forbidden Planet, 13, 142
Ford, John, 131, 142; *Fort Apache*, 147, 207n23; *The Searchers*, 115
Fordism, 8
Frankenheimer, John. See *Manchurian Candidate, The*
Frankenstein, or The Modern Prometheus, 4–5, 6
Frankenstein (James Whale), 5
Foucault, Michel, 205n15

Gaddis, John Lewis, 166
Gannon, Charles, 30
genre hybridity, 9–11, 16–17, 48–49
Genter, Robert, 90, 97
Giant Claw, The, 155, 161–62, 179
GI Bill, 98, 109
Goin, Peter, 137
Gojira, 53, 129

Gordon, Bert I., 185
Gothic tradition, 4–6, 48, 132, 149, 185

Halberstam, David: *The Coldest Winter*, 15, 205n17, 214n1; *The Fifties*, 29, 139
Halliburton, 187–88
Hammer Films, 102–3, 185, 213n12
Hantke, Steffen: "Bush's America," 219n6; "Cloverfield," 199; "Military Culture," 190; "The Road Movie," 215n9; "Science Fiction and Horror," 218n1
Harris, Mark, 209n1, 211n14, 213n10
Harris, Shane, 191, 218n2
Harvey, David, 201
Haskin, Byron: *Conquest of Space*, 9; *Robinson Crusoe on Mars*, 157, 176; *War of the Worlds*, 14, 195
Heartbreak Ridge, 208n31
Heffernan, Kevin, 51, 212n5
Hendershot, Cynthia, 203n7
Hersey, John, 206n20
Hidden Persuaders, The, 91
Hiroshima, 66, 70, 79, 206n19, 207n25
His Dark Materials, 194
historical displacement, 14
Hoberman, J., 133, 136–37, 147–48, 207n23, 212n4, 215n7, 216n13
Hollings, Ken, 11–13, 91, 191
Homeland Security Act, 191
Hooper, Tobe, 196
HUAC, 90
Hubbard, L. Ron. *See* Scientology
Huntington, John, 169–72, 175

I Am Legend: film, 199, 201; novel, 111, 217n7
I Married a Monster from Outer Space, 14, 44, 85–87, 105–6, 159, 197
Indian captivity narrative, 132, 212n4, 214n5
Innocents, The, 185
interpellation, 49–58, 86, 146

Interstellar, 209n1
Invaders, The, 88
Invaders from Mars, 14, 44–45, 55, 75, 87, 89, 107–10, 196, 215n12
Invasion of the Body Snatchers, 14, 45, 53, 55, 87, 89, 110–14, 211n2, 213n14
Invasion U.S.A., 9, 44, 62, 67–83
Island of Lost Souls, 5
It Came from Beneath the Sea, 129
It! The Terror from Beyond Space, 198
I Was a Teenage Frankenstein, 211n1
I Was a Teenage Werewolf, 211n1

Jacob's Ladder, 114
Jancovich, Mark, 8–9
Japanese internment, 141
Johnson, Chalmers, 24
Journey to the Center of the Earth, 156
Judgment at Nuremberg, 28

Kaes, Anton, 43
Kahn, Herman, 13
Kansteiner, Wulf, 41
Kaplan, E. Ann, 41
Kaplan, Fred, 11, 43, 166, 217n9
Katzman, Sam, 58
Kennedy, John F., 45, 171, 181, 189, 207n22, 211n16, 218n11
Kerry, John, 189
King, Stephen, 6, 87, 201–2, 211n2
Kinsey, Alfred, 91–92
Kitses, Jim, 132, 134, 214n6
Klein, Christina, 167–68, 181
Klein, Naomi, 201
Kneale, Nigel, 102–4
Korean War, 15, 63–64, 70–71, 73, 79–80, 90, 97–98, 205n17, 211n18, 212n4, 214n1
Kosofsky, Eve, 93
Kristol, William, 191
Krushchev, Nikita, 13
Kubrick, Stanley, 186, 209n3

Land Unknown, The, 157
Last of the Mohicans, The, 159
Latham, Rob, 215n12
Lawrence, John Shelton, 204n9
Leane, Elizabeth, 159–60
Ledbetter, James, 19, 186–89
Lenihan, John H., 133
Lethem, Jonathan, 219n5
Let There Be Light, 209n33
Lev, Peter, 132
Lewis, Tom, 125
Life magazine, 20, 21–22, 98–99, 193, 200, 204n12, 206n20, 213n9
Lingeman, Richard, 97, 99, 119–20, 206n19
Lockheed Martin, 22
Lord of the Rings, 194
Lost World, The, 45
Lowenstein, Adam, 43
Lucas, Blake, 136, 214n4
Luce, Henry. *See* American Century
Luciano, Warren, 8, 58, 61–62, 67, 72

MacArthur, Douglas, 22–23, 31, 189
Manchurian Candidate, The, 90
Manhattan Project, 31, 131–32, 139–42, 190
Man in the Grey Flannel Suit, The, 94, 100, 212n6
Mars Attacks, 196
Matheson, Richard, 9, 111, 199, 217n7
May, Elaine Tyler, 94, 96
McCain, John, 189
Menzies, William Cameron. *See Invaders from Mars; Things to Come; Whip Hand, The*
Merrill, Judith, 125
MIG fighter plane, 71
military: careers, 22–23, 189; iconography, 4; metaphysics, 20, 59, 82; remilitarization, 15
Mills, C. Wright, 19–21, 44, 59, 164
Mist, The, 201

Monolith Monsters, The, 129, 143, 146–47
Monsters versus Aliens, 199
Moore, Michael, 186
Mystery Science Theater 3000, 44, 195

Nadel, Alan, 78–79, 167, 183
napalm, 204n12, 213n13
National Guard, 60, 210n8
National Security Act, 32, 191
New Deal, 26, 83
Newman, Kim, 197, 204n10, 211n17
Niagara, 115
Night of the Demon, 10, 185
Night of the Eagle, 185
Nitze, Paul, 26, 205n16
Nixon, Richard M., 166, 189, 195, 196
NSC 68. *See* Nitze, Paul
nuclear tourism, 137–39
nuclear weapons, 28–40, 74–75, 121–23, 206n19; "tactical," 33; testing, 137–38, 206n21, 207n24

O'Donnell, Victoria, 13, 60, 129
Office of Wartime Information (OWI), 42, 48
Old Gold cigarettes, 98–99
On the Beach, 34–35
Operation Crossroads, 158, 162
Operation Ivy, 181
Outer Limits, The, 14, 210n6; "The Architects of Fear," 116–18; "The Brain of Colonel Barham," 117–18

Pal, George, 57, 153, 169–72, 216n3
Palumbo, Donald, 170–72, 216n4
Panic in the Year Zero, 34, 125
Peace Corps, 218n11
Pearl Harbor, 25, 76
Pearl Harbor (movie), 194
Peeping Tom, 185
Plan 9 from Outer Space, 58, 62–64
Planet of the Vampires, 198

Pleasantville, 197–98
post-traumatic stress disorder (PTSD), 105–6, 196
Power Elite, The. See Mills, C. Wright
Presentation of Self in Everyday Life, The, 91
Prince, Stephen, 40–41, 186, 191, 209n32
propaganda, 47–48, 57–58, 69
Psycho, 185
Psycho Beach Party, 196

Quatermass Experiment, The, 102–4
Quatermass 2, 148, 185, 213n12
Quatermass Xperiment, The, 102–4, 185

Rabkin, Eric, 203n1
RAND Corporation, 11
Rebel Without a Cause, 173
Red Dawn, 32
Red Nightmare, 144, 151
Renzi, Thomas, 170
Resident Evil, 198
Rocketship X-M, 58, 66
"rollback," 25
Rosenberg, Aaron, 30
Russell, Harold, 101, 104

Said, Edward, 205n14
Schatz, Thomas, 15, 204n9
Schlosser, Eric, 33
School of the Americas, 218n11
Scientology, 91
Sebald, W. G., 42–43
Seed, David, 90
Shapiro, Jerome, 35, 132
Shapiro, Michael J., 210n11
Shaw, Tony, 203n8; and Denis J. Youngblood, 68, 69
Shelley, Mary. *See Frankenstein, or The Modern Prometheus*
Simak, Clifford, 125, 214n2
Skal, David, 209n4

Smith, David A., 212n3
Sobchak, Vivian, 8, 203n3
Sontag, Susan, 135, 203n4, 216n3
South Pacific, 157
Star Trek, 55
stock footage, 61–62, 210n10, 210n11
Strategic Air Command, 9, 36, 38, 124, 207n26
sublime, 6–8, 136

Tales of Tomorrow, 22
Taxi Driver, 114
technoscience, 5, 203n2
teenagers, 57, 173–74
Telotte, J. P., 60, 203n4, 216n2
These Are the Damned, 173
Thing from Another World, The, 13, 51–52, 53, 159–61, 179, 204n11
Things to Come, 209n3
Thirty Seconds over Tokyo, 124
This Island Earth, 7, 216n5
Thriller, 9
Time Machine, The: George Pal, 10, 162, 153–55, 172–80, 182–83; H. G. Wells, 45, 169–72
Time Travelers, The, 45, 168
Titus, Costandina A., 66, 207n25
Tompkins, Jane, 135–36, 149
Top Gun, 194, 208n31
Transformers, 194
trauma, 40–44, 209n33, 214n15
True Confessions, 85
Truman, Harry, 3, 210n6; doctrine, 50, 163–64
Tudor, Andrew, 5, 8, 12, 203n5, 213n14
Turse, Nick, 186
Twelve O'Clock High, 9, 36, 37, 39–40, 124, 204n9
Twenty Million Miles to Earth, 129
20,000 Leagues Under the Sea, 10, 45, 60, 203n4, 210n7, 216n2
Twilight's Last Gleaming, 215n10

Twilight Zone, The, 9, 214n15; "The Monsters Are Due on Maple Street," 126, 144; "The Thirty-Fathom Grave," 116; "Where Is Everybody?", 115–16

"ugly American," 216n1, 217n9
United Nations, 165

V-2, 58–59
Valantin, Jean-Michel, 59
Van Vogt, A. E., 198
Verne, Jules, 156–57
veterans, 97–98, 114–20, 212n8, 213n10
Vietnam War, 114, 120, 154, 187–88, 204n11
Village of the Damned, 173
Vint, Sherryl, 160

Walpole, Horace. See *Castle of Otranto, The*
War Game, The, 34
War of the Worlds: H.G. Wells, 148; Byron Haskin, 156, 195; Steven Spielberg, 195
Warshow, Robert, 135–36, 149
Washington, George, 76
Welcome to Mars. See Hollings, Ken
Wells, H. G., 148, 153, 156, 169–72
Wells, Simon, 176
Westad, Odd Arne, 24, 26–27, 164, 165, 205n14
Westerns, 132–37, 206n23
Westfahl, Gary, 169
Wetmore, Kevin, 43
Whip Hand, The, 143–44
Why We Fight: Frank Capra, 57, 187; Eugene Jarecki, 186–87
Wilcox, Francis, 168
Wild One, The, 173
Williams, Tony, 204n11
Wills, Gary, 140
Wilson, Sloan. See *Man in the Grey Flannel Suit, The*
Wilson, Woodrow, 163

Worland, Rick, 42, 47–48, 209n1, 209n2, 210n6
World, the Flesh and the Devil, The, 34, 217n7
World War II, 15, 42, 77–78, 80–83, 96–100, 123–24
Wylie, Philip, 22, 34, 121–24, 127
Wyler, William: *The Best Years of Our Lives*, 28, 100–101, 115, 204n9, 213n11; *The Memphis Belle: A Story of a Flying Fortress*, 124

Yucca Flats, 31

Zinn, Howard, 79, 80–83, 164, 213n13

www.ingramcontent.com/pod-product-compliance
Lightning Source LLC
Chambersburg PA
CBHW030620230426
43661CB00053B/2079